Science & Technology

QUESTIONS & ANSWERS

Science & Technology

PHYSICS · CHEMISTRY · BIOLOGY
MEDICAL TECHNOLOGY · EARTH SCIENCE
TRANSPORT AND SPACE TRAVEL · INFORMATION TECHNOLOGY

**Dr. Alexander Grimm · Dr. Christoph Hahn · Ulrich Hellenbrand
Dr. Ute Künkele · Horst W. Laumanns · Ralf Leinburger**

Bath New York Singapore Hong Kong Cologne Delhi Melbourne

Contents

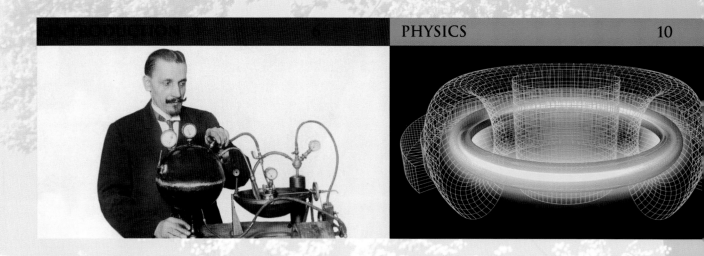

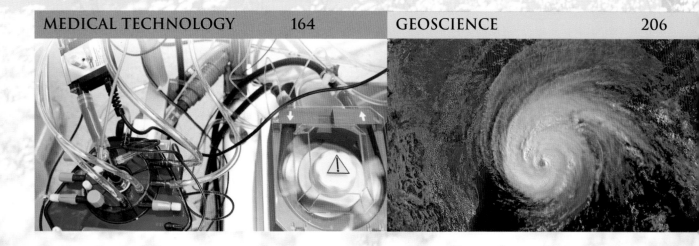

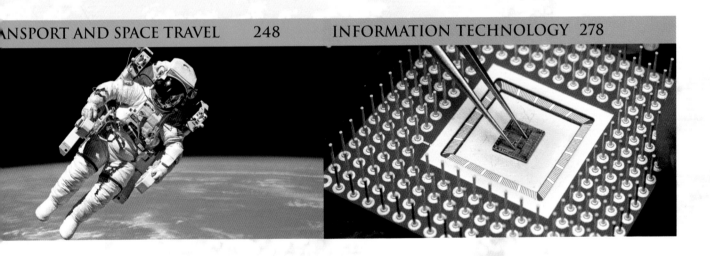

INTRODUCTION

Meteoric developments in the natural sciences are leading more and more quickly to further discoveries about the basis of human life. These are followed by technical achievements, the results of which change our everyday lives completely through new processes and instruments. Anyone who wants to understand the world and wishes to join in the dialogue, therefore, needs to know about these developments.

This superbly illustrated volume, based on the question-and-answer principle, should help to fill in knowledge gaps, to brush up on and augment existing understanding, to find out something new, and to make the structure of a world that is daily becoming ever more complicated more accessible. Scientific and expert authors answer over 500 questions on natural science and technical phenomena that define and have a lasting effect on our everyday lives. At the same time they impart basic knowledge about the living and inanimate world of nature, about substances and the smallest components of our planet, as well as the actual state of research and development of technologies relevant to the future—technologies we cannot imagine doing without.

Electricity is just one of the numerous elementary topics in the field of physics, which explores inanimate nature.

Biology is the science of the living world of nature and consequently encompasses all aspects of life and the interaction of living things with one another.

The collection of questions within individual chapters has been designed in such a way that existing knowledge may be tested but, at the same time, there is ample opportunity to deepen one's understanding in the area in an easy yet comprehensive way. As the individual questions and answers within a particular topic are presented completely and clearly and not built up consecutively,

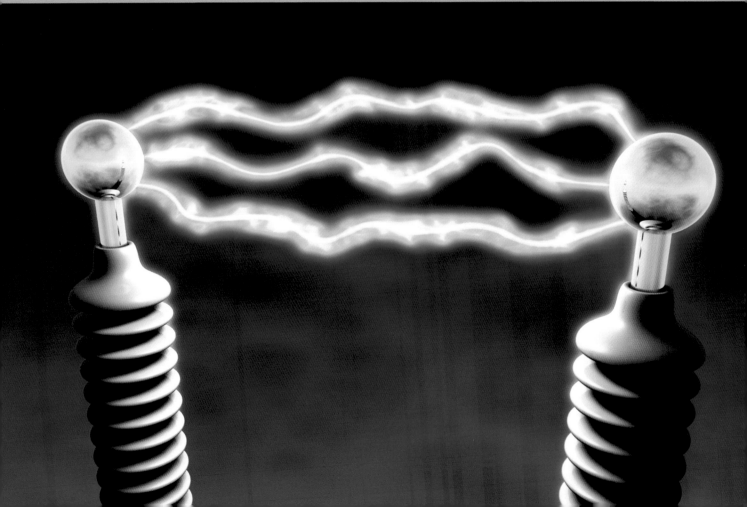

the volume may also be used selectively as a work of reference. Furthermore, a detailed index at the back of the book makes it possible to pick out the information that is needed on a certain topic.

The order of the seven chapters reflects the interleaving of scientific knowledge with the development of new technical products. First the three classic natural sciences—physics, chemistry, and biology, which are very closely connected—are introduced: physics is concerned with inanimate nature, its characteristics, its structure, and its changes as well as the forces that cause these changes; chemistry explores the chemical elements, the substances and compounds; and biology concerns the living natural world. Following this comes the chapter on medical technology, which is based on and developed from the findings of the three sciences named above. The next chapter, geoscience, is concerned with how the Earth's systems function, and gives insight into, among other things, the branches of geology and geography, soil science and mineralogy, as well as meteorology and geoecology. This chapter is followed by two further technical chapters on topics that have a profound influence on everyday life today: transport and space travel, with questions and answers on discoveries with regard to means and options of transport; and information technology, covering all the different aspects of communication such as cell phones, PCs, and the internet, an area in which new products have altered everyday

Above: Mercury is just one of many elements that chemistry (the theory of the structure, behavior, and changes of substances) examines.

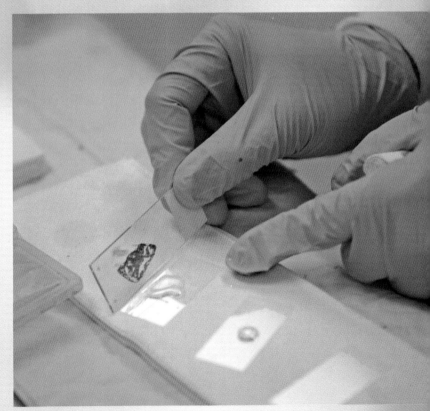

The advances that have recently been made, and are still to be made, in medical technology are groundbreaking both in diagnosis and in therapeutic treatments.

life fundamentally and in a lasting way for children as well as adults within the space of very few years.

Some of the questions raised may remind readers of their own time at school, for example, of physics lessons: What is the relationship between force and energy? What is friction? Are there smaller particles than atoms? How is electricity produced? What is light? In addition, however, exciting phenomena or the physics edifice of ideas, such as quantum physics or the Big Bang theory, will be explained, which go beyond "classroom science."

The chemistry chapter is devoted to atoms and their chemical reactions, and explains the periodic system, the process of fire, the composition of water as well as the importance of the ozone layer. However, questions about chemical products in everyday use will also be answered here, covering soap and detergents, dyes, batteries and accumulators, light bulbs and neon strip lights, fertilizers and explosives, synthetic materials, silicone, ceramics, sugar, oil, gasoline, and much more.

The biology chapter deals with the biodiversity of microorganisms, with plants, animals, and human beings, their interaction with one another as well as the consequences of environmental and climate change. In this chapter the reader will find information about the foundation and origin of life on Earth and the latest developments in research, about cells as elements of all living things and the opportunities and risks of genetics and genetic engineering, about the processes of evolution (mutation, heredity, learning) and the achievements in bionics (in which humans use nature as a model to design mechanical systems, for example in aircraft manufacture), and also about ecology and biotopes and the harmful and useful characteristics of bacteria and fungi.

The questions about the current status of medical technological development concern the fields of pharmacy (the manufacture of medication), diagnostics (e.g. X-rays and their varied potential uses, electroencephalography (EEG) and electrocardiography (ECG), ultrasound, laser, and endoscopies), and therapy (e.g. communication aids to improve daily life, such as hearing aids, Braille tables, and talking computers). Besides this, the reader is given information on dental technology and dentures, transplants and implants, plastic surgery, and aids for the support of internal organs, such as dialysis machines and cardiac pacemakers. In addition,

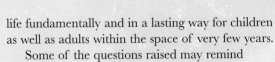

Weather phenomena such as tornadoes are just a small aspect of geoscience, which encompasses the fields of geology, geography, mineral resources, agricultural technology, and geoecology.

there are plenty of facts about technical equipment and security systems within the hospital setting as well as pathology's remits.

The geoscience section contains facts worth knowing about the Earth's origins, the forces of nature and ice ages, water as the basis of life, the atmosphere, and climate and weather. There is also information on mineral resources, on the way different power plants function, and on alternative energy sources. In addition, there are comprehensible explanations of aspects of agricultural technology and instruments and scope of remote sensing, whether by satellite or GPS (Global Positioning System).

The transport and space travel chapter is dedicated to every form of human locomotion— on land, on water, and in the air. Along with explanations of the classic means of locomotion, such as bicycles and automobiles, trains, ships, and airplanes, this chapter also contains facts on the most recent related technical discoveries of the past decades. Subjects such as transport routes (roads, bridges and tunnels) and airports and their security are discussed here along with aspects of space travel and the limits of deep-sea diving.

Finally, the information technology chapter presents the world of radio, television, computers, and the internet. It contains explanations of the most important aspects of transistors, cell phones, microchips, DVDs, USBs (Universal Serial Bus), the www (worldwide web), DSLs (Digital Subscriber Lines), and MP3s as well as

The transport and space travel chapter answers all sorts of questions on human locomotion on water, on land and in the air.

semiconductors, operating systems, electronic smog, security while browsing the web, and the digital age of music.

This wealth of exciting topics is not only presented in a comprehensible question-and-answer format, but is also made clear and vivid with the aid of photographs, graphics, and illustrations. Numerous information boxes on further aspects of a topic amplify the explanations. In this way, general knowledge and a more profound understanding are brought to readers of all ages and backgrounds, making the book enjoyable for all.

The latest television technology is just one facet of information technology, which embraces some of the most key aspects of our modern society, including, among other things, cell phones, computers, and the internet.

Universe

Perpetual motion

Thunderstorms

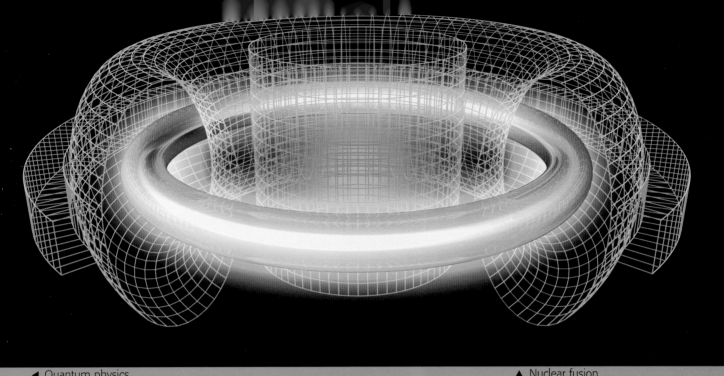

PHYSICS

The science of physics seeks to explain "how things basically function." Physics describes phenomena and processes in nature and derives from them generally applicable laws, theories, and models. In comparison with chemistry, which is concerned with how chemical reactions alter the properties of substances, physical processes include, above all, changes in matter and energy within space and time. This applies to all quantity fields, from subatomic elementary particles and a ball that moves in the Earth's field of gravity right up to our entire cosmos.

Force and energy   Electricity

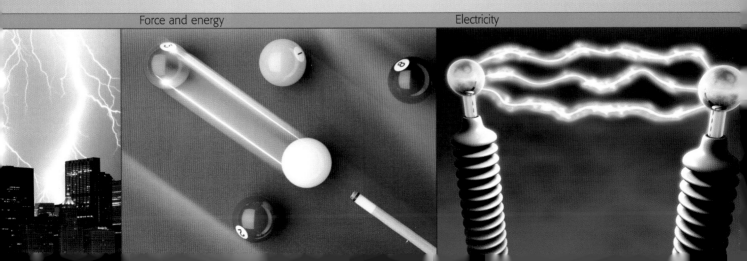

PHYSICS: THE SCIENCE OF INANIMATE NATURE

Stylized model of a
lithium atom.
Three electrons
revolve around the
atomic nucleus
(not true to scale).

What is physics?

Physics is the science of inanimate nature. It is diametrically opposed to biology, which is concerned with living things. Physics seeks to explain natural phenomena and processes or events, such as lightning (electricity). Questions about the origin of the world, the creation of the cosmos as well as the properties or characteristics of time and space are also core themes in physics, which deals with such issues as the

structure of matter, the forces and energy that affect our world, or questions such as: "What is heat?" "Why does an airplane fly?" "How can you throw a ball furthest?" In principle, some parts of the fields of chemistry (the science of substances), geology (the science of the Earth's crust), or meteorology (the science of weather phenomena) belong to physics but are dealt with as fields in their own right for historical reasons and for reasons of practicality.

Solar cells convert light into electrical energy. Humans can use the electricity produced.

Who was the first physicist?

The Greek mathematician and inventor of mechanical devices, Archimedes (circa 285–circa 212 BC) is generally considered to be the first physicist. He was well ahead of his time and introduced the basic theory of statics, formulated the principle of the lever, and discovered the principle of buoyancy. And it is the Archimedes Principle that says that an object floating on water has the same mass as the water it displaces. He was also the first person to describe the ratio of mass to volume i.e. density.

Which famous physicist of the present day is the successor to Sir Isaac Newton?

Stephen Hawking (born 1942) holds the prestigious seat of Lucasian Professor of Mathematics at Cambridge University, which was established in 1663. His most famous predecessors were, among many other well-known physicists and mathematicians, Sir Isaac Newton (1643–1727), Sir George Stokes (1819–1903), and Paul Dirac (1902–1984). Hawking, who is almost completely paralyzed and confined to a special wheelchair, became famous for his studies on black holes.

How does physics influence our lives?

Apart from the laws of nature to which we are subject, the science of physics influences our daily lives by providing us with technological advances and, not least, by shaping our conception of the world. Nowadays, for example, every child knows that the Earth is round and that it orbits the Sun, and that the Sun in its turn is part of the Milky Way, which we can

Technology thanks to physics

Apart from its theoretical side, physics has many practical applications, as the recognized laws benefit humans in the shape of technology. Even a simple lever to lift weights uses the discovery of a law of physics (the principle of the lever); the system of pulleys is a refinement of the same principle and has relieved humanity of the great burden of lifting the heaviest objects. In principle, all the technology that is in use today comes as a result of discoveries in physics from the use of an ax to chop wood in the forest, to the rich sound of stereo systems, to televisions and DVD players, nuclear power plants and solar panels, cars and rockets.

see at night as a hazy band in the heavens. Physics has largely taken over from religion in articulating modern human beings' conception of the physical world. What is more, physics does not just formulate discoveries but also continues to analyze them, asking questions such as: "Why is the Earth a sphere?" "Why does it revolve around the Sun?" "Why is the Sun so bright and hot?" In this way, every answer throws up new questions, so that physicists and other natural scientists, out of curiosity and urgency, will push ahead in the future to find out more—and in more and more precise detail—about the world, in order to understand and explain its events.

Sir Isaac Newton (1643–1727) formulated the law of the force of attraction between objects. Force is measured in newtons (N) in recognition of his work.

FORCE AND ENERGY: INVISIBLE YET EFFECTIVE

What is force?

If force has an effect on a movable object, the object will accelerate. The result of the effect of force is therefore always a change in velocity. On stationary objects, if not just a single force but several forces are acting on an object at the same time, these may sometimes cancel each other out. For example, if a book is sitting on a table, the net force is zero, i.e. the gravitational force is equal and opposite to the force the table exerts on the book.

What is energy?

Energy can be considered as stored force. If a bow is pulled tight, for example, force is needed to do this. This force is stored as energy in the bow; since the bow is elastic, it will shoot back to its old form when it is released. The energy is transferred to an arrow that is placed in the bow, and the string is drawn

back. As soon as the string is released, the arrow is accelerated and is given kinetic energy (the energy that moving objects have). If this arrow is shot vertically into the air, its kinetic energy decreases as it flies higher because of the force of the Earth's gravitational pull. It will stop for a brief moment, the apparent end of its kinetic energy. However, the energy has not vanished but remains, so to speak, "hidden" in the arrow. This hidden energy is called potential energy, which becomes kinetic energy again as the arrow falls. The higher the arrow was shot into the air in the first place, the faster it will be traveling when it reaches the ground again.

Energies can thus change from one type of energy into another. Potential energy, after the drawing of the bowstring (bow stress), changes into kinetic energy (flight of the arrow), which reverts to potential energy (when the arrow

In billiards the force of the blow by the cue is transferred to the playing ball. Clearly, force (as well as power) also involves direction.

In archery, bending the bow and tightening the bowstring first of all store energy. This energy is transferred to the arrow when the bowstring is released.

achieves maximum height), and finally becomes kinetic energy once more as the arrow falls to Earth.

Which forces occur in nature?

Strictly speaking, there are only four fundamental forces in nature: gravity (gravitational force), the electromagnetic force (charges and magnets), and the strong and the weak nuclear forces (forces on the subatomic level). It is predominantly gravitational force and electromagnetic force that determine our everyday lives.

What forces are at work when a person lifts an object?

On the one side, of course, the Earth's gravitational force on the object. Gravitation acts on the object, trying to make it fall downwards. On the other side, the force that the person transfers by way of his or her hands in lifting the object. The hands consist of atoms (see page 18), as does the object. When the hand and the object come into contact with one another, their electron shells repel one another reciprocally due to their electrical charge. A person must exert a greater force upwards in order to overcome gravitation and lift the object. A net upward force will accelerate the object upwards. When the two forces are equal in magnitude and opposite in direction the object is stationary.

What is the difference between nuclear power and nuclear energy?

Nuclear forces (strong interaction), among other things, act like glue to hold together the atomic nuclei. On the one hand, nuclear energy is considered to be the energy which is stored in the atomic nucleus due to nuclear forces, and on the other, it is regarded as the energy created by nuclear fission in nuclear power stations, i.e. the end product in the form of heat or electricity.

Can energy disappear?

No, energy is always constant and can only be converted into other forms of energy. Kinetic energy is often seemingly "swallowed up" by friction, for example, if an object's movement is slowed. However, if this happens, heat results, which is also a form of energy even if it is not available for movement.

Gas contains chemically stored energy. This is released by the burning of fuel in a car engine, which produces the necessary energy to drive the vehicle.

MATTER: THE SUBSTANCE OUR WORLD IS MADE OF

Does matter have force?

Yes, all matter gravitates towards all other matter. The force at work here is called gravity or the gravitational force. The bigger the mass, the greater the gravitational force between it and other matter. The mass of the Earth is so great that all objects are firmly attached to its surface but, on the other hand, it is so small that a person can easily pick up a stone. However, if a stone is thrown into the air, its flight is resisted by gravity and it soon falls back to the ground. Incidentally, the force of the stone on the Earth is the same as the force of the Earth on the stone. Since the mass of the stone—in comparison with the mass of the Earth—is tiny, however, the effect of the stone on the Earth is not noticeable.

People clearly sense the rapid changes in direction and speed of a roller coaster only because of inertia.

Scales measure the force with which matter is pulled by the Earth. Thus, it is not the actual matter (or mass) that is measured, but the weight of the matter.

Would it hurt more to be hit by a stone in space than on the Earth?

If a large mass is immobile, it needs a great deal of force to move it. Inversely, it is difficult to stop a moving mass. This inertia is a fundamental property of matter—the greater the mass, the more inertia it has. As the inertia and not the weight needs to be stopped, it makes no difference whether we are hit by a stone in weightless space or on the Earth.

Is gravity the strongest force?

No, at any rate not over short distances. Planet Earth weighs approximately $13{,}170 \times 10^{21}$ lb (6×10^{24} kg), but a small magnet exerts a greater pull on a piece of iron than the unimaginable great mass of the Earth does. However, if the magnet is moved just a few inches away from the piece of iron, the iron will fall to the floor.

Over greater distances, the actually weak gravitational force is unbeatable. The Earth is 93 million miles (149 million km) away from the Sun but the Sun's gravitational pull is so strong on the Earth that the Earth revolves around it elliptically. No magnet would still have an effect at this distance.

Immense amounts of energy are needed for a space shuttle to be able to escape from the gravitational force at the Earth's surface and go into orbit around our planet.

A LOOK INTO THE MICROCOSMOS: WHAT DOES MATTER CONSIST OF?

For how long have we known what matter consists of?

At one time it was thought that the world consisted of four basic elements: fire, water, earth, and air. Matter can burn (fire), fluids can be squeezed out of many objects (water), often steam occurs in heating (air), and matter may be in many cases hard like stone (earth). The Greek natural philosopher Democritus (460–371 BC) was one of the first people to imagine matter as something completely different, namely that it consisted of tiny, indivisible and moving particles, called atoms. These, according to Democritus, get stuck to one another, blend and form infinite varieties of combinations and forms, and this was his explanation of the endless diversity of matter. It was not until much later (1906) that the British physicist Ernest Rutherford proved the existence of atoms in experiments and, as a result, proved that Democritus' assumption was correct in principle.

Are atoms the smallest building blocks of matter?

No, the smallest are quarks and electrons—atoms can, as we now know, be split. Protons and neutrons, which make up the atomic nucleus, are believed to be formed from three quarks each, in varying arrangements. The electrons, for their part, form an electrically charged shell around the nucleus. If an atom were magnified by a factor of 100,000,000,000, it would have a diameter of $\frac{1}{25}$ in (1 mm) and the electron shell would correspondingly be approximately 300 ft (100 m) from the nucleus. The electrons themselves would appear at this magnification as tiny specks of dust hardly visible to the human eye. The atom is thus a huge expanse of empty space—a minute nucleus in the middle of the vast emptiness of the electron shell.

The movement of elementary particles is demonstrated by the production of traces in a so-called bubble chamber. The paths of charged particles are curved due to an applied magnetic field.

How much does an atom weigh?

The lightest atom is the hydrogen atom, weighing just 1.66×10^{-27} kg (written out: 0.00000000000000000000000000166 kg!). Iron and uranium are heavier than hydrogen by factors of 55.8 and 238 respectively, but even these atoms are unimaginably light by our everyday standards of measurement.

What is the task of neutrons?

Protons in the atomic nucleus repel one another because they are all positively charged. They could

The natural philosopher Democritus (460–371 BC) was the first person to proclaim atoms as basic elements of matter.

Atom

Atomic nucleus

Neutron

Proton

Stylized atom: an atomic nucleus with positively charged protons (red) and neutral neutrons (blue), surrounded by the atomic shell.

not be held in a restricted space, therefore, if a second attractive force were not effective between them, i.e. nuclear forces or so-called strong interaction. Although neutrons are uncharged, they provide the required attractive force to bond the atomic nucleus together.

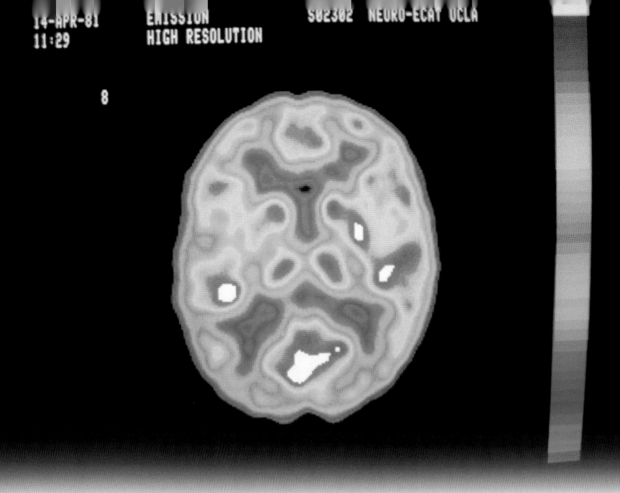

ENERGY AND MATTER:
TWO SIDES OF THE SAME COIN

Positron Emission Tomography (PET) uses antimatter to represent in colors the varying blood supply to different areas of the brain.

Can matter change into energy?
Yes, that is possible. In nuclear fission, as carried out in nuclear power stations, the fission fragments are lighter than the initial nuclei. The tiny difference in mass is converted into energy and is sufficient to produce electricity or—in the worst-case scenario—the destructive effect of a nuclear bomb.

What is antimatter?
Antimatter is a form of matter whose atomic building blocks, antiatoms, consist exclusively of antiparticles, namely positrons, antiprotons, and antineutrons. It is constructed in exactly the same way as ordinary matter, except that the individual particles have an inverse charge.

How much energy is there in mass?
The formula for this is world famous: $E = mc^2$. This means that energy is the mass multiplied by the square of the speed of light (approximately 186,000 miles/s or 300,000 km/s). Thus, if 1 kg of matter is converted entirely into energy,

approximately 9×10^{16} joules are released. That would correspond to the energy of 1,500 Hiroshima atom bombs!

What happens if matter collides with antimatter?
The reaction is many times stronger than in nuclear fission, as a collision between matter and antimatter results in the complete obliteration of both. The entire mass is converted into energy. The explosion that would be triggered by large masses of matter and antimatter meeting would be unimaginable.

Can energy change into matter?
Yes, energy can be spontaneously converted into matter. In such a process, equal parts of matter and antimatter are created. If the antimatter particles that are produced collide with their equivalents of matter (e.g. a positron with an electron), these are converted again into pure energy in the form of radiation.

How was matter created?

Matter was created from the energy of the Big Bang. Theoretically, matter and antimatter should have been created in the same amounts. This was fortunately not the case; otherwise all matter would have been reconverted into energy. More matter than antimatter must therefore have been created in the Big Bang, and from this tiny surplus of matter, all the planets, stars, and galaxies were created.

Antimatter can also be of practical use

It may sound very odd, but antiparticles are used in medicine—in Positron Emission Tomography (PET) to detect tumor activity. In this process the patient is given an injection of radioactive fluorine-18 solution that is principally deposited in tumor tissue. There it decays rapidly (see "What forms of radioactivity are there?" page 26) and as each nucleus decays, it gives out a positron (antielectron) that, together with an electron, reverts to energy. In doing so, two photons of gamma radiation are emitted in opposite directions. Our bodies are practically transparent to gamma radiation. With the aid of a detector, the direction in which the gamma radiation penetrates the body can be plotted for each pair of photons and this indicates the location of the tumor. The procedure is quite safe for the patient, as only the smallest amounts of radioactive material are used. PET was developed and came into use in the 1970s. Its greatest advantage compared with older techniques is the extremely low radiation levels to which the patient is exposed. There is one disadvantage, however; the procedure is extremely expensive. As the isotopes required for the procedure have only a short half-life, they need to be produced in a particle accelerator located nearby.

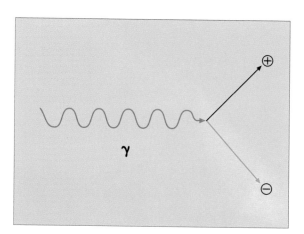

A gamma quantum (photon, wavy line) is converted into an electron (blue arrow) and a positron (antielectron, black arrow). Energy condenses to matter.

Testing a nuclear bomb in Nevada, USA. The destructive quantity of energy is released by nuclear fission.

CURRENTS: FROM THE FLOWING STREAM TO THE AIRPLANE IN FLIGHT

What does a stream have in common with fine sand?

Both can flow. If fine sand is placed in a downward-sloping channel, all the grains will roll downwards. As they do this, they bump into one another and this action affects their individual paths but all in all the sand flows downhill. Water consists of many smaller individual particles—water molecules—which moreover exert a lower frictional force on one another. Water therefore flows more rapidly than sand even on shallow inclines. However, owing to friction with surfaces beneath the water, a stream flows slowest at the bank or at the bottom. Therefore, through this (albeit lower) frictional force, the molecules near the bank also slow the molecules situated in the middle of the stream. Thus the stream flows most quickly in the middle. Physicists also call this internal friction viscosity.

At around 3½ miles (5.6 km) long and 16 sq miles (41 sq km), the Mer de Glace or "Sea of Ice" glacier (Mont Blanc, France) is the fourth-largest ice stream in the Alps.

Daniel Bernoulli (1700–1782) and his effect

The Swiss physicist, mathematician, and doctor Daniel Bernoulli established the principles for hydro- and aerodynamics in 1738 and thereby created the foundations for numerous technical applications. The so-called Bernoulli effect describes how rapidly flowing liquids or gases have a lower pressure than slower flowing ones. Among other things, this effect is the reason why airplanes fly (see page 268).

Why is road traffic viscous?

A driver naturally avoids coming into contact with other cars and brakes before an accident occurs. We not only apply the brakes if a slower car changes lanes, in order to avoid going into them, but we also keep a watchful eye on the fast lane, for we know that approaching drivers fear

A traffic jam on the expressway. Even after the cause of the traffic jam (e.g. an accident) has been cleared, vehicles can be slow to get moving due to backup effects.

that another car could swerve and also change lanes. This interaction between cars is in some ways similar to the friction that occurs between molecules. In fact, the calculations and predictions regarding traffic and possible backups follow the laws of fluid mechanics in physics. Road traffic is thus viscous in the physics sense of the word.

Why do backups form if too many cars are on the road?

The cause lies in the reaction time of the drivers. If all cars, even those at small distances apart, were to drive equally quickly and, on braking, all the other drivers were to react straight away, and subsequently all were to simultaneously accelerate again, traffic would flow even if there were a great many cars on the road. Due to delays in our reaction times, however, it does not work like that—and the resulting effect is a backup, which can lead to total gridlock. To avoid this happening, modern traffic management systems try to minimize backups at the outset by the use of early warning signs.

How does a sailing ship sail into the wind?

A sailing ship can only sail into the wind up to a certain angle, as the wind otherwise simply pushes the boat off course. Modern racing boats are able to sail into the wind up to an angle of 35 degrees. The sail deflects the wind, and this causes the ship to move forwards. However, in deflecting the wind, force is transferred to the boat, which tends to make it move in a sideward direction. For this reason, sailing ships are equipped with a large fin-like keel that counters the sideways thrust with necessary frictional resistance enabling them to stay upright.

Sailing ships use air currents deflected by the sails to generate their forward movement.

THE PARTICLE ZOO AND QUARKS: SPLENDIDLY COLORFUL

Martin L. Perl (born 1927) explains in his laboratory in Stanford, USA, how free quarks could theoretically be proved.

Are there smaller particles than atoms?

Yes, because atoms consist of the atomic nucleus and a shell of electrons. The atomic nucleus is composed of protons and neutrons. It is currently thought that these in turn consist of three so-called quarks. Quarks and electrons are elementary particles, i.e. they cannot be reduced into further, even smaller, particles. As well as quarks and electrons there are a few other elementary particles (see the information box on page 25), in particular, neutrinos, muons, and bosons. Bosons are force-carrying particles, as photons for the electromagnetic force, as gluons for the strong force, as W^+, W^-, or Zo for the weak force, and as gravitons for gravitation. All other particles are made up of quarks and are not elementary particles in the strictest sense. Neutrinos and muons do not convey forces but exist as free particles.

Where did quarks get their name from?

The expression is English in origin. The physicist and 1969 Nobel Prize winner Murray Gell-Mann discovered and gave the quark its name, inspired by James Joyce's novel *Finnegans Wake*. The name is from a poem about King Mark, in which it says: "Three quarks for Muster Mark! Sure he hasn't got much of a bark and sure any he has it's all beside the mark." James Joyce was famous for coining new words and for elaborate distortion of language. The term "quark" was based on Joyce's neologism, as until that time the word "quark" did not exist in the English language. It is believed to be a nominalization of the archaic "to quark" (to caw like a crow).

Model of elementary particles (overall view)

PARTICLE		REST MASS IN KG	LIFETIME	ELECTRICAL CHARGE	SPIN***
Electron	e	9.198×10^{-31}	stable	−1	0.5
Electron Neutrino	ν_e	$< 5.4 \times 10^{-36}$	quasi stable*	0	0.5
Muon	μ	1.908×10^{-28}	2.2×10^{-6} s	−1	0.5
Muon Neutrino	ν_μ	$< 5.4 \times 10^{-31}$	quasi stable*	0	0.5
Tau	τ	3.1986×10^{-27}	3×10^{-13} s	−1	0.5
Tau Neutrino	ν_τ	$< 5.4 \times 10^{-29}$	quasi stable*	0	0.5
Up quark	u	$2.7 - 8.1 \times 10^{-30}$	variable	2/3	0.5
Down quark	d	$9 - 15.3 \times 10^{-30}$	variable	−1/3	0.5
Charm quark	c	$1.8 - 2.52 \times 10^{-27}$	variable	2/3	0.5
Strange quark	s	$1.44 - 2.79 \times 10^{-28}$	variable	−1/3	0.5
Top/Truth quark	t	$3.042 - 3.222 \times 10^{-25}$	variable	2/3	0.5
Bottom/Beauty quark	b	$7.2 - 8.1 \times 10^{-27}$	variable	−1/3	0.5
Photon	γ	0	force carrier**	0	1
Zo Boson		0	force carrier**	0	1
W+ Boson		ca 1.6×10^{-25}	force carrier**	1	1
W− Boson		ca 1.44×10^{-25}	force carrier**	−1	1
Gluon		0	force carrier**	0	1
Graviton		0	force carrier**	0	2

* Neutrinos can merge, or rather change their properties, on account of a quantum effect (neutrino oscillation).

** Force carriers transmit forces that are stable until they are absorbed by the interacting particle.

*** Spin corresponds to the rotation of a particle around its own axis. Gravitons rotate quickest.

Murray Gell-Mann (born 1929), the "father of the quark." His research on elementary particles and their interactions was rewarded with the Nobel Prize for Physics.

Inspection of a pion detector in Fermilab's particle accelerator, one of the largest of its kind.

Why are there no individual quarks?

Quarks hold onto one another tightly. So much energy would need to be used to prise them apart that this would be sufficient to form two new quarks, a quark and an antiquark, which is exactly what happens in a separation attempt.

If one tries to separate a quark from a proton (which consists of three quarks), for example by striking it with another particle, the energy is converted into more quarks. The proton survives and a meson is produced (a particle made up from a quark and an antiquark).

Mesons are extremely unstable and change back into energy after about 10^{-8} seconds. The attempt to isolate a quark is therefore futile.

Are there particles that have no mass?

Yes, for example the photon that makes up light and transmits the electromagnetic interaction. Since photons contain a great deal of energy and energy corresponds to mass, they are said more exactly to have no rest mass. Other zero-mass particles are the gluon and the graviton.

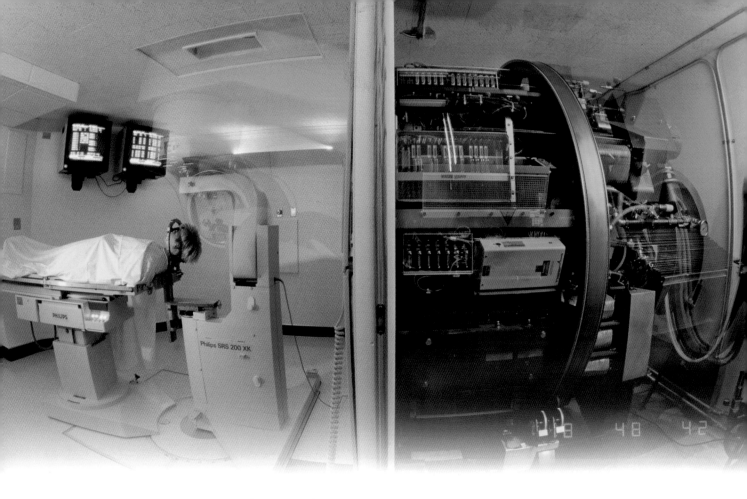

RADIOACTIVITY:
FAMOUS AND INFAMOUS

Irradiation of a brain tumor with gamma rays, which are produced with the aid of a small particle accelerator (linear accelerator).

What is radioactivity?

If a substance is radioactive, it consists of unstable atomic nuclei which alter when energy is released until they are stable. In this way, the released energy can be emitted directly as short-wave light radiation or as particles that carry kinetic energy. If particles are released, the composition of the atomic nucleus changes and therefore the radioactive substance also changes.

What forms of radioactivity are there?

There are three main types of radioactivity. Firstly, there is alpha decay. This is when heavy, unstable atomic nuclei spontaneously release a small helium nucleus (two protons and two neutrons). The individual particles of the large nucleus are loosely bound, as the cohesive nuclear force is only effective over short ranges (less than the core diameter). If two protons and neutrons accidentally

Alpha decay: a helium nucleus, consisting of two protons and two neutrons, is emitted from a large atomic nucleus.

What does half-life mean?

Cesium[137] is a beta ray emitter with a 30-year half-life, which means that in the course of 30 years, half of the cesium is converted into Barium[137]. A further 30 years later, half of the remainder will have decayed again. From 1 lb (450 g) of cesium there will be 4 oz (112 g) still remaining after 60 years, after 120 years 1 oz (28 g), and after 240 years 1/16 oz (7 g). The cesium that was released in the Chernobyl reactor accident is therefore, despite its relatively short half-life of 30 years, still present and will have an appreciable effect on the environment for decades.

come close together within the core, they will bind to each other more tightly. The resulting energy difference is released in the form of kinetic energy (see page 14), i.e. the alpha particle is flung off from the nucleus. Second, we have beta decay. In the case of a large surplus of neutrons in the nucleus, a neutron can, by emitting an electron, convert spontaneously into a proton. The electron

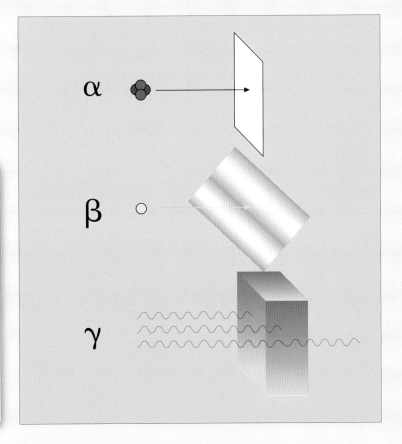

Radiocarbon dating

Living tissue contains large amounts of carbon (^{12}C). In nature, a carbon isotope may sometimes occur with two additional neutrons (^{14}C). It is formed in the atmosphere, inhaled by plants and animals, and incorporated into the cells. When a tree dies, the entire metabolism is halted and no more ^{14}C is absorbed. The existing ^{14}C within the wood is radioactive and decays to nitrogen. As this is no longer replaced by new, inhaled ^{14}C, the age of the wood can be determined on the basis of the ratio of the normal ^{12}C to ^{14}C. Thus, the older the wood is, the less ^{14}C occurs in it. As the half-life of ^{14}C is known to be 5,730 years, this method allows conclusions to be made about the age of items of historical interest such as wooden artifacts, plant remains, or animal bones.

is flung off from the nucleus. Similarly, in a surplus of protons, a proton can become a neutron. In this instance, however, a positron (antielectron) with a positive charge is released. Third, there is gamma decay, in which only surplus energy is emitted in the form of short-wave, energy-rich radiation.

Above: A sheet of paper stops alpha radiation. A thin sheet of metal, on the other hand, is needed to stop beta radiation, whilst gamma radiation is only absorbed by solid lead.

How dangerous is radioactivity for people?

The danger depends on the type of radiation. Alpha particles are not able to travel very far in the air and they would not penetrate paper. Humans' topmost skin layer, which is dead, holds this sort of radiation at bay. However, if a source of alpha rays is swallowed—by eating contaminated food, for example—then the energy-rich particles hit the living cells directly and can cause damage to them in the form of cell changes (possibly cancer-forming). Beta radiation can travel several feet through the air, making its way through the topmost skin layer and in this way enters the body, but its effect is small. Gamma radiation, on the other hand, is very dangerous; being rich in energy and having zero rest mass, it completely penetrates the body.

Marie Curie (1867–1934) discovered radioactivity in her laboratory.

NUCLEAR POWER STATIONS: USED NUCLEAR FISSION

Why does nuclear fission supply energy?

Large atomic nuclei are more loosely constructed than smaller atomic nuclei, as the nuclear force that holds them together is effective only over very short distances. The repulsion of the proton charges, on the other hand, has an effect at greater distances. If a large, heavy atomic nucleus is split into two smaller ones, the individual particles within the two individual nuclei will move closer together, as they all stabilize each other by means of the nuclear force. At this point potential energy is released.

What is the fuel of a nuclear power station?

The most well-known fuel is uranium, which occurs in nature in three forms that differ from one another in terms of the number of neutrons. The most common is ^{238}U, which makes up just over 99

percent of uranium found in nature, but it cannot be easily split. The less common, fissionable ^{235}U comprises just 0.7 percent of uranium found in nature. The third, ^{234}U, is too rare (0.0055 percent) and so is not used in nuclear power stations.

Why is nuclear fission so dangerous?

During the fission of ^{235}U, two smaller new atomic nuclei and three emitted neutrons are created. If a neutron strikes a ^{235}U atomic nucleus, this is split again and emits three new neutrons. If two or three neutrons strike other nuclei causing them also to split, then a sort of avalanche results, a kind of explosive chain reaction (which is what happens in an atom bomb). In a nuclear power station, on average only every third neutron is allowed to strike a ^{235}U nucleus so that the reaction proceeds steadily. Usually, only a maximum of 7 percent ^{235}U is therefore contained in the fuel rods (the remainder consists of the harmless but radioactive ^{238}U). The neutrons are more likely to cause fission if they are made to move more slowly (known as "moderating" the neutrons). This is done by surrounding the fuel rods with deuterium ("heavy water"). However, this

Atomic waste reprocessing plant in La Hague, France. The radioactive material is stored in secure and very stable containers.

Common reactor types

Light-water reactor: here the fuel rods are cooled by normal water. Water intercepts comparatively large amounts of neutrons, which is why the fuel rods must contain sufficient uranium-235 (^{235}U)—up to 7%.

Heavy-water reactor: heavy water consists of oxygen and two deuterium nuclei (instead of hydrogen nuclei). Heavy water does not intercept neutrons as well as ordinary water does, hence only fuel rods with a lower amount of ^{235}U (from 0.7%) are needed for energy generation. The production of heavy water is, however, expensive.

Fast-breeder reactor: here, during the nuclear fission process, fissionable plutonium is produced from the unusable uranium-238 (^{238}U). Fast breeders thus generate at least a third more energy out of the fuel rods. However, plutonium is very dangerous and can be used for making nuclear weapons. There is therefore the additional danger of misuse of this reactor type.

must be controlled carefully to avoid a chain reaction leading to an explosion.

Above: A uranium mine in Saskatchewan, Canada. Uranium is extracted from the mined rock.

How does a nuclear power station produce electricity?

The released energy heats up water to produce high-pressure steam, which drives a steam turbine. The turbine turns a generator, which produces electricity. Water is used to condense the steam as part of the steam cycle. This is done in cooling towers where only vapor is emitted so, at least in this regard, nuclear power stations are environmentally friendly.

Why is atomic waste dangerous?

Uranium is radioactive and, due to its extremely long half-life, is a problem that will remain for hundreds of years. The fission products are also radioactive and long-lasting. Spent fuel rods present a huge potential danger. There is still no completely safe way to dispose of them even today and this is why the use of nuclear energy is so controversial. The risks of running a nuclear reactor (which uses a braked chain reaction, without which an explosion would occur) are considered by many to be incalculable.

The cooling tower of a nuclear power station in Middletown, Pennsylvania. During the night of March 28, 1979, there was a major hazardous incident. The cost for the long-term management of the damage came to almost one billion US dollars.

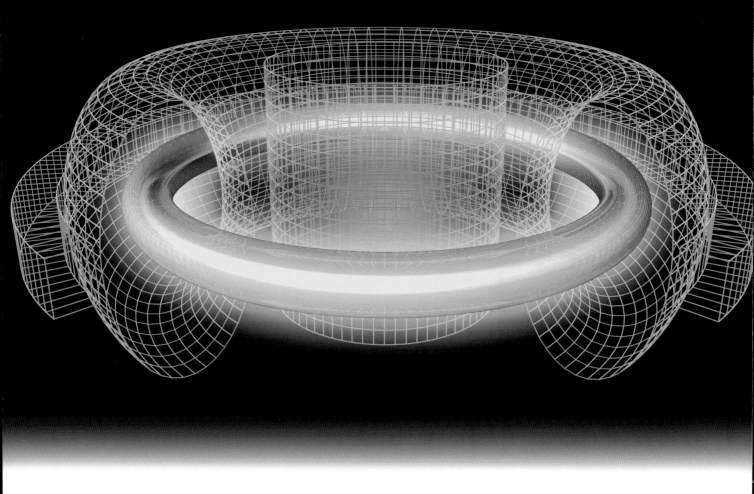

NUCLEAR FUSION: ENERGY SUPPLIER OF THE FUTURE?

The core of a fusion reactor. The plasma is so hot that it must be suspended by powerful magnets.

What is nuclear fusion?

Nuclear fusion means the joining of two atomic nuclei to achieve a new, larger nucleus. To make this possible, the repulsion of protons of both nuclei needs to be overcome before the nuclear forces can stabilize the new nucleus. For this, high pressure and high temperatures are needed.

Why does nuclear fusion supply energy?

Two individual small atomic nuclei are somewhat heavier than their sum after fusing. The difference is emitted as energy. Nuclear fusion is therefore the opposite process to nuclear fission of larger nuclei. Light nuclei generate energy by fusion, while nuclei that are heavier than iron produce energy by fission.

Indirect use of nuclear fusion

Solar cells capture sunlight and convert its energy into electricity. Solar cell technology is, however, not without its detractors, since arsenic and cadmium telluride (used in place of silicon), which are harmful to health and the environment, are used in the manufacture of some thin-film solar cells.

Do we already live by nuclear fusion?

Yes, although that may sound at first astonishing. Our existence actually depends on it. The Sun radiates light and its warmth is produced by nuclear fusion in its inner core. Inside the Sun, it is hot enough in extreme pressure to create, over several stages, helium from hydrogen. Plants absorb the Sun's energy through their leaves by way of chlorophyll and convert the energy of the absorbed light into chemical energy in the form of sugar. All animals feed on this sugar, either directly as herbivores or indirectly, when they eat the meat of herbivores.

Is nuclear fusion technically usable?

Yes, although its application has been viewed very skeptically since it was first used in the construction of the hydrogen bomb (first great explosion, 1952). Its development for peaceful purposes, i.e. energy generation, is much more challenging (see the information box). One difficulty is the need to steadily maintain the required high pressure and temperature. Theoretically it is possible, but in practice it is still too energy-consuming to be viable.

Are there any fusion reactors yet?

No, it is still not technically feasible to generate more energy from the fusion than is required to initiate the fusion process. A first trial reactor is in the planning stage and should go into service in the south of France in 2016. It is a joint project between the EU, the USA, China, India, Japan, Korea, and Russia.

Is nuclear fusion dangerous?

In principle, no, because the fusion reaction would come to a standstill in the case of reactor damage. In a nuclear (fission) power station, the reaction must constantly be held in check, whereas in fusion the reaction must be kept running

Future prospects

If the challenges of nuclear fusion were to be overcome, future energy supply problems would be solved. The production of electricity in an environmentally friendly way would be feasible, and would also open up the possibility of replacing inefficient combustion engines with electric motors. The emission of greenhouse gases globally would be markedly reduced. However, some problems are yet to be solved and the cost of the generated electricity is expected to be very high so renewable energy sources could still dominate in the long run.

artificially. Furthermore, relatively little radioactivity occurs during fusion in comparison with that at nuclear power stations.

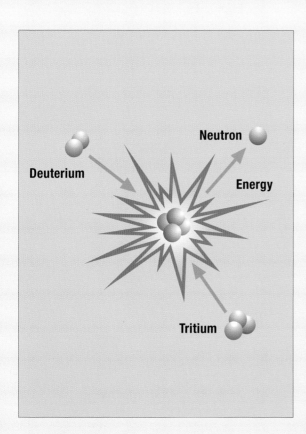

Above: In fusing deuterium and tritium to a helium nucleus, a neutron (red) and energy are released.

Below: The Sun is a gigantic, natural fusion reactor and pure energy: in a mighty explosion (top of picture) gas is emitted from the fireball (a "protuberance").

CHARGE, FIELDS, VOLTAGE, ELECTRICITY: SIMPLY ELECTRIFYING!

What is electric current?
Electric current consists of negatively charged electrons flowing through a conducting material, for example an electrical cable. The positively charged protons in the material, on the other hand, remain tightly bound in the atomic nucleus. In a plasma, however, the positive charges are also mobile and contribute to the electric current, for example in a lightning strike.

Why does wire become hot when electricity flows?
In a conductor the flowing electrons are slowed continuously when they jump from atom to atom. Their kinetic energy is converted into heat, which heats the wire (and, for example, lights the filament of a bulb). The deceleration of electrons is called electrical resistance. An object with great resistance is called an insulator.

How is electricity produced?
If a conductor is moved through a magnetic field then a current of electricity will flow through the

Small artificial flashes. The voltage produced by a generator is sufficient to allow a current to flow through the air.

What do volt and ampere mean?
Ampere (A) refers to the measure of electric current, i.e. the number of electrons that are flowing through the conductor per second. It was named after André-Marie Ampére, one of the discoverers of electromagnetism. A volt (V) is the measurement of the driving force that causes current to flow. The driving force is called voltage. People's skin has a high resistance, so that practically no current can flow through it at low voltage. However, if the voltage is high enough, the current can pass through the skin and this can be life threatening, as the entire nervous system functions by electrical impulses. The result is an electric shock that may influence the heartbeat and lead to ventricular fibrillation (potentially fatal, abnormal heart contractions).

conductor. This is how direct-current generators and alternating-current alternators work. For example, a bicycle dynamo, which is a small generator, has a small wheel that is usually turned by the tire. This wheel spins a wire-wound rotor that is between magnetic poles, and a current is

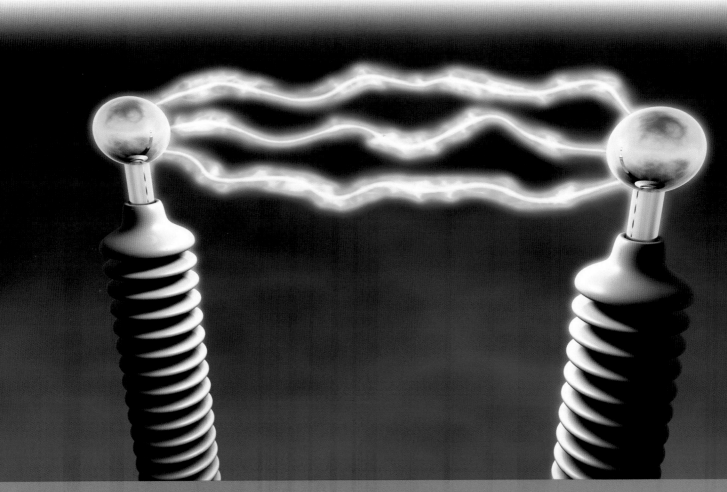

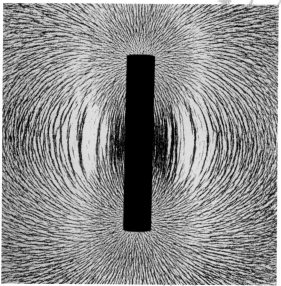

In a magnetic field, iron filings arrange themselves in the direction of the effective force. The resulting lines point to the magnet's poles.

produced. Large power plants work on the same basic principle.

What is alternating current?

Alternating current is an electric current that reverses its direction at regular intervals. The number of direction changes per second is measured in hertz (Hz). In alternators, the turning of the conductors creates alternating current. The turning produces a cyclical change of direction, which is reflected in the direction of flow of the current produced, i.e. the current flows to and fro. Direct current flows in only one direction and is generated, among other things, by batteries. In this process, current is chemically stored and on connection to a circuit flows continuously until the battery is fully discharged or "flat."

What is a magnet?

A magnet produces a magnetic field that always has two poles (north and south) and attracts iron or other magnetic materials. If two like poles are brought together, they repel one another, while opposite poles attract. As the Earth has a magnetic field, a compass needle always aligns itself so that its magnetic north pole points towards the magnetic south pole of the Earth and vice versa. Similar to these "permanent" magnets are also electromagnets, where a wire is wrapped around an iron core, producing a magnetic field when current flows through the wire. These electromagnets can be turned on and off (by switching the flow of current), which is not possible with a permanent magnet.

How does a Faraday cage function?

Electricity cannot penetrate into the interior of an enclosed space if the casing can conduct electricity. The electricity just flows around the exterior of the casing. During a thunderstorm, therefore, you are probably in less danger inside a car than outside it, despite the existence of windows, as interruptions to the casing do not allow lightning to penetrate the interior of the car. However, hands should not be placed outside of the window nor should they even touch the exterior of the bodywork if lightning strikes the car. The surface current would strike the hand or arm and cause an electric shock.

In high-voltage power lines, the applied voltage is between 110,000 and 380,000 V.

THUNDERSTORMS: A MAJOR PHYSICAL EVENT

Thunderstorm over Chicago, Illinois. Lightning conductors conduct the current safely from the rooftops into the ground to prevent damage to high-rises.

How does a thunderstorm originate?

In a thundercloud, strong updrafts dominate, which transport moist air rapidly to great heights. Here, countless tiny droplets of water are formed, which freeze into hailstones at greater heights. The updrafts prevent the stones from falling for a period of time so that the droplets increase in size, constantly meet, collide, and rub together. The rubbing induces a build-up of static electrical charge. The raindrops and hailstones are usually negatively charged and these negative charges—the electrons—are carried with them when they fall. At lower air levels the drops or hailstones evaporate or melt respectively. In this way charge is constantly transported from the upper cloud level to the lower, across which electrical tension (i.e. voltage) increasingly builds up.

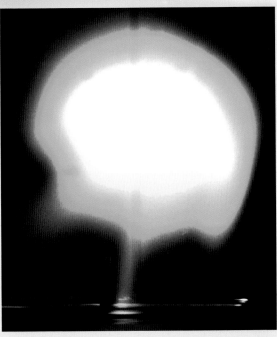

Ball lightning in the laboratory—or more exactly, ball lightning-like plasma clouds produced by a team of plasma physicists from the Max-Planck Institute for Plasma Physics in Garching, Munich, and from the Institute for Physics at the Humboldt University in Berlin.

When does lightning begin?

When the voltage that has been built up is big enough to break through the air resistance, electricity flows in the form of lightning. Theoretically, electric fields of 900 kV/ft (3,000 kV/m) would be needed to cause air to conduct, so that would suggest a voltage of many million volts. In practice, it needs electric fields of only about 60 kV/ft (200 kV/m). The difference might be explained by the fact that, instead of normal air, freely moving charged molecules (ions) are also present, which aid the flow of current. The exact conditions are still unclear, but there is some suggestion that cosmic radiation might be a possible trigger.

Does all lightning strike the ground?

No, around 90 percent of lightning flashes jump from cloud to cloud or cloud layer to cloud layer and never reach the Earth. In heavy rain, however, the negative charges are also brought to the ground and lightning can then accordingly strike the ground.

How hot is a lightning flash?

The energy of an impulse is so great that the air in the lightning channel is heated up to about 54,000°F (30,000°C). The heated air expands rapidly and produces a loud bang, which is heard as thunder.

Why is thunder heard after the lightning is seen?

The light of the lightning flash spreads at the speed of light—186,000 miles/s (299,792,458 km/s), while the speed of sound is 769 mph (around 343 m/s). The speed of lightning itself is about 18,600–62,000 miles/s (30,000–100,000 km/s). The long rumble of thunder is due to the length of the lightning bolt, with one end being further away than the other from the listener's ear. The sound of the thunder may also be diffused by echo effects. If the number of seconds between the lightning and thunder are counted and divided by 5, the distance of the thunderstorm can be estimated in miles (or in kilometers if divided by 3).

How much current flows in a lightning bolt?

On average, a current of 20,000 A flows in a lightning bolt, even if the bolt lasts for only a split second. 50 mA is enough to be fatal for a human.

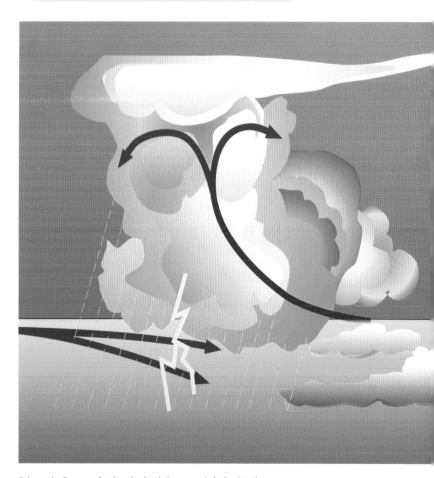

Schematic diagram of a thundercloud. Strong updrafts lead to the formation of an anvil-shaped storm front that is several miles high, and to an intake of air (blue arrow) at the front of the storm.

LIGHT: THE ELECTROMAGNETIC SPECTRUM

What is light?

Light is electromagnetic radiation, such as that emitted by the Sun, which acts like a wave in a frequency range that the human eye can perceive. At the same time, light also acts like a stream of particles, which are called photons (hence the expression "beam of light"). Electrons can be shot out of atoms and molecules can be split simply by the impact of a photon striking them. A film in a camera is exposed in this way; the light splits the silver bromide into silver and bromine. The silver darkens the film and a negative is created.

Small water droplets in the air produce a rainbow. The yellow-white sunlight is dispersed by refraction into the colors of the spectrum.

Can you sail with light in outer space?

Theoretically yes, even though it may sound crazy! The photons (particles of light) produce a small bump when they strike a surface. The transmitted force per bump is minuscule, but it has an effect due to the almost complete lack of friction in the vacuum of outer space. If you were to fit a light but gigantic sail in front of a small object, it would be continually accelerated by the sunlight. The mass would need to be minimized, as otherwise the object would be too inert to react promptly to the acceleration. However, you can only be pushed by light. Tacking, i.e. changing directions, as with the "terrestrial" sailing boats (see page 23), would not work due to the lack of friction in outer space.

What are colors?

The human eye can detect light wavelengths between about 380 and 780 nm. Short-wave light appears blue, long-wave light red. However, the eye can detect only a very small part of the whole electromagnetic spectrum. Infrared radiation, microwaves, and radio waves also belong to this spectrum but are too long for us to see. At the other end of the spectrum are ultraviolet radiation, X-rays, and gamma radiation, which are also not visible to the human eye because of their short waves.

How does X-ray radiation X-ray the body?

In the same way that glass is transparent to visible light, the body is more or less transparent to X-rays. Denser structures such as bones absorb more of the X-rays, reducing the degree of film exposure. Contrast media are sometimes used to obtain a differentiated X-ray film of internal

organs. Such media absorb the X-rays to colorize and illustrate certain tissue structures for the X-ray radiation. The energy that transports the short-wave X-ray radiation can, however, have a harmful effect on the body and bring about potentially cancerous cell changes, so it is advisable to avoid them unless necessary.

How does a microwave oven work?

Microwaves are absorbed by water and heat it up by exciting the molecules to vibrate. This process produces strong frictional heat, which heats up the food from the inside out. The appliance itself and special microwave crockery are not excited by the microwaves and remain cold.

What does VHF mean?

VHF is the abbreviation for "very high frequency" and refers to light with wavelengths between 1 and 10 m (radio frequency 30–300 MHz). VHF radio transmissions are thus transmitted with short-wave electromagnetic radiation, as opposed to the longer waves of visible light. Apart from radio programs, television programs also used to be transmitted via television antennae in this wavelength range.

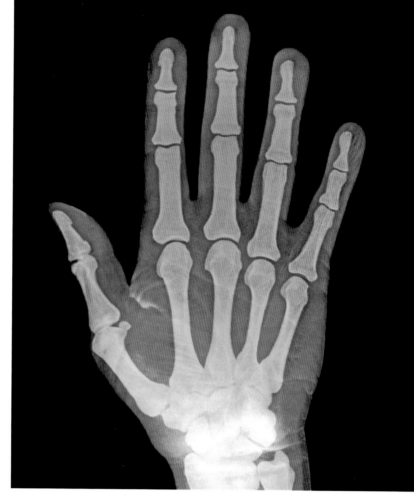

Above: An X-ray picture of a hand. X-rays help medical diagnoses by making the inside of the body visible.

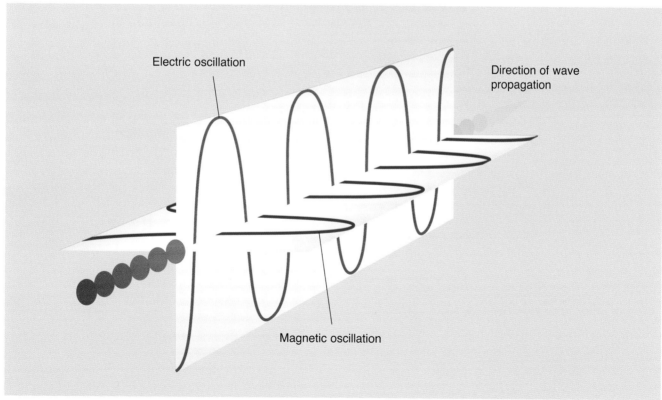

Light: a double wave—one electric and one magnetic.
That is why light is also called electromagnetic radiation.

OPTICS: MAGNIFIERS AND LASERS

How long have lenses been around?

As early as the 3rd century BC, Archimedes observed that transparent crystals could refract light beams. Refraction means the bending of a light ray as it passes from air to another medium. The degree of refraction depends on the material and the angle at which the ray strikes. With the correct grinding and shaping of the right material, we can produce a lens that focuses light on a specific point. In earlier times lenses were manufactured from expensive crystal but nowadays glass or plastic serve equally well. Archimedes is said to have used crystal as a vision aid and consequently to have invented lenses. However, it was actually not until the 11th century that the Arabic scholar Abu Ali al-Hasan Ibn al-Haitham developed the laws of light refraction. His publications led to the invention of glasses.

How does a telescope work?

A telescope consists of at least two lenses. The first, especially large lens (the objective lens) gathers the light and focuses it to form an image. This lens is shaped in such a way as to bring only very distant objects into sharp focus, i.e. it has a long focal length. Objects that are near appear blurred. A second, smaller lens (the eyepiece or ocular lens) magnifies the image. Large telescopes use a gigantic parabolic mirror instead of an objective lens to focus the light by reflection and produce the image.

How does a microscope work?

The basic principle is the same as the telescope. However, the objective lens is shaped in such a way that it focuses on objects that are close by, i.e. it has a very short focal length. The lens is small and very convex in order to produce the necessary magnification. The maximum meaningful magnification is about 1,200 times. Light waves resolve only specimens that are greater than 0.3 µm. This means that magnification at 1,000 times corresponds to 0.3 mm on the image that is produced. All smaller specimens are blurred. If the image, which is produced by the lens, is artificially magnified still further by stronger eyepieces, no new information will be forthcoming. This is the same as with a blurred photograph that

is further enlarged with a magnifier—the picture just becomes even more blurred.

What is a laser?

The term "laser" is an acronym for Light Amplification by Stimulated Emission of Radiation. A laser produces a focused light ray of a single color, i.e. light of the same wavelength. Laser rays are produced via a carrier substance such as crystal or gas. Here an effect of quantum physics, namely stimulated emission, is used, in which a single beam of light, or rather its corresponding photon, triggers the emission of further photons in a kind of chain reaction. The light waves of the laser beam bounce back and forth in phase, while being further energized by an external energy source. In medicine, lasers are used first and foremost as delicate cutting instruments. The heat created by them closes fine blood vessels by sealing them, which prevents wounds from bleeding afterwards.

However, lasers are also indispensable in many other areas of everyday life. Just a few examples are CD and DVD players, laser printers and copiers, and barcode readers at the supermarket as well as the use of laser instruments in range-finding, data communication via fiber optic cables or in light shows (e.g. pop concerts). Powerful laser beams are also used in industry for cutting materials, even metals.

The largest telescope in the world is currently the W. M. Keck Observatory on Hawaii. The mirror measures 33 ft (10 m) in diameter and can be distorted to compensate for air disturbance.

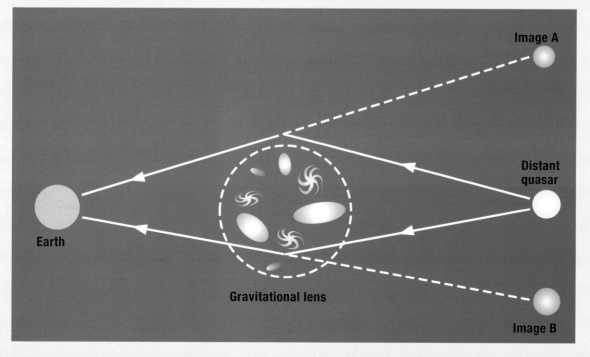

Image A

Distant quasar

Earth

Gravitational lens

Image B

A schematic representation of a gravitational lens. Between a distant quasar (bright, extremely distant nucleus of a galaxy) and the Earth, a galaxy cluster can be seen (center), which refracts the light from the quasar. In this way, two or more images of the quasar can be seen (Image A and Image B).

THE NATURE OF HEAT AND DISORDER

What is heat?

Heat is a measurement of the speed of the individual particles that make up matter. The atoms and molecules of a cooler object are slower than those of a hot object. If they are brought into direct contact with one another, the faster particles of the hot object strike those of the cold object. By the striking of the particles one against the other, the kinetic energy is distributed, i.e. the slow become quicker and the quick become slower until all the particles have roughly the same speed. For heat to be examined in detail, the properties of all the individual molecules must be taken into account. This can only be done through statistical calculations, which can therefore make the formulation of heat calculations at times very laborious.

The molecules of hot liquid move so quickly that the ones richest in energy (hottest) can leave the binding fluid in the form of vapor, and thus we get a steaming cup of hot tea or water.

Why does ice melt when heated while eggs become hard?

In solids such as ice, the molecules are bound together. If energy is supplied to the individual particles, they will move more and more rapidly. Eventually the bonds that hold them as a solid are not strong enough to hold the excited molecules and they start to break apart and flow. The result is that the solid becomes liquid. This is a physical process. A raw egg, on the other hand, becomes solid when heated due to a chemical change taking place in the molecules. The heating process breaks up the enormous egg-white and yolk molecules in places, which then strike each other with increased energy due to the heat. These molecules bind together more readily and in a different way, resulting in the hardening of the egg white and yolk.

How does a refrigerator work?

The heat is transferred from the inside of the refrigerator to the outside by using a compressor to pump a special fluid around a closed circuit. The fluid evaporates into a gas within an evaporator inside the fridge, absorbing heat. The heat is then rejected by the condenser outside the fridge as the gas condenses back into a liquid.

Does the world become more and more disordered?

In principle, yes. More energy is needed to build up ordered structures than is needed to destroy them. The molecules of a crystal, e.g. sugar, form a lattice effect and have a high degree of order. If a spoonful of sugar is put into a hot cup of coffee, it will rapidly dissolve and the structure gives way to a

Why does blowing on hot food cool it down?

When food is hot, it means that the food molecules are moving rapidly. Heat escapes from the food by various methods. Some of the hotter water molecules in the food may have enough kinetic energy to "boil" off and escape as a vapor. Also, air molecules that come in contact with the food will absorb some energy, speed up and then move away by natural convection, or by faster, forced convection if a person is blowing on the food. In the food, e.g. in a bowl of soup, only the slower molecules remain, and consequently the average speed of all the remaining molecules decreases and the soup cools down. The same principle cools us down if we stand wet in the wind. Water evaporates from the skin and in so doing the quickest molecules pass over to the gas phase first. The wind carries them away and the remaining water on the skin is colder than before.

A refrigerator cooling unit. Freon®, a gas harmful to the ozone layer, was used as a coolant until the 1990s. Modern refrigerators are cooled with butane or tetrafluorethane.

Temperatures in our universe: from hot to cold	
	Temperature °C (°F)
Big Bang	10^{32} (1.8 × 1032)
Sun's core	12.8 (23.0) million
Earth's core	6,700 (12,100)
Sun's surface	5,504 (9,939)
Surface of Venus	464 (867.2)
Boiling point of water in normal air pressure	100 (212)
Freezing point of water in normal air pressure	0 (32)
Lowest temperature on Earth (Vostok, Antarctica)	−89.2 (−128.56)
Surface of Pluto	−229 (−380.2)
Cosmological radiation	−270,425 (−454.765)
Lowest produced temperature in a physics laboratory	−273,1500001 (−459.67)

chaotic distribution of molecules in the coffee. To put the sugar back into its ordered crystalline form would only be possible with the addition of lots more energy to evaporate, refine, etc. Due to inefficiencies of energy conversion, more energy would be required (and more disorder created) to bring order back to the sugar than would be gained by the sugar itself in becoming crystalline again. Hence disorder in the universe—called entropy by physicists—increases slowly but surely.

Steam locomotives convert the heat of a gas (in the boiler) into mechanical energy.

Above: A schematic representation of hot liquid in a pot. The hotter the liquid, the quicker the individual particles move. The quickest particles can leave the bond of the liquid and cross to the gas phase.

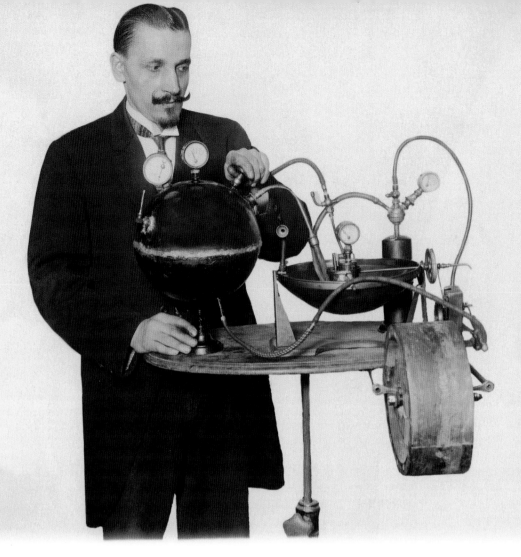

THE DREAM OF PERPETUAL MOTION

There have been countless attempts to patent a perpetual motion machine, but even the most complicated machines cannot flout the laws of nature.

What is a perpetual motion machine?

A perpetual motion machine is a machine that, once set in motion, would run forever without a supply of energy. This pipe dream of countless inventors and hobbyists could solve all the energy problems of the world, if the machine were, for example, an energy-supplying engine. There are three kinds of perpetual motion: perpetual motion type 1, in which the energy, which the machine should supply, is mechanically produced; perpetual motion type 2, where the energy is generated from the temperature of the surroundings; and perpetual motion type 3, which continues indefinitely but does not supply any excess energy.

Who was the first person to have the idea of the perpetual motion machine?

Tradition has it that the earliest records of the construction of a perpetual motion machine come from the 8th century. The Indian astronomer Lalla had the idea of a wheel driven by liquid mercury, which could change its center of gravity and thereby push itself. Leonardo da Vinci (1452–1519) was also preoccupied with the idea of a perpetual motion machine but he soon came to the conclusion that it was theoretically impossible to construct one.

Generating energy from nothing: dream or possibility?

Even a vacuum has a basic amount of energy, which is why minuscule fields or pairs of particles-antiparticles can spontaneously form, although they disintegrate extremely rapidly. To tap into this so-called "flickering" of the vacuum to generate energy from it is the subject matter of sci-fi novels, which visualize a future scenario in which a huge potential of usable energy is available. Since, however, in reality there are only minuscule fluctuations, which produce just a few elementary particles, a technical use is unfortunately unimaginable.

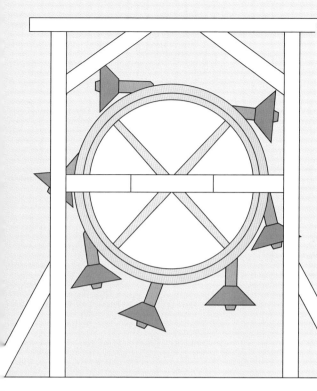

Villard de Honnecourt outlined this perpetual motion device around 1230, but it did not work.

minimal but it is not zero. Frictionless conditions are known only in the microscopic field. So-called superconductivity (frictionless flowing current) or superfluidity (also known as quantum fluids) close to temperatures of absolute zero (−459.67°F −273.15°C) belong to this field. However, to reach these low temperatures where such effects occur, and above all to shield them from external warming, energy would have to be expended. This form of perpetual motion machine is thus impracticable.

Are perpetual motion machines at least theoretically conceivable?

No, at least not the perpetual motion machines of type 1 and 2. A machine based on type 1 contravenes one of the cornerstones of physics, the theory of conservation of energy, which states that the total energy of a sealed system is constant. Energy can be converted into other forms, for example kinetic energy into heat, but it does not produce energy from nothing. A perpetual motion machine based on type 2 would also be inconsistent, as it would extract its energy from the heat of its surroundings. However, heat cannot transmit itself under its own impetus from a cooler to a hotter object. To do that, energy is necessary, and more energy than is ultimately generated. A type 2 perpetual motion machine would come to a standstill as soon as the surroundings cooled down.

And what about the chances for a type 3 perpetual motion machine?

Such a machine is at least theoretically conceivable. However, in this case braking friction, which converts kinetic energy into heat, throws a spanner into the calculations. Even the Earth on its orbit around the Sun does not represent a perpetual motion machine, for it is constantly slowed down when it collides with the tiniest particles in space. Of course the effect is

Even Newton's pendulum does not move endlessly. The energy transfer from sphere to sphere does not proceed without frictional loss and heat generation.

IT'S GETTING COLD: EXOTIC PHYSICS AT ABSOLUTE ZERO

Can temperatures drop indefinitely?

No, for temperature is simply the measure of the kinetic energy of the particles that make up matter. If particles are slowed down more and more—i.e. an object cools down—at some point they would all stop moving (vibrating). There would be no condition colder than this. In reality, particles cannot be slowed to a complete stop, since the electrons could no longer maintain their distance from the atomic nucleus. There is, however, a minimal energy that they can have, so-called zero-point energy. This state is reached at $-459.67°F$ ($-273.15°C$) and thus marks absolute zero, which is expressed with the thermodynamic unit 0 K on the Kelvin scale. 273.15 K is exactly 0°C on the Celsius scale.

What are superconductors?

Superconductors are conductors in which electrical current can flow without resistance. Normally, the electrons strike the atoms of the conductor as well as one another, which makes the conductor resistive. If a conductor is cooled to a very low temperature, its atoms "vibrate" less, which means that two electrons can travel together in a kind of coupled pairing, and this prevents them colliding with one another and with the atoms. For most conductors this state is not reached until a few degrees above absolute zero. There are, however, so-called high-temperature superconductors, which have superconducting properties in "warmer" temperatures and for which cooling with liquid nitrogen (boiling point $-320.44°F/-195.8°C$) is sufficient. The low temperature superconductors are used technically for the production of very strong and stable magnetic fields and are used in medicine, for example in MRI scanners, or as magnetic lenses in particle accelerators such as the one at DESY (Deutsches Elektronen-Synchrotron, a research center for elementary particles) in Hamburg. High temperature superconductors are being used for power transmission and may have potential for use in nuclear fusion reactors.

Can magnets fly?

A magnetic field induces flowing current in a superconducting coil. In the coil, which at its

A magnet hovers above a superconductor. The energy that is necessary to start the current flow in the superconductor is in the magnet's magnetic field.

Sir William Thomson, Baron Kelvin of Largs (1824–1907), also known as Lord Kelvin, founded modern thermodynamics.

simplest is a closed ring, the current produces its own magnetic field, which repels that of the other magnetic field. Thus a magnet above a superconducting ring hovers, since the magnetic field produced by the current flow in the superconductor repels it.

Bose Einstein Condensate: identically connected atoms

Single atom gases can, with sufficient pressure and extremely low temperatures, be formed into a very unusual state: the so-called Bose Einstein Condensate (BEC). This is where all the atoms are in the same quantum state and they react like a single particle. Bose and Einstein predicted and formulated this phenomenon in the 1920s, but it was not until 1995 that this matter state was reached in experiments. To do it, the atoms were pre-cooled by laser and then caught in a magnetic-optic trap.

More fluid than fluid: what is superfluidity?

If helium is cooled to absolute zero, it first becomes fluid at nearly −452.02°F (−268.9°C). If it is cooled even more, the fluidity alters and loses its viscosity, meaning that it suddenly flows without internal friction. This superfluidity shows effects that are hardly imaginable: it completely wets any container and could escape through a hole in the lid of the container, which means that it can flow upwards! Other molecules can swim and rotate frictionless in this superfluidity, behaving as they would in a vacuum. This effect is used in modern physics for spectroscopy (analysis of matter through its reaction to light, for example absorption of different wavelengths). In addition to helium, only the lithium isotope ^{6}Li can assume the state of superfluidity.

A tank with cooled helium. Liquid helium can reach the state of superfluidity, a frictionless fluid.

EINSTEIN'S THEORY OF RELATIVITY: A SMALL REVOLUTION!

Is everything relative?
No, and that may sound surprising. Many quantities behave relatively to each other, for example speed and place, but there is one absolute quantity: the speed of light in a vacuum.

What does relative mean?
If I see an object approaching me, there are three basic possibilities: first, I am stationary and the object is moving towards me; second, the object is stationary and I am moving towards it; third, we are both moving towards each other. Who is still and who is moving can only be decided with regard to a fixed reference frame, for example a tree at the side of the road. If the tree is stationary relative to me, then I know I am stationary and the object is approaching me. It could also be argued that the tree is moving with the Earth's rotation and

therefore it is not a suitable reference point as I am also moving together with the Earth. The ultimate consequence means that it cannot be decided who or what is moving, but this statement can apply only with reference to arbitrarily definable frames of reference—thus relative to them.

What does time have to do with speed?
The time of an object passes all the more slowly the faster it is moving; and also its mass increases with the speed. Both effects are only observable at very high speeds way beyond our level of experience, but they are measurable with accurate atomic clocks placed in rockets. At close to the speed of light, time would pass very slowly and it would even stop if the speed of light were able to be reached. If an astronaut flies away from the Earth at close to the speed of light and

One of the first atomic clocks, from 1955. Nobel Prize winner Charles H. Townes (born 1915) explains the difference between it and a normal electric clock.

The young Albert Einstein (around 1905) at the time of publication of his theory of relativity.

returns—after what for him would be a short period—it could be that hundreds of years had already passed on Earth.

How high is the greatest possible speed?

The speed of light in vacuum is unbelievably 186,000 miles/s (299,792,458 km/s). Nothing travels faster than this, and matter cannot quite reach that speed.

Why can't time go backwards?

At speeds less than that of light, time travels forwards. At the speed of light, it stops. To move backwards it would have to move at more than the speed of light. However, as matter can only ever be slower than light because the energy to get closer and closer to the speed of light becomes enormous, time also moves for it in only one direction—forward. Logic also precludes time travel into the past. Otherwise the sequence of events could be changed retroactively. For instance, say you travel back in time and prevent your parents from getting to know one another by going with your father to play bowls; you would never have been born, so how can you go bowling with your father? Retrospectively, if you thus ceased to exist, then you would not have gone bowling and your parents would have got to know one another. You would still have been born and would then once again prevent your conception. The resulting endless circle is an insoluble paradox that would throw the world out of kilter.

What is the space-time continuum?

The three dimensions—height, breadth, and depth—are bound together with the fourth dimension—time—to a continuum, space-time for short. As even physicists are unable to imagine these four dimensions in a concrete way, they explain space-time as a thin rubber skin. Matter directly affects space-time; a large mass dents it to some extent. Stars have the effect of pebbles in it; they form a relative hollow in this rubber skin and stretch it a little.

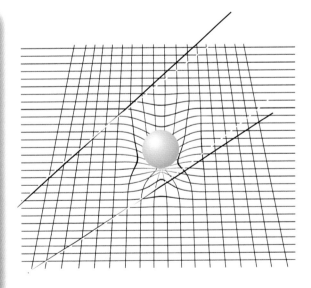

Light rays are bent by gravitation fields, here by a sun. The black line shows the path of a straight light ray, the yellow line the actual light ray.

OUR SOLAR SYSTEM

The comet Hale-Bopp, one of the brightest comets of the 20th century. The tail consists of gas (blue) and fine dust (turquoise).

How many planets orbit the Sun?
Following the new definition in 2006, eight planets belong to our solar system: Mercury, Venus, Earth, Mars, Jupiter, Saturn, Uranus, and Neptune.

How old is the Earth?
Around 4.6 billion years ago our solar system, and along with it the Earth, was created from a huge cloud of gas and dust. In comparison with the universe, which is 13.7 billion years old, the Earth is comparatively young.

What is a planet?
A planet is a heavenly body that orbits the Sun and shines with reflected light. It must have sufficient mass available to be almost spherically shaped through its own gravitational force and it must have cleared its elliptical orbit of other similar objects, by binding smaller objects (moons) to it by its gravitational force, or by absorbing impacts. The International Astronomical Union (IAU) adopted this definition on August 24, 2006. As a result, Pluto lost its former status as a planet, as it has not been able to clear its orbit of other objects.

Why does a comet have a tail?
Comets are small celestial bodies that come so close to the Sun that they partially evaporate and, besides gas, also lose small dust particles. The pressure of the sunlight pushes this fine cloud of gas and dust away from the Sun. The observer receives the impression of a comet nucleus (the object itself) with a distinct tail. Comets either orbit the Sun on a highly elliptical path, or they are travelers who have lost their way in the solar system and pass close to the Sun. Organic

The planets in our solar system

Planet	Diameter km	Mass kg	Density g/cm³	Distance from the Sun	Orbital period (length of year) D=day, Y=year	Rotation period (length of day) M=minute, H=hour, D=day
Mercury	4,878	3.302×10^{23}	5.427	0.387	87.97 D	58 D, 15 H, 36 M
Venus	12,103.6	4.869×10^{24}	5.243	0.723	224.7 D	243 D, 0 H, 27 M
Earth	12,735	5.974×10^{24}	5.515	1 AU	365.26 D	23 H, 56 M
Mars	6,794	6.419×10^{23}	3.933	1.524	686.98 D	24 H, 37 M
Jupiter	138,342	1.899×10^{27}	1.326	5.204	11.86 D	9 H, 55 M
Saturn	114,174	5.685×10^{26}	0.687	9.582	29.457 Y	10 H, 47 M
Uranus	50,533	8.683×10^{25}	1.2	19.201	84 Y	17 H, 14 M
Neptune	48,865	1.024×10^{26}	1.638	30.047	164.8 Y	16 H, 6 M

* 1 AU (astronomical unit) is the distance from the Earth to the Sun, which is 92.6 million miles (around 149 million km).

Saturn and its famous rings. The atmosphere in the image has been colored in order to show fine structures more clearly in contrast.

molecules have been discovered in comet nuclei (so-called snowballs). It is thus debated whether comet impacts might be a source of the beginning of life on Earth.

Are there other solar systems?

Yes, in the Milky Way alone there are anywhere between 100 billion and 500 billion stars and beyond that hundreds of billions of other galaxies all with many millions of stars. In a radius of about 300 light years around the Earth, approximately 7 percent of the stars examined were found to have planets. So far, however, scientists have only been able to make out relatively large and heavy planets, so the percentage may be much higher.

The center of the Milky Way, our galaxy, in the constellation Sagittarius. Dark dust clouds obscure the view of the hot nucleus.

The Oort cloud: is it responsible for waves of extinction on Earth?

On the edge of our solar system are the remains of the objects from which the planets were created. Countless objects, from the size of dust particles to massive chunks of ice and rock, revolve around the Sun at a distance of three light years. The objects of the Oort cloud are distributed around the solar system on a kind of spherical dish. Oort serves as a reservoir for comets and meteorites (chunks of rock). Around every 30 million years the Earth experiences a wave of extinction of species. It is possible that an object with the same period of revolution, for example a still undiscovered planet or a very faint asteroidal companion of the Sun (brown dwarf), pulls numerous chunks of rock from the cloud into the interior of our solar system. This increases the probability of large meteorites smashing into the Earth. This, together with the climate change that followed, and the dust thrown into the atmosphere, darkening the sky, is assumed to have happened around 65 million years ago and was responsible for the extinction of dinosaurs among other things. However, up to now there is no clear evidence to support it.

THE UNIVERSE:
IN THE BEGINNING WAS A BANG

When was the universe created?

The Big Bang occurred 13.7 billion years ago and an unimaginable amount of energy was released. As time was also created in the Big Bang, the question of how the world looked beforehand makes no sense—there is no beforehand. The Big Bang cannot be imagined as a simple explosion that took place in a space, since space was also created at that moment. One theory proposes that space may have expanded at more than the speed of light at the beginning. Neither mass nor energy can move faster than light in space, but the theory does not contradict the theory of relativity (that the space-time continuum expanded with more than the speed of light), since space consists of neither mass nor energy.

Does the Big Bang have an echo?

Yes, at least as light, since sound cannot spread in outer space (for sound needs a carrier, such as air, which is lacking in outer space). The remains of the radiation created by the Big Bang have since

cooled to 2.725 K (to just under $-454°F/-270°C$). What we have is therefore just a cold afterglow. This cosmological radiation was predicted theoretically in the 1940s but was only discovered in 1964 quite by chance by Arno Penzias and Robert Woodrow Wilson. They received the 1978 Nobel Prize for Physics for the discovery.

Record-breakers

The temperature at the beginning of the universe was about $10^{32}°C$ with a density of 10^{94} g/cm^3. These are very large numbers, e.g. 10^{32} means 1 followed by 32 zeroes. In comparison, the density and temperature in the Sun's core are low: 2.8 million °C and 150 g/cm^3. During expansion, the universe cooled very rapidly. At the age of 10^{-33} seconds it was "only" $10^{25}°C$ hot, thus cooler by around a factor of 10 million. After one second the temperature of the universe was only 10 billion °C.

How did the world develop after the Big Bang?

The first quarks and electrons came into being after 10^{-33} seconds. Protons were formed later, each having three quarks, and eventually the first simple atoms were formed, each from a proton and an electron. The early universe therefore consisted mainly of hydrogen gas. Due to their attractive force, huge gas clouds concentrated more and more densely together and collapsed, forming the first stars. The clouds were so huge that billions upon billions of galaxies—consisting of billions of stars—were created. Nuclear fusion occurred within the stars and the first light elements (e.g. helium) were formed. Nuclear fusion inside stars can create only light elements. Anything that is heavier than iron must have been created through the enormous internal pressure of exploding stars. Thus our Earth consists of recycled stardust.

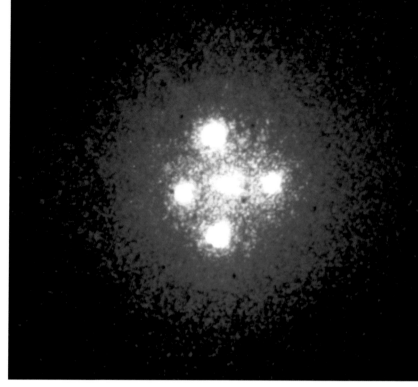

Above: A quasar is distorted into four individual images by a gravitational lens. The point in the center is the object (galaxy) whose mass is bending the light.

Quasars: by now extinct

The first galaxies shone a lot brighter than their counterparts of today. As they look "quasi" (almost) like a star through a telescope, they are called quasars. They are seen only at remote distances (several billion light years), since they no longer exist today, having turned into normal galaxies. However, their light is still on its way to us. So, when we look at them, we are in fact seeing far back into the past.

Left: Detail of Omega Nebula. The gas cloud consists mainly of hydrogen, the basic element of our universe.

Timeline of the universe

Time	Temperature	Event
0 seconds	10^{32} K	Big Bang
10^{-36} seconds	10^{27} K	Separation of the strong interaction
10^{-33} seconds	10^{25} K	Formation of quarks
10^{-12} seconds	10^{16} K	The four fundamental forces are separated
10^{-6} seconds	10^{13} K	Quarks bind, protons and neutrons form
10^{-4} seconds	10^{12} K	Neutrinos uncouple, antiprotons and antineutrons are annihilated
1 second	10^{10} K	Positrons (antielectrons) are annihilated
10 seconds	$< 10^9$ K	Formation of atomic nuclei
400,000 years	ca 3,000 K	Formation of stable atoms with electron sheath, decoupling of cosmological radiation
1 billion years	ca 2,500 K	First galaxies (quasars) are formed
9.2 billion years	ca. 30 K	Earth is formed
13.7 billion years	2.7 K	Human beings emerge

BLACK HOLES, WORMHOLES, SPACE EXOTICA: SCIENCE FICTION OR REALITY?

A huge black hole in the center of a galaxy. The huge mass of the black hole bends space-time.

What is a black hole?

A black hole is a celestial body with extremely high density. Its gravitation near the surface is so great that everything, even light, is attracted to it and cannot escape it. For the Earth to turn into a black hole, it would need to be crushed to a ball measuring around $1/3$ in (9 mm) in diameter.

Are there black holes in nature?

Yes, there are many of them. The most famous are Cygnus X-1 in the Cygnus constellation and Sgr A in the Sagittarius constellation. Sgr A is an enormous black hole in the center of the Milky Way—its mass is equal to more than 3 million solar masses.

As black holes are literally black, they cannot be observed directly. However, their gravitational field accelerates charged matter so strongly even

at remote distances that they send out high-energy X-radiation, which can be observed. A sort of aura of X-radiation thus appears around black holes.

How does a black hole form?

Nuclear fusion inside a star produces great pressure through released energy. This pressure counteracts the star's own gravity.

If nuclear fusion ceases—when the star has used up all its fuel—the pressure drops and the star implodes. If the star is heavy enough, the momentum of the implosion is sufficient for the electrons inside the star to be pushed into the atomic nuclei and initially neutrons are formed. If the counterpressure of the neutrons among themselves stops the collapse, then a neutron star is formed. If the counterpressure is insufficient, the neutrons also disintegrate and the star collapses to a black hole.

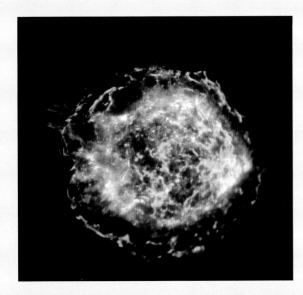

Cassiopeia A, a supernova remnant in the constellation of Cassiopeia, emitting energy-rich X-radiation. A black hole could be the cause.

During the implosion, nuclear fusion reignites at the outer edge of the star as hydrogen is still available there as fuel. This surge of energy allows the outer areas of the star to explode while the core continues to collapse. This star explosion is called a supernova.

Can black holes explode?

Yes, at least that is what the famous physicist Stephen Hawking (born 1942) suspects. The reason for this is the spontaneous formation of matter-antimatter particle pairs in the black hole's gravitational field.

If they form right on the border, from which nothing else can escape the black hole, it is possible for one particle to be thrown back into the black hole and the other one flung away from it. For an external observer, a black hole thus theoretically emits individual particles from time to time, which form so-called Hawking radiation. As matter cannot be formed from nothing, the mass of the black hole must decrease by the mass of the emitted particle. If nothing more falls into the black hole from the outside, it must therefore become more mass depleted over time, until it falls below a critical density and then the black hole explodes.

Wormholes could theoretically form if a mass stretches the space-time continuum so far that it merges with the other side of the continuum. For this to happen, the other side—antigravity—must also stretch.

CREEPY: DARK MATTER

Is there a world beyond the world?

"There are more things in heaven and Earth [...] than are dreamt of in your philosophy."

Shakespeare's quote is readily cited as confirmation of an invisible world beyond our imagination. Mystics believe that unknown forces exist, such as invisible energies or fields. But how is this viewed by modern physics? Here, too, we speculate about worlds that are invisible to us, about parallel universes (such as are described in science fiction literature), about alien dimensions or dark matter.

However, physicists have a much harder time than mystics, since they must search for evidence for their theories or explain them plausibly through known natural phenomena. The evidence for alien space dimensions is still to be found but, if string theory is correct, we will be able to discover it in the next few decades with the aid of particle accelerators.

Is matter missing in the universe?

In all likelihood, yes. If we observe other galaxies through telescopes, we can, thanks to the Doppler Effect (see information box), infer the speeds of individual stars. But there is a problem: it would seem that the matter of the galaxies that is visible is not sufficient to hold the stars together; they are too quick.

Matter can of course be concealed in dark gas clouds, rock, planets, or in very faint dwarf stars (brown dwarfs). However, by even the most generous projections, this cannot explain the high speeds of the stars.

In the Coma Cluster in Berenice's Hair, the mass of the galaxies would have to be 400 times larger than what has been observed for the galaxies themselves as well as the cluster of galaxies to be stable.

Doppler Effect

This is a phenomenon that everyone knows. If a police car with its siren approaches you, you hear the siren much higher at that point than later when the car has gone past. The speed alters the wavelength of the sound. On approaching, the sound waves become shorter, and on moving away they become longer (with respect to the ear of the listener). A similar effect occurs with radiated light, but this is discernible only at very high speeds. Thus, the faster an object moves away from us, the redder (long wave) the light that is radiated or reflected from it. Vice versa, when an object approaches, the light becomes more blue (short wave).

Dark matter: the solution to the problem?

Another attempted explanation for the apparently missing matter in the universe is the theory of dark matter. Dark matter (according to the theory) is only in contact with the rest of the universe by

Bernard Sadoulet with his WIMP detector in Berkeley, California, USA. WIMPs are low-mass particles, such as neutrinos, which contribute to the universe's "missing mass."

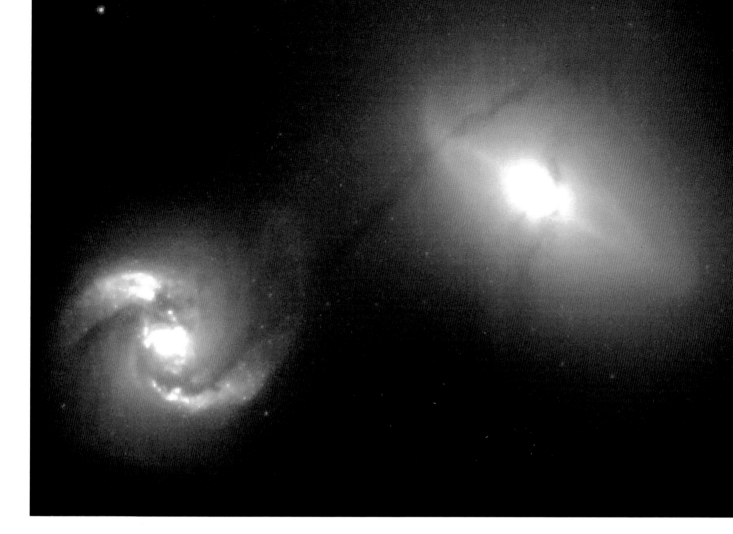

means of gravity and therefore cannot radiate light. The counterpart to dark matter is dark energy, which is, among other things, responsible for the expansion of the universe. It is possible that the world even consists mainly of dark matter and dark energy: 73 percent dark energy, 23 percent dark matter, 3.7 percent normal matter and energy, and 0.3 percent so-called neutrinos. In this distribution, the known laws of nature in their hitherto accepted form would still be valid, though we would be living in a world that for the most part would remain completely invisible to us. It is hoped in future years that the effects of dark matter can be proved with new particle accelerators, since up to now there is no evidence for its existence.

A section of the sky, seen through the Hubble space telescope. The image on the right is the actual image. On the left is the same section with 37 artificial stars superimposed using a computer. If dark matter existed in the form of faint dwarf stars (red dwarfs, brown dwarfs), many additional objects should be observable in the image on the right. Dark matter must therefore exist in a different form.

Above: NGC 1409 (right) and 1410 (left), two nearby galaxies that are closely connected by their gravity. They collided around 100 million years ago. Since then, the larger galaxy has sucked matter from the smaller one—the flow of matter is clearly recognizable as the diagonally running dark line (cold gas). The hazy mist connecting the two galaxies is made up of many galaxies.

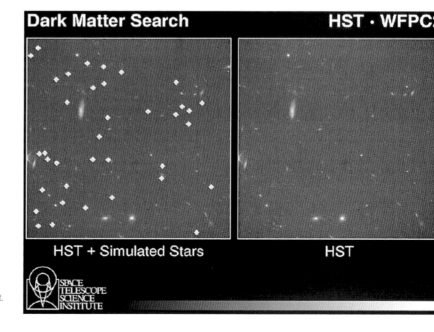

QUANTUM PHYSICS: WHEN NATURE TAKES A LEAP

A wall of 30 cobalt atoms arranged in a ring, taken with a force microscope. Each individual atom was exactly positioned to configure this ring. With this technology, it is hoped that extremely small circuits for quantum computers will soon be developed.

What is the famous quantum leap?

The well-worn expression "quantum leap" in everyday terms signifies a breakthrough or an especially big step in development. But what actually is a quantum leap? In everyday experience, all quantities are continuous. It is true that we measure time in units (e.g. seconds, hours), but time itself does not seem to jump but rather flows continuously. All other quantities, too, such as length, force, or energy, seem continuous to us. In nature, however, with respect to quantities there are always only multiples of a minuscule elementary unit or basic building block. As the elementary units are incredibly small, we do not feel their effects in our everyday world. Looked at in extreme detail, the world corresponds to a chessboard on which the figures can only jump from square to square and cannot be positioned between two squares. The leap from one field to the other, i.e. a quantum leap, is therefore actually extremely short, just 10^{-35} m in length. The advertising industry would do well to reconsider the use of the term when promoting improvements to a product, since a "quantum leap" in terms of quality would be minimal, hardly even noticeable.

Is the world made up of particles or waves?

"Both" is the spontaneous answer that we would like to give—matter is made up of particles, light of waves. However, light can produce a direct push or impact at certain points as if it were made up of particles. These elementary particles that move with the speed of light are called photons. And what about matter? Imagine a wall with two tiny slits in it. If this wall is bombarded with electrons, they are either reflected or they fly through one or other of the cracks. Actually, they fly through both cracks simultaneously, exactly the way a wave on the surface of the water can simultaneously pass through two

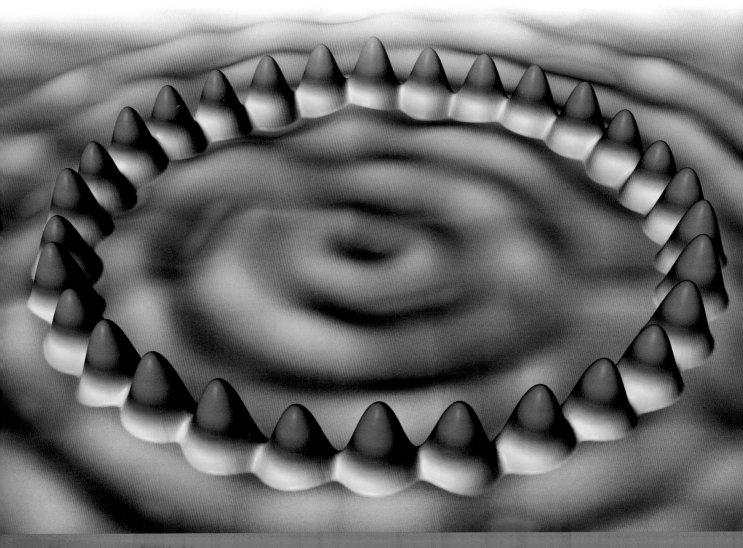

Richard Feynman (1918–1988), one of the leading quantum physicists of the 20th century.

The dream of "beaming"

Beaming means scanning an object and measuring the position and velocity of all the subatomic component particles in order to reconstruct this object exactly in a different location. Instead of the object, only the information about the object would be conveyed from one place to the other. Due to Heisenberg's Uncertainty Principle, this is an impossible dream. However, the Austrian quantum physicist Anton Zeilinger (born 1945) has succeeded in beaming individual photons.

Richard Feynman (1918–1988), who worked intensively with quantum mechanics, said, "I think you can say with certainty that no-one understands quantum mechanics."

Are all measurements inexact?

Yes, and this is even a law of nature, at least on the quantum level. The Heisenberg Uncertainty Principle states that it is not possible to measure exactly both the position and velocity of a particle at the same time. It may be explained like this: if an attempt were made to confine a tiny particle, for example an electron, in a very small space with the aid of force fields, the velocity of the particle would then be all the more indeterminate. The result would be that the electron could become so quick that it could break out of its prison, unless extremely strong fields were available to hold it. If it is successfully confined, it can suddenly emerge on the other side of the prison even though it actually should not be there. This electron behavior is also called the tunnel effect.

separate arches under a bridge. The wave is, after all, not a moving point but a broad front. These electron waves are real—they are used, for example, in electron microscopy. However, if you examine the exact path of each electron with a measuring device, the wave collapses and you actually see only particles. This characteristic is mind-blowing for the human imagination to visualize. It was no surprise that the famous physicist and Nobel Prize winner

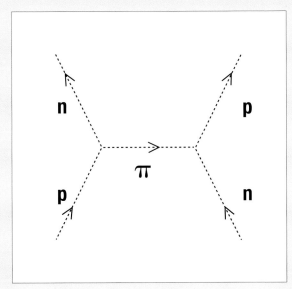

The Feynman diagram of pion exchange (π^+) between a proton (p) and a neutron (n), which convert into one another.

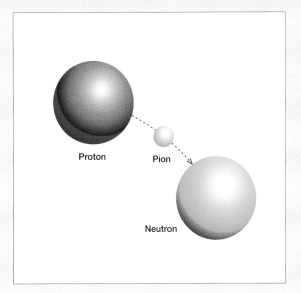

A graphic representation of the Feynman diagram. The proton sends a pion to the neutron and yields its charge. It thus becomes a neutron and the neutron becomes a proton.

The Earth and its moon, here causing a solar eclipse, are only tiny elements in a complex universe.

THE SEARCH FOR THE THEORY OF EVERYTHING (TOE)

Is there a theory of everything?

Perhaps, anyway the scientific world is looking for it. But is not nature too complex and rich in structure to allow itself to be squeezed into a single formula? Take matter, for example. It is made of the most diverse molecules and atoms, substances and compounds, but the bottom line is that it is fundamentally formed from quarks and electrons. Moreover, matter can be converted into energy. So if photons (as carriers of light) and quarks and electrons are transferable into one another, they can be combined in a unified theory. Meanwhile, of the four known fundamental forces of nature, three can be combined into one theory: electromagnetic force, the strong nuclear force, and the weak nuclear force. Up to now only gravity cannot be included. If it were, we would have a theory for all the forces of nature and could express a theory for everything. Nevertheless, nature would not allow itself to be "calculated" since, as a result of the Heisenberg Uncertainty Principle, the exact starting point for future calculations is not arbitrarily measurable.

What is the principle of least action?

The principle of least action is a basic principle of mechanics. In school we learn that a ball's flight curve is a parabola, which can be calculated using the law of the force of gravity. It can also be expressed thus: the chosen path of an object is the one for which the sum of the kinetic and potential energy of each point along the path gives a minimum value. In other words, the path of least effort is chosen. The potential energy at every point along the flight path depends on the gravitational field. That is the problem with these kinds of formulae. They can be expressed simply enough, but to calculate them in real-life situations, the so-called boundary conditions (such as the type of gravitational field) must be known. The necessary mathematics for it is, to some extent, so complicated that in schools it is preferable to teach the parabola as trajectory.

How many dimensions are there?

The theory of relativity describes four dimensions (three spatial—length, breadth, depth—and time). However, new theories act on the assumption of

10 or 11 dimensions. This is the result of a simple-sounding idea. It would be very convenient if all matter and particles were only based on one single fundamental element. Imagine a tiny piece of thread that had different characteristics depending on which way it swung—this way it's a quark, this way an electron, that way a photon. If we try on the basis of this idea to express the known effects of quantum mechanics by means of fewer formulae, then the equations are only solvable if we accept that the world is based on not just four dimensions but on 10 or 11. These additional dimensions would be hidden and would occur only in the extreme microcosm. The "string" (as physicists call it), on the other hand, oscillates in all dimensions. There is still no experimental evidence for the string theory. Moreover, the underlying mathematics is so complicated that some parts of the theory are still not calculable with our current state of knowledge. If string effects could be successfully shown in experiments, great advances would be made in the search for the theory of everything.

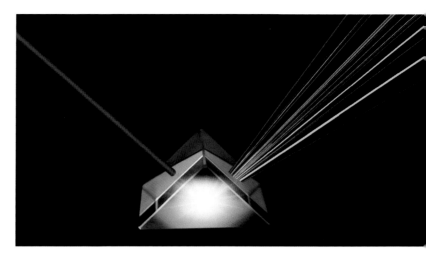

A light ray is fractionalized in a prism into its component parts. The refraction depends on the color (wavelength) and its speed within the glass.

Light always takes the quickest route

How simple it is to summarize optics. Light moves quicker in air than in glass. If the path of a ray of light passes partly through air and partly through glass, then the shortest way is not necessarily the quickest, which leads to the phenomenon of refraction.

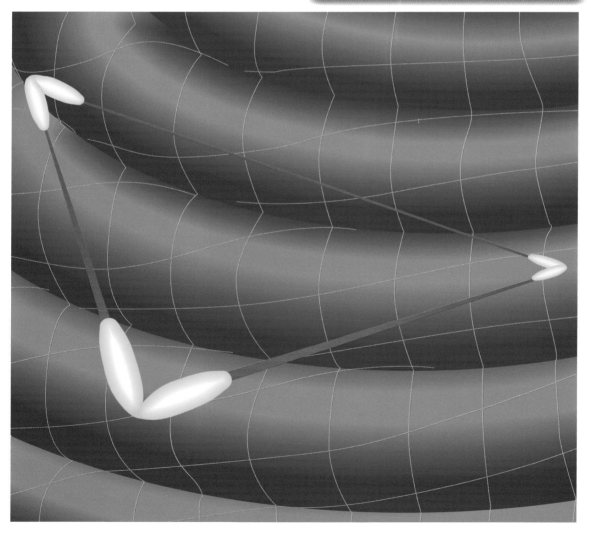

A hypothetical detector of gravitational waves, which are bending space. The three laser beams would be deflected by the waves and thus no longer reach their destinations.

NOW FOR PHILOSOPHY:
WHY WAS THERE A BIG BANG?

What is the meaning of the universe?

Many religions try on the basis of a history of creation to discover a meaning for the world. Did God create the Big Bang and with it the entire universe, and since then watch how it developed? The biggest problem when pondering the Big Bang is the lack of belief that space as well as time came into being with the Big Bang. And where did it all *originally* come from? It could hardly have all come from nothing. Or did it? Modern science understandably has difficulties with this point. This is where modern cosmology, with its partly revolutionary ideas, begins. Cosmology is a branch of physics that tries to explain the history and structure of the universe. It cannot answer the question of the meaning of the universe, however, as this represents a subjective view of the world.

The Creation of Adam painted by Michelangelo around 1508–1512. In the biblical creation, God created man in his own image.

Where does uncertainty begin?

Nowadays, physicists believe the structures of the universe and its history of development can be properly explained and reconstructed. If it is assumed that the universe was created in the Big Bang, however, then the first 10^{-33} seconds would still seem to be in the realm of the purely theoretical, since space is supposed to have expanded at speeds faster than light during this so-called "inflationary phase."

Are there alternatives to the Big Bang hypothesis, the "creation from nothing?"

Yes, there are several theories. One very interesting approach is the so-called ekpyrotic universe, which physicists Paul Steinhardt and Neil Turok thought up. Their theory is based on the acceptance that space has ten dimensions, as also postulated by the

Detail of the Orion Nebula, the birthplace of many young stars.

string theory. To put it in a nutshell, at least two cold, virtually empty, four-dimensional universes—branes—exist side by side. 13.7 billion years ago one of the branes, which was moving along a fifth space dimension, collided with a second. In the collision, the entire kinetic energy of the striking brane was converted into radiation, matter, and expansion of space. Due to quantum effects, the brane's movement became wavy through the fifth dimension, which is why the collision did not take place all at once. This explains the fluctuation of cosmological radiation. According to the theory, then, the Big Bang was not "creation from nothing," but rather an effect produced by two colliding branes. The advantages of this hypothesis are clear: there is no inflationary phase at the start of space expansion and the world is not born at one single point with infinite density and temperature that came from nothing, and furthermore time exists before the collision. The whole basic consideration of the ekpyrotic universe (see information box), however, rests on the unproved string theory, and so it remains in this respect pure hypothesis. And the philosophical question about the whys and wherefores also remains unanswered, for we are simply left with yet another question: "Where did the original branes come from?" For the time being, finding the answer to this question will continue to be the task of religion and philosophy.

What does ekpyrosis mean?

Ekpyrosis is an ancient Greek expression meaning "out of the fire." The idea already existed in Germanic/Nordic mythology as Ragna Rök, an apocalyptic battle in which the known world will burn and be consumed in flames, and a new, different world will be created. The old gods go down with the old world and new gods will come to rule over the new.

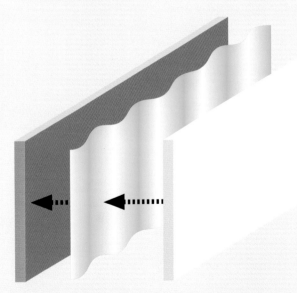

Schematic representation of the collision of universes ("branes"), as postulated in the theory of an ekpyrotic universe. The wavy blue line represents a brane, which is being pushed by the brane on the right towards the brane on the left, with which it collides.

Sugar

Periodic table

Phosphate and sulfur

19 K Potassium	20 Ca Calcium	21 Sc Scandium	22 Ti Titanium	23 V Vanadium	C Chro
37 Rb Rubidium	38 Sr Strontium	39 Y Yttrium	40 Zr Zirconium	41 Nb Niobium	M Molyb
55 Cs Cesium	56 Ba Barium	La-Lu Lanthanum	72 Hf Hafnium	73 Ta Tantalum	V Tung
87 Fr	88 Ra	Ac-Lr	104 Rf	105 Db	S

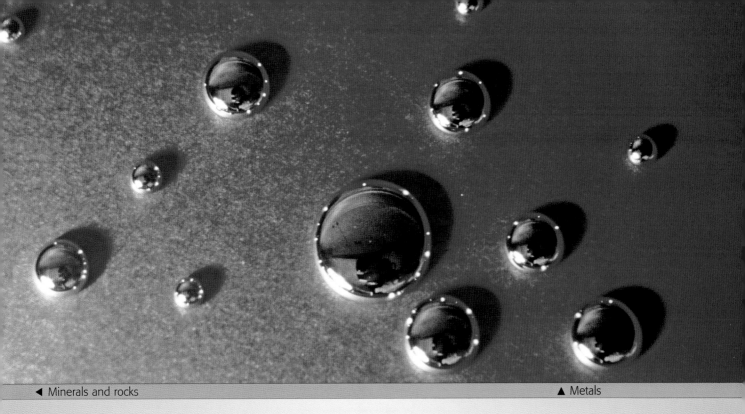

◄ Minerals and rocks

▲ Metals

CHEMISTRY

Chemistry is the science of substances. Substances are made up of atoms, which can form complex compounds when merged together. Chemical reactions are present in every aspect of our lives, be it metal, which rusts by its reaction with oxygen, sugar, which is burned in our bodies as energy, or gasoline in a car engine. All too frequently, chemistry is associated with synthetic materials. Such a view, however, excludes a large part of our environment. For no matter what it is—stick or stone, air or water, animal, plant, or human—everything is made up of chemical elements and compounds.

Atoms

Acids and bases

CHEMISTRY: THE WORLD OF SUBSTANCES

What is chemistry?

Chemistry is the science of the composition, properties, and reactions of the substances that make up our world. The substances, or matter, are made up of atoms, the basic units of matter. Electron sheaths are responsible for the properties of atoms and molecules. So you could describe chemistry in one sense as atomic physics, which, however, should not be confused with nuclear physics, which mainly studies the properties of the nucleus of the atom.

Why is chemistry an independent discipline?

The boundaries between the fields of physics and chemistry are actually not easy to define. Parts of chemistry overlap with atomic or molecular physics. Chemistry, especially organic chemistry, is concerned also with the structures of life, while physics explores inanimate nature. However, even here physics intervenes, namely in the specialist field of biophysics. Chemistry has proved so technically and economically significant by its production of new substances (e.g. synthetic substances or the refining of raw materials such as crude oil into gasoline) that it is traditionally defined as a discipline in its own right.

Is chemistry unhealthy?

The expression "it's full of chemicals!" is often heard whenever additives in food are being discussed in a negative way. In this instance, chemistry is being reduced to the production of preserving agents or even pesticides. However, the human body is nothing other than a large chemistry laboratory in a way; we burn sugar, convert fatty acids, alter substances, for example protein, which is coagulated in the stomach, and in this way utilize the nature of substances, as all creatures do. So it cannot be said that chemistry is unhealthy, since we cannot live without chemical processes. Our metabolism itself (from the Greek *metabole*, "change") is by definition chemistry in its literal sense.

It is not negative that humans have learned to manufacture known as well as new substances. However, technical applications can have negative effects, for instance in the form of gigantic chemical factories damaging the environment, and that does not need to be the case. A neutral view of chemistry and its possibilities helps to

Not a witches' cauldron but the colorful world of chemistry. Liquid passes to the gas phase when heated.

differentiate the positive from the negative aspects and to recognize the enormous value and use of chemistry for humankind.

Which chemical process did humankind particularly advance?

Fire! What would have become of humankind if it had not discovered fire? Fire is none other than a chemical reaction, for example of wood with oxygen in the atmosphere as it is heated to its ignition temperature. So, the first people who were able to kindle fire could be described as the first chemists. Of course they did not know the processes behind making fire, but they knew how to make use of it.

The economic factor

Chemistry was economically rather unimportant for a long time, until towards the end of the 19th century when the first synthetic dyes were developed for the textile industry. The demand was huge, since many of the natural pigments, which came from the cultivation of plants for their colors, were prohibitively expensive. The chemical industry grew rapidly. The ability to synthesize substances became a key factor in the new economy, which went far beyond dyes. Whether for detergents, novel inventions (such as celluloid, the basis of the film industry), or the successes of modern pharmacology, chemistry has become indispensable in all aspects of our modern life.

A variety of chemicals in the laboratory. The individual containers must be labeled accurately. Caustic and other dangerous substances are identified by their warning labels.

Dyes in powder form. Many of the common dyes (e.g. for textiles) are produced synthetically today.

THE DREAM OF GOLD: FROM ALCHEMY TO MODERN CHEMISTRY

Were alchemists magicians?

Many stories and myths surround the ancient alchemists. Of course they did not work magic but in principle they were the precursors of modern chemistry, for the aim of the alchemists was to change substances into one another. Mainly metals took center stage. So they searched for ways to produce precious metals like gold from base metals. To do this, they tried to discover the properties of substances and understand their composition in order that they could manipulate them. The gained knowledge was kept secret, which made alchemy an esoteric doctrine. Thus, alchemy acquired the mystique of the occult and magic.

Where does the expression "alchemy" come from?

Alchimia is the Arabic expression for alchemy. This may be borrowed from the ancient Egyptian word *kemet*, meaning "black country" or "black earth." This word also referred to the country of Egypt itself, as the earth there became darker and darker due to flooding by the Nile. The Greek word *kimia* is used in the sense of smelting. Alchemy was therefore understood to be either the art of smelting or (which is more likely) the art of the black country (meaning "of ancient Egypt").

What is the Philosopher's Stone?

The Philosopher's Stone was a dream of all alchemists; they searched for a substance that could be used to change base materials, especially metals, into precious metals such as gold and silver. They believed that materials consist not just of physical matter but also of principles such as "noble" and "base." It was said that with the aid of the Philosopher's Stone the principle of "noble" (or "precious") could be conferred on any substance.

What is the connection between mercury (quicksilver) and gold?

In the periodic table of chemical elements (see page 72) mercury follows on directly from gold and always has only one proton more.

Detail from *The Alchemist's Studio* by the Flemish artist Jan van der Straet (1523–1605).

The alchemists knew neither the periodic table nor the internal composition of matter. What they saw as special in mercury lay in the fact that it was the only metal that was fluid at room temperature. For a long time it was thought that all metals were made up of a mixture of sulfur and mercury, what we call alloys today. The doctor, naturalist, and philosopher Paracelsus (1493–1541) added salt as a third element in order to be able to explain non-metallic substances, too. Fundamental religious principles played a role here, namely the triune aspect of the Christian god. Naturally, alchemists were just as unsuccessful at producing gold by mixing sulfur with mercury as they were at finding the Philosopher's Stone.

When did alchemy die out?

The Renaissance heralded the end of alchemy, when there was a desire to be free of irrationalism and to throw out all mysticism that was incapable of proof. Instead of sham attempts at making gold, the purely scientific observation of substances came into being. This period was the birth of modern chemistry. In a sense, the death knell was sounded in the middle of the 18th century by the French chemist Antoine Laurent Lavoisier (1743–1794).

He established that oxidation increases the weight of metal. To do this, he experimented with mercury oxide, removed the oxygen, and oxidized the mercury again. As the newly produced mercury oxide weighed just as much as the substance he started out with, he recognized the absorption of oxygen and with it the underlying chemical reaction.

Gold. This precious metal is still coveted today and is correspondingly valuable.

Mercury is the only metal that is fluid at room temperature. This property fascinated alchemists.

THE ATOM:
A HARD NUCLEUS
WITH A SOFT SHELL

An artistic representation of an atom with electrons revolving around the nucleus.

Can atoms be seen?

No, with a diameter of just 0.00000001 mm they are far too small for that. These days, however, it is possible to scan them. To do this, an atomic force microscope uses a fine needle with a tip that is made up of a single atom. The surface of the object to be examined is scanned with this fine tip. If the needle is directly above an atom, both the electron sheaths repel one another. In the space between two atoms, however, the needle can penetrate deeper into the object before it strikes the next atom. Since no needle can be cut finely enough, it is manufactured chemically—by etching. The precision movement of the needle from atom to atom takes place via materials that bend slightly, dependent upon an applied electrical voltage. Only in this way can the needle tip be positioned exactly.

What does an atom have in common with an onion?

An onion is made up of several interleaved skin layers or sheaths. In the same way, electrons form several shells around the atomic nucleus. The electrons in an atomic shell can only exist within defined energy levels; this is an effect of quantum mechanics, which, put simply, states that they can only exist at certain distances from the atomic nucleus. Niels Bohr proposed this atomic model in 1913. He also established that the number of electrons in an individual atomic shell varies. The innermost shell has space for only two electrons, the second and each further shell (apart from a few exceptions) have space for eight electrons.

What are orbitals?

Orbitals represent a further development of Bohr's atomic model. Electrons are in reality not pure particles but possess wave properties as well. An electron can be imagined as a hazy cloud. As soon as you try to measure the exact position of an electron, the charge cloud disappears and the electron is suddenly an immeasurable, almost point-shaped, particle. However, it is possible to calculate the probability of where electrons would

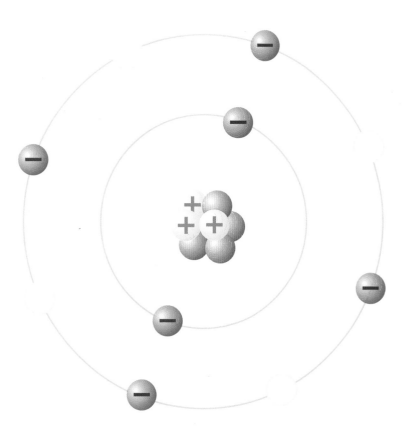

A carbon atom. On the outer electron shell there are still four places free for more electrons (marked as white circles). The atomic nucleus is made up of six protons (positively charged, three of them are visible in the picture) and six neutrons (neutral) each.

best be located, if they were measured, or rather seen. The areas with the greatest probability of locating an electron correspond exactly to the distances of the Bohr shells or orbitals. The Bohr model represents only a simplified approximation of the actual shape of an atom but it does explain many chemical properties of elements.

What is a chemical element?

Chemical elements correspond to the different atoms occurring in the natural world. The chemical properties of the atoms are defined by the number of protons in the atomic nucleus. Gold is made up of atoms with 79 protons. The atomic nucleus of oxygen has eight protons, hydrogen has only one. The atomic shell has exactly as many electrons (negative charges) as the nucleus has protons. Thus, atoms have an overall zero charge since the positive and negative charges cancel one another out.

Niels Bohr (1885–1962) in 1925. The Danish physicist and Nobel Prize holder developed the shell model of the electron sheath.

How many elements are there?

To date there are 117 recognized different elements. 93 elements occur naturally. However, many can be produced only in the laboratory and most of these are short lived. Americium is an exception. Elements with large nuclei, such as uranium or plutonium, are frequently unstable and decay radioactively.

What are ions?

Ions are atoms that have lost one or several electrons or have one or several too many. Light, for example, can knock individual electrons out of their shells (orbitals). Due to their charges, ions have different chemical properties from neutral atoms.

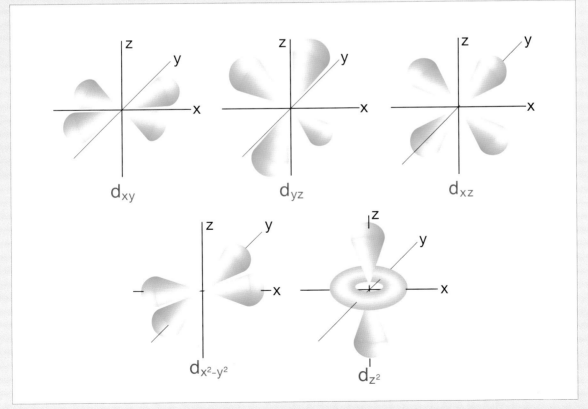

Visual representation of the orbital model. Electrons are not only point-shaped particles but can also appear as waves or as a charged cloud. The possible forms of these charged clouds (orbitals) are represented here. The three space dimensions are labeled x, y, and z. The individual possible orbitals are labeled d (d_{xy} is, for example, the name of an orbital in the x-y level).

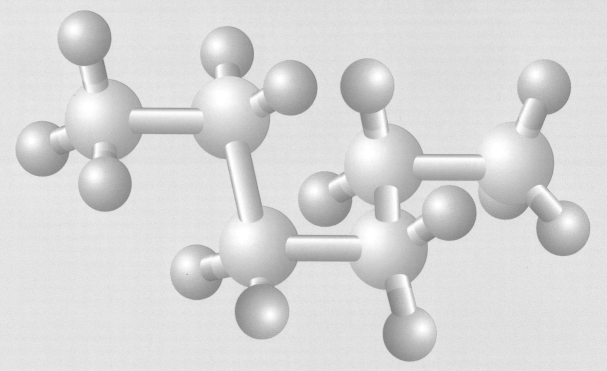

The hexane molecule, a hydrocarbon, is made up of six carbon atoms (blue) and 14 hydrogen atoms (green). It is used in industry as a solvent.

CHEMICAL REACTIONS: HOW ATOMS BOND

What are molecules?

It could be said that most atoms are very sociable because they form small aggregates that are referred to as molecules. The electron shells of the atoms involved are responsible for binding them together or "compounding" them. Substances, which are made up of molecules, are called chemical compounds.

Why do atoms stick together?

The shells of an atom's electron sheath each have an exactly defined number of places for electrons. Atoms are always anxious to completely fill the outermost shell. The outermost shell of chlorine atoms, for example, has exactly one space free for an electron. Sodium, on the other hand, has its outermost shell occupied by only one single electron, while its next deeper shell is complete. So it gives its electron to the chlorine, and both thus complete their outermost shells. With the handing over of the electron, the sodium becomes positively charged and the chlorine atom becomes negatively charged—both have now become ions. And that is how sodium chloride (cooking salt) is produced. The chlorine and sodium ions attract one another but repel among themselves. This necessitates a regular three-dimensional arrangement called a crystal lattice. Each grain of salt is such a lattice.

Cl

Cl

Cl_2

Chemical bonding of two chlorine atoms. The two outermost electron shells, here represented as orbitals or charged clouds with electrons sitting in them, each still have exactly one place free. The atoms amalgamate the two individual electrons and share the shell, so that it is complete for both.

In molecules, the atoms are closer bound than is the case with crystals. This happens, for example, through sharing electrons. Chlorine (as already described) is missing an electron to complete its outermost shell. Two chlorine atoms are able to help each other out here by letting their electron sheaths overlap.

Which atoms dislike each other?

The saying "the chemistry has to be right" applies equally to science as it does to people, if two atoms are to bond. If the electron sheaths cannot complement one another, bonding the atoms is not normally possible.

How big do molecules become?

The smallest molecules, for example chlorine, oxygen, and hydrogen gas, are made up of just two atoms. Molecules can, however, form long and complex chains, and in principle these can be endless. An example of a very big molecule is our genetic substance DNA. It is made up of more than 100 billion atoms and is for this reason one of the biggest natural molecules. They cannot be seen with the naked eye, but with the aid of a microscope they can be identified as chromosomes in the cell nucleus.

Can molecules break up?

Yes, mainly large complex molecules, and also when being heated they have a tendency to do so because of the increased kinetic energy created by colliding with each other. Radioactivity can also damage molecules. Alpha particles (like small cannon balls) can do considerable harm, for example to DNA. For the most part, our body repairs the DNA damage itself, but the affected cells can die or might lead to cell changes or proliferation, such as in cancer. Molecules can also be split or fragmented by other molecules or atoms fighting with them over the allocation of electrons. So one compound can change into another.

Is concrete a chemical compound?

No, because it is a mixture of cement and gravel and is not made up of homogeneous molecules. Even the main ingredient in cement is simply a combination of calcium, aluminum, and iron compounds, so-called oxides.

When the cement mix solidifies, the individual molecules do indeed link up to many small crystals to form a solid structure, but it is still not a homogeneous compound but rather a mixture of materials.

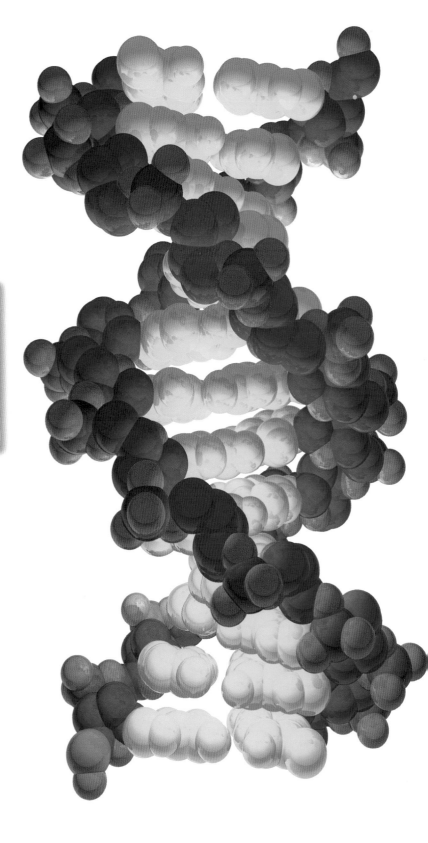

DNA, one of the biggest molecules occurring in nature, looks like a distorted ladder. The rungs, here represented in light blue, store the genetic information of life.

THE PERIODIC TABLE OF ELEMENTS: ORDER IN DIVERSITY

What does the periodic table of elements mean?

The periodic table of elements tries to order the natural elements on the basis of their chemical properties. The atoms strive to occupy their outermost shells completely with electrons. The first shell has space for just two electrons, and all the other shells (bar some exceptions) have space for eight. The natural elements can now be sorted on the basis of the occupation of their outermost shell. Each proton in the nucleus corresponds to one electron in the sheath. The third element, for example lithium, has three electrons, i.e. the innermost shell is full and the next outer shell is occupied by one electron. We can now count thus: with every additional proton in the nucleus of the following elements, the second shell is further filled until the tenth element, neon, completes the shell—with two electrons in the innermost shell and eight in the second.

Then the next round begins: sodium, the eleventh element, has once again just one electron in the outermost shell (now the third shell), and argon, as number 18, completes the shell again. In this way the elements are incorporated into an eight-column table. The elements positioned below one another in a column in this table have similar properties to each other as they have the same number of electrons in their outermost shells. These columns are called main groups.

What are noble gases?

Noble gases have exactly enough electrons to fill their outermost shells. For this reason they do not form compounds readily and they form no molecules, so they are available atomically. They make up the eighth main group in the periodic table (consisting of helium, neon, argon, krypton, xenon, and radon).

Element symbol / **Element name** — Fe (Iron)

Fe Solid elements
Hg Liquid elements
Tc Radioactive elements
He Gaseous elements

The periodic table of elements groups the chemical elements according to their properties—similar elements are positioned one below the other. The light-colored columns are the eight main groups; the blue- and green-colored ones are known as the subgroup elements. The main groups differ chemically from one another quite considerably, whereas the subgroups (metals, without exception) are often quite similar to one another.

The elements of the seventh main group, those that are lacking an electron to fill their outermost shell—chlorine, fluorine, bromine, iodine, and astatine—bond together with elements of the first group to form salts (e.g. chlorine and sodium give cooking salt). They are called halogens (from the Greek *halo*, "salt"). The rows of the table are called periods and are made up of elements with the same number of occupied electron shells.

What are subgroups?
From the fourth period it becomes more complicated, as here shells are at first left out during the allocation and only later filled up after the second electron has been placed in the outermost shell. The filling up changes nothing in the outermost shell, which is why these elements are so very similar. They are invariably metals. Precious (or noble) metals such as gold, silver, and platinum are also subgroup elements.

Who invented the periodic table of elements?
The periodic table of elements was developed by two chemists independently of one another

and almost simultaneously. Dmitri Ivanovich Mendeleev presented it in 1869 in Russia and just pipped the German chemist Lothar Meyer to the post. The latter published his table in 1870. The first periodic table contained only the main groups. Over time it was added to, piece by piece, as new elements were discovered.

Airships such as zeppelins, here the *Los Angeles* in 1923, were filled with hydrogen or helium, as these gases are much lighter than air and provide uplift.

Dmitri Ivanovich Mendeleev (1834–1907), the inventor of the periodic table. Element number 101, mendelevium, was named in his honor.

What is an isotope?
As well as charged protons, atomic nuclei are also made up of uncharged neutrons. The same element can therefore have nuclei of differing atomic masses, depending on the number of neutrons. These different forms of atomic variations of an element are called isotopes. In chemistry, isotopes are usually unimportant, as their equal valency means that they do not differ from one another chemically. However, physically their properties are often markedly different. Many isotopes are radioactive.

AGGREGATE STATES OR THE DIVERSE FACES OF MATTER

Water is heated to boiling point. The liquid passes over into the gas phase, here seen as water vapor.

What are aggregate states?

The solid, liquid, and gaseous aggregate states describe the different manifestations of substances. For example, at room temperature oxygen is gaseous, water is liquid, and iron is solid. The aggregate state depends firstly on the substance and secondly on outside influences such as pressure and temperature—even iron can be smelted and vaporized, given the right conditions. At normal air pressure, iron must be heated to 4,982°F (2,750°C) before it actually begins to boil and afterwards vaporize. Water of course boils at 212°F (100°C), while oxygen crosses over from the liquid to the gas phase at −297.346°F (−182.97°C).

How many aggregate states are there?

Along with the three classic phases—solid, liquid, and gaseous—three more aggregate states can be identified. The most well known is plasma, a hot gas whose atoms are ionized by impacting each other and thus losing one or more electrons. Other aggregate states are superfluidity and the Bose Einstein Condensate (see page 45).

A mixture of ice and a watery liquid, in this case Bourbon whiskey. The ice cools the drink to 32°F (0°C), the melting point of water.

What is a gas?

A gas is made up of molecules or individual atoms, which can move completely freely. Based on temperature—which is nothing other than a measurement for the kinetic energy of the component particles—the individual molecules collide repeatedly and are thus dispersed into any space that is available to them. The higher the temperature, the more rapidly the individual molecules move, and the lower the external pressure, the more freely they can move. The smaller and lighter the molecules are and the less force they exert on one another, with which they could adhere to one another, the sooner they pass into the gas phase. Helium is the noble gas with the smallest atoms. The atoms also exert very low bonding forces on one another. Thus, helium is already gaseous at −452.074°F (−268.93°C). Correspondingly, it can be frozen to a solid only under very high pressure.

Can ice turn directly to a vapor?

Yes, this is called sublimation. Water sublimates only under very low external pressure. Frozen carbon dioxide passes directly into the gas phase under atmospheric pressure at −109.3°F (−78.5°C). It is called dry ice (as opposed to "water ice") because it vaporizes "dry," i.e. it shows no liquid phase.

Is glass a liquid?

As strange as it may sound, basically yes. If glass is heated it does not begin to pass over directly from a solid to a liquid state, but first becomes softer in order to become more and more liquid at an increased temperature. The heating reduces only what is known as viscosity. Conversely, the glass becomes steadily tougher as it cools until it is practically solid. Thus glass is an extremely viscous liquid that behaves like a solid.

What is snow?

Snow is a loose accumulation of small ice crystals. There is air between the individual crystals. Ice and air have a different refraction index, which is why the light within snow is scattered in all possible directions (by refraction). Hence, though snow appears white, it is actually opaque.

Sulfur, an anomaly

Sulfur is made up of ring-shaped molecules. At 246.2°F (119°C) it melts to a yellow liquid. From 320°F (160°C) the rings break open and form long chains. Thus, sulfur becomes increasingly viscous. Between 392°F (200°C) and 482°F (250°C) the chains screw up into balls and the sulfur becomes very viscous, almost like rubber. If it is heated further, the chains begin to break up and the sulfur gradually becomes runny again. At 833°F (445°C) the fragments are finally so small that the sulfur passes into the gas phase.

Magnification of a snowflake. The angulated structure of this small ice crystal reflects the angle of the water molecules.

FIRE: WHEN OXIDATION GAINS MOMENTUM

Why does wood burn?

Wood consists mainly of carbon. If wood burns, the oxygen in the atmosphere joins with the carbon of the wood. Oxygen tries to attract two electrons so that its outermost electron shell is completed. The outermost shell of the carbon is half full with four electrons. If two oxygen atoms bind with one carbon atom then the aim is achieved: the four electrons complete the two oxygen atoms to form carbon dioxide. Since the oxygen in the atmosphere is present almost exclusively in the form of O_2 molecules, energy must first be supplied so that the bonding in the oxygen molecule is broken apart. Only then can a new, more favorable compound be formed. The energy difference is given off as heat and enables the further reaction of other oxygen molecules with the wood. The energy quantity is so great that the surplus heat in the form of flames can be released outward.

Once ignited, the reaction continues until the entire carbon store is used up. A fine ash is left over at the end: the residual substances of the wood.

Why does wet wood not burn?

Water absorbs the heat energy released during burning like a sponge. This energy is used to break up the hydrogen bonding and allow the water to evaporate. Oxygen now lacks the energy to dislodge new carbon atoms from the wood. Thus, if the wood is too wet the fire goes out or cannot be ignited in the first place.

What does oxidation mean?

The expression "oxidation" comes from oxygen (oxides are oxygen compounds). Originally, reactions were denoted as oxidation when oxygen was incorporated and as reduction when oxygen was yielded. However, it seems more consistent to define the reaction type generally by the transfer of electrons, so if a material is oxidized then electrons are removed and if it is reduced then electrons are added. Thus, oxygen does not necessarily have to be involved in oxidation. Frequently, oxidations and reductions are abbreviated to "redox reactions."

Dry wood is oxidized by means of atmospheric oxygen accompanied by the release of heat energy. The wood burns, as in this campfire.

Rust is a known problem with iron, as can be seen here in this pipe. On the left it can be seen in its original state, and on the right it is completely rusted through. The chemist would say that the iron is oxidized to iron oxide.

What do fire and rust have in common?

Both are oxidations. So, for example, in the case of fire the carbon oxidizes, and in the case of rust a metal oxidizes (e.g. iron). The process of rusting is normally much slower than burning. If the metal has a large surface, however, where it can react with oxygen, it catches fire and burns quickly. Hence iron wool really ignites.

What is corrosion?

It could be assumed to be the same as rusting, as corroded metal is initially simply rusty. Chemically speaking, however, this assertion is not entirely correct. Generally, by corrosion we mean the slow deterioration of a substance through exposure to other substances in the surrounding area. This can happen in the form of oxidation (rusting) but other reactions can also corrode a substance, for example acid.

Why does hydrogen make hair blond?

Hydrogen does not dye hair blond; this assertion is more of a linguistic shortcut. It is hydrogen peroxide, not hydrogen, that is used to make dark hair lighter. Hydrogen peroxide, H_2O_2, easily loses a single oxygen atom to pass over into the more stable form of H_2O, namely water. However, single oxygen atoms are extremely aggressive and oxidize the dark hair pigment, melanin, which due to the reaction simply becomes colorless.

Christina Aguilera celebrates the Grammy she has just won (February 2007). Her peroxide blond hair color is not natural. Bleaching with hydrogen peroxide produced it.

MATCHES, FIREWORKS, DYNAMITE: FROM THE HIGHLY COMBUSTIBLE TO THE EXPLOSIVE

The red match head lights the moment it is rubbed against a convenient surface—usually the match box. The energy is released through the reaction of phosphorus with a sulfur compound.

Why does a match light?

The head of a match contains a sulfur compound (e.g. antimony trisulfide) and potassium chlorate. Potassium chlorate oxidizes sulfur compounds accompanied by the release of great energy quantities. To begin the reaction, the match is pulled over a friction surface that contains red phosphorus, which reacts immediately and also extremely forcefully with potassium chlorate. The oxidation of the phosphorus, which comes to rest on the match head during friction, releases enough energy to activate the oxidation of the antimony sulfide. The match lights. Originally, there were matches whose heads were made up of red phosphorus and potassium chlorate directly. They would light on any sort of friction surface but also reacted just on pressure. These sorts of matches could catch fire anywhere, for example in someone's trouser pocket, and are therefore no longer in use.

What does dynamite have to do with the Nobel Prize?

Many explosive mixtures hold the danger of self-igniting at the slightest supply of energy. In earlier days, nitroglycerine, an extremely dangerous and unstable liquid with high explosive force, was used for blasting in the mining industry. The Swedish chemist and industrialist Alfred Nobel (1833–1896) researched nitroglycerine and by coincidence discovered that it was feasible to bond it in a solid. Thus, in 1866 he invented dynamite, which does not react to vibration. The demand in mining was enormous, especially for diamond mines. Nobel rapidly earned a fortune from his patent. In his will he founded a trust, which awards prizes to those who through their discoveries have performed a great service to humanity. The Nobel Prizes have been conferred annually since 1901 in physics, chemistry, peace, medicine, economics and literature.

Blasting of a high-rise. If the explosives are positioned correctly, the building collapses in upon itself without damaging neighboring buildings.

What is an explosion?

An explosion is a reaction in which a great deal of energy is released very rapidly similar to when a match is lit. As long as the energy can be discharged, i.e. the reaction takes place in the open, it fizzles out usually in the form of heat.

However, if more energy is released than can be given off through heat transfer, then the surplus is discharged in the form of a shock wave and kinetic energy of the associated object or of objects nearby. This makes explosions dangerous. If the reaction mixture is confined in a solid container, the discharge of energy of otherwise harmless mixtures is prevented and energy thus builds up until the container is blown apart. Of course gunpowder burns powerfully in the open air, but it is to a large extent harmless. Within the solid casing of a firecracker, however, it can be dangerous.

Interesting facts

• The first matches were invented in the 6th century in China.

• In the 13th century, bombs containing gunpowder were used as weapons in China.

• In 1285, the Syrian Hasan al-Rammah described the manufacture of gunpowder and its use for firearms.

How does a firework rocket work?

Firecrackers contain explosive mixtures of material, which are lit by a fuse. The first reaction takes place in a solid, downward-opening casing. The pressure is discharged through the opening and the recoil sends the rocket high into the air. The actual explosion then takes place in the air in a second chamber. As a pure explosion in the air would be only loud and not particularly attractive for the spectator, substances such as verdigris, sodium, magnesium, and potassium permanganate are added to the mixture, which make colorful flames when lit.

Firecrackers are a loud, colorful, and peaceful use of explosive materials.

CATALYSTS ARE USUALLY TINY

What is a catalyst?

A catalyst promotes a chemical reaction by reducing the quantity of energy needed for the activation of the reaction. It is itself not used up during the reaction. Catalysts are usually tiny. Even individual molecules or atoms can function as catalysts. Most people have heard of catalysts either because of the common figurative use of the term, or because they know something about cars—all modern cars have a catalytic converter, a complicated technical device in which catalysts are contained.

Can sugar burn?

Sugar must usually be very intensely heated to burn. It is actually impossible to light it with a match; if you hold a flame to sugar for a long time it will simply melt and caramelize. However, there is another trick. If the sugar is sprinkled with a little plant ash (e.g. from a cigarette or cigar) and lit with a match, it catches fire and burns with a hissing noise. The ash is preserved and serves as a catalyst for the reaction.

What are enzymes?

Enzymes are proteins that serve as catalysts in living cells. They lower the energy needed to start chemical reactions and thus facilitate a controlled metabolism. Without these small silent helpers, living cells would quickly die off, as the entire metabolism would collapse. Enzymes can also be used technologically for bio-reactions, for example in fermentation processes, which are started with the aid of bacteria or fungi such as brewer's or baker's yeast.

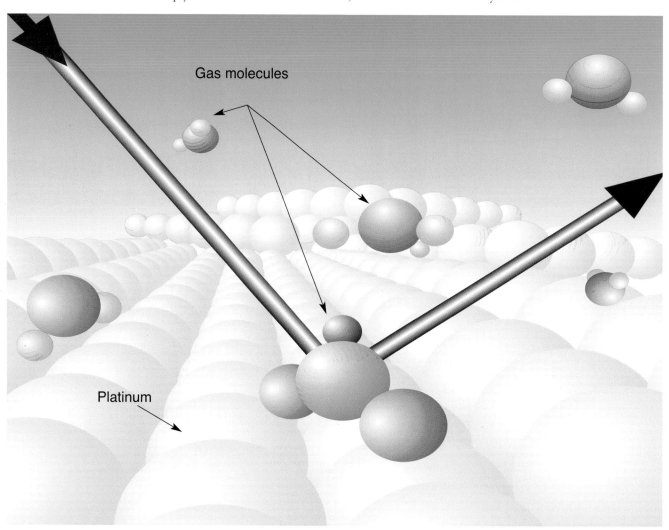

Gas molecules

Platinum

A gas composed of different molecules flows along a platinum surface. The platinum has the effect of a catalyst. If a molecule combines with the platinum, it can react more easily with other elements of the gas, for example with hydrogen or oxygen. After the molecules have been converted, the bond with the platinum is released. Exhaust gases are decontaminated in this way.

Why does an apple turn brown when exposed to the air?

When an apple is cut up, some of the cells are always injured and cutting brings the cell content into contact with the oxygen in the atmosphere. Oxygen molecules do not react by themselves as their outermost electron shells are already filled up, but the enzymes contained in the apple cells catalyze the reaction, so that oxygenation occurs and the apple turns brown. The brown coloring of the apple does not make it any less edible.

As the color does not look aesthetically pleasing to most people, however, apples are aerated with antioxidants to slow down this reaction; it then takes a lot longer for the apple flesh to change color.

Above: In cheese manufacture, rennet (a mixture of two enzymes or biocatalysts) is added to the milk to make it coagulate.

The pineapple effect

If you eat a fresh, slightly unripe pineapple you can find that your tongue feels furry. This effect occurs as a result of the protein-splitting enzymes in the pineapple fruit. These can also become active in the oral cavity while you eat. Unripe pineapples, especially the hard core of the fruit, are particularly rich in enzymes and sometimes have this unpleasant effect.

The flesh of an apple turns brown after it is bitten into. This reaction is caused by enzymes (catalysts) in the apple.

COLORFUL CHEMISTRY

Why are colors colored?

Colors depend on the wavelength of light. White light is really a mixture of all visible wavelengths. With the aid of a prism, which refracts the individual wavelengths to varying degrees, the individual color components are separated, as occurs in a rainbow. Objects very seldom produce light themselves; most just reflect the light with which they are lit. If an object is lit with white light but nevertheless appears red to us, then the other, non-red wavelengths are evidently not reflected by it. The quantum properties of electrons are responsible for this. Depending on their freedom of movement within the molecules, they can absorb photons with wavelengths that match their own. If reflected light is examined, the chemical properties of the lit object can thus be ascertained, i.e. its composition.

Why are blue jeans blue?

Denim was developed as a sturdy fabric for work trousers. Since dark trousers are less susceptible to staining than lighter colored ones, the material was dyed. Indigo dye, known as a colorant since ancient times, was used in the 19th century for coloring uniforms and was known and valued for its stability in light and colorfastness in washing. Although at the end of the 19th century (at the birth of denim, so to speak) there was still no suitable method for the synthetic manufacture of indigo dye, it was produced naturally in vast quantities from the

---

Interesting facts

There is an ancient work method associated with indigo blue dye. Indigo is a challenging dye to use because it is virtually insoluble in water. The dye first had to be converted into soluble indigo white, which is actually yellow, by dissolving in stale urine, which causes a process called reduction. The textiles could then be soaked in the diluted indigo white solution. This was afterwards turned back into the blue dye by oxidation, by laying the material flat upon the grass in the Sun. A lot of oxygen was built up in the grass by photosynthesis and this oxidized the indigo white to indigo blue.

Dyes in diluted solutions. Thanks to modern chemistry, practically any shade of color can be manufactured today at a reasonable price. In earlier times, natural materials had to be obtained which were often rare and very expensive.

Thanks to the hardwearing material, blue jeans are still best-sellers today. Nowadays jeans are manufactured in every color under the Sun.

indigo plant and was traded for a good price. Blue jeans are still dyed indigo blue today.

Is all food coloring synthetic?

Not necessarily. The well-known yellow color of rice in Spanish paella is produced from a natural plant extract, namely saffron. This is found in the

> **Interesting facts**
>
> • 120,000 blooms are needed to make 2.20 lb (1 kg) of saffron. The flowers are harvested by hand.
>
> • At around 20 US dollars per 0.035 oz (1 g), saffron is almost as expensive as pure gold.
>
> • Ink was in use in ancient Egypt 3,000 years ago.
>
> • Iron-gallus ink, which was already being made 2,300 years ago by extracting the essence of oak apples with iron sulfate, is still in use today as a permanent ink.

deep red stigma of a special species of crocus. As well as natural dyes, for example turmeric (yellow), chlorophyll (green), and carotenoids (yellow/red), there are many synthetic food colors in use today, for example azorubin (E122, blue). All permitted food colorings, even the natural ones, have what is known as an E number, a defined labeling system for food additives. So E140 is none other than natural chlorophyll.

Saffron, one of the most expensive spices, dyes food yellow even though it is actually red in color.

FROM IRON TO STEEL: THE PERFECT MIXTURE

What is an alloy?

An alloy is the mixture of a metal with one or several other chemical elements. These may, but do not have to, be other metals. Unlike in a chemical compound, the elements involved are not bound to each other. By using an alloy, an attempt is being made to optimize the properties of a metal. For example, soft metals can be hardened or the susceptibility to corrosion can be avoided.

Most church bells are still made of bronze. They generally have a mixing ratio of 75–80 percent copper to 20–25 percent tin.

How did people discover the use of alloys?

It was probably by chance that humans discovered, about 8,000 years ago, that coppery ores released a liquid in a hot fire and that they solidified again when they cooled. However, copper has the disadvantage that it is very soft, so it was not suitable for making utilitarian objects such as axes. After tin was discovered, humans soon attempted to mix copper and tin together in a liquid state. The result was bronze, which proved to be a lot more durable and stable than copper. Bronze was subsequently used to make decorative and utilitarian objects, as well as weapons. This discovery brought about an end to the Stone Age and the beginning of the Bronze Age. The use of bronze has been documented since 3300 BC.

What is steel?

Steel is an iron alloy with an impurity of less than 2 percent carbon. Iron was discovered around

1000 BC and replaced bronze in the manufacture of tools. Charcoal furnaces were not developed until the 12th century, but these were able to reach the required temperatures to melt the iron completely and burn up the surplus carbon. The subsequent development of steel marked an important technical advance. Not only did work tools such as axes became more durable than the older iron or bronze utensils, but so did weapons, for example swords. This was a decisive factor in the power struggles of medieval Europe; the outcome of some battles was decided on the basis of who had the harder and more powerful steel weapons.

Steel is normally more durable and harder than iron and its properties are dictated by the choice of suitable impurities used in the alloy. A content of 10.5–13 percent chromium makes steel rust-free, for example, as a thin layer of chromium oxide forms on the surface and prevents atmospheric oxygen from damaging the steel beneath. If 2 percent molybdenum is mixed into the alloy, the steel in addition becomes resistant to hydrochloric acid and thus is better protected from corrosion. Other constituents in modern steel manufacture are nickel, manganese, cobalt, and niobium.

Liquid steel in a steelworks. Due to great heat, more than 2,732°F (1,500°C), workers must wear protective clothing.

Above: Peaceful use of iron. Iron axes were harder and more durable than the earlier bronze tools.

ACIDS AND BASES:
REALLY CAUSTIC

Lemons taste sour. Citric acid is responsible for this. It is found not only in lemons but also as a product of metabolism in all living cells, although not in such high concentrations as in citrus.

Why do lemons taste sour?

Normally, a taste is perceived by taste buds situated on the tongue and transmitted to the brain. However, what are the taste buds reacting to if the signal says "sour?" They are reacting to ions, electrically charged atoms or molecules, and in this particular case H_3O^+ ions, i.e. water molecules (H_2O) to which an individual proton (a hydrogen ion, H^+) is attached. The positive charge causes a momentary opening of what is known as an ionic channel in the nerve cell of the taste bud. It is like the flip of a switch that registers a small electrical short circuit. The charge flows and the short electrical impulse is transmitted to the brain as information. The citric acid in a lemon forms the H_3O^+ ions, and they are what give us a sour taste in the mouth.

What is an acid?

Acids are substances that give up a proton or hydrogen ion to its reaction partner in chemical reactions. Thus, in water (H_2O), H_3O^+ ions are produced. Substances that intercept and bond protons are called bases. If a base is dissolved in water it releases OH^- ions. One OH^- and one H^+ ion together result in H_2O, i.e. water. Thus, acids and bases neutralize each other.

What is pH value?

The pH value is a measurement of the amount of free H_3O^+ ions dissolved in water. The usual scale goes from values of 0 to 14. A pH value of 7.0 is neutral, i.e. the liquid contains as many H_3O^+ ions as OH^- ions. Values below 7 are acid, values above 7 are alkaline.

Why are acids and bases corrosive?

Free protons or H_3O^+ ions are highly reactive. They are able to split molecules spontaneously or alter them structurally by the transfer of a proton. The same applies to bases, as OH^- ions are also profoundly reactive.

Powerful acids are usually stored in glass containers, as glass is resistant to most acids.

the water molecules to form H_3O^+ ions. The associated base is NaOH (sodium hydroxide or caustic soda). This dissolves in water to Na^+ and OH^-. OH^- and H_3O^+ result in two H_2O molecules (water), while Na^+ and Cl^- together result in NaCl, sodium chloride, i.e. cooking salt. Salts are thus always products of an acid-base reaction.

Interesting facts

• Glass is resistant to most acids, but hydrofluoric acid (HF) manages to corrode even glass.

• Vinegar is also an acid.

• Concentrated sulfuric acid, in addition to its acid property, also acts as an oxidizing agent, which makes it especially dangerous.

• Super acids such as fluorosulfuric acid can be a thousand times more acidic than concentrated sulfuric acid. In water their effects are somewhat dampened, as the amount of H_3O^+ ions in water is limited.

• The strongest known acid is so-called magic acid (a mixture of fluorosulfuric acid and antimony pentafluoride). It is a billion times more acidic than concentrated sulfuric acid.

What does salt have to do with acid?

Hydrochloric acid (HCl) is one of the best-known acids. HCl is the compound of one chlorine atom (Cl) with one hydrogen atom (H). If HCl is dissolved in water, the two atoms are released from one another, but chlorine gains an electron from the hydrogen. Thus, H^+ ions are formed that bond with

Are salts acid or alkaline?

Neither, as salts are end products after the exchange of a proton between acid and base. They can neither release nor accept another proton. Salt water is therefore not corrosive (unlike hydrochloric acid or caustic soda).

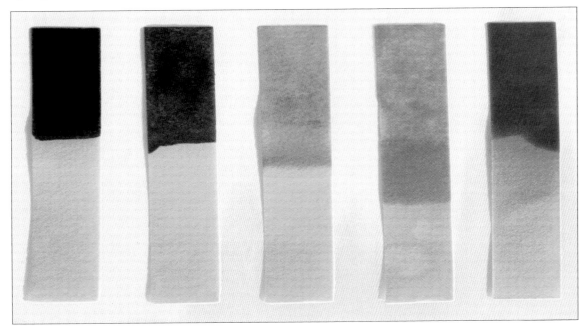

Litmus changes its color depending on acid level. With litmus paper it is possible to determine the acid level of a solution quickly and easily.

CLEAN THANKS TO CHEMISTRY: FROM SOAP TO WASHING POWDER

What is soap?

Soaps are the salts of fatty acids, and potassium or sodium bases. In ancient times, people recognized that the mixture of vegetable ash (alkaline) and oil (acid) had a cleaning effect. For a long time, the Romans were considered to be mollycoddled because they used soap, as most people used pumice stone to clean their skin, but gradually soap caught on. Soap is particularly effective against fatty dirt. These days soap is manufactured principally from vegetable fats such as palm oil, olive oil, and coconut oil, and from animal fats such as bone fat, tallow, and lard.

What are surfactants?

Surfactants are materials that reduce the surface tension of water, thereby making it easier for the water to wet the clothes' fibers. Another property of surfactants is their dual nature. They can interact at one end of the molecule with fats (hydrophobic, water repellent) and at the other end with water (hydrophilic, water-loving). Fat does not dissolve in water due to the hydrogen bridge bonds; fats cannot break them open and establish close contact with water molecules.

Why does soap wash?

Soaps are made up of surfactants, which bond fatty dirt particles with their hydrophobic ends. Surfactants settle together and form hollow balls in the water. The hydrophilic (water-absorbing) ends of the surfactants form the outer surface, which is why the ball dissolves in the water; the hydrophobic (fat-bonding) ends are oriented inwards. Thus, the dirt particles are sealed in and can be washed away with the tiny surfactant hollow ball in the washing water or removed from the skin.

What is the difference between hard soap and soft soap?

First and foremost they are distinguished by their consistency, and soft soaps are produced from potash salts (e.g. potash and fatty acids) while hard soaps are made of sodium salts (e.g. soda).

Modern detergents produce a brilliant white wash. To do this, a whitening agent is added to the cleaning surfactants. Light areas of the material are dyed while color areas remain virtually untouched.

Do detergents damage the environment?

Generally speaking, yes. However, their harmfulness has already been significantly reduced. Soaps have the disadvantage that they flocculate in hard (calciferous) water and no longer have sufficient washing power. Thus, for a long time phosphates were added to detergents to soften the water. They entered the environment via wastewater. Phosphates are strong fertilizers and encourage growth of algae and bacteria in the watercourses which, in their turn, use up the diluted oxygen in the water with the result that, due to lack of oxygen, permit only certain forms of life. In the US, the debate has been ongoing since the mid 1980s and states have adopted various measures concerning the use of detergents containing phosphates. Modern detergents contain improved surfactants in place of soaps; these do not need phosphate water softeners to increase their washing power. However, detergents are still environmentally damaging, as surfactants—due among other things to their fat-dissolving properties—have an impact on water habitats and disturb the natural balance. To minimize such impact, surfactants are microbiologically degraded in wastewater treatment plants. They can be removed to a large extent but unfortunately it is not possible to remove them completely.

What are liquid soaps?

Liquid soaps are made from especially short-chain fatty acids. Unlike classic soaps they do not react as a base and are often promoted as pH-neutral in advertising. The advantage of pH-neutral wash lotions is that they are kinder to skin; if soaps are too aggressive, skin problems can arise, such as sensitivity and dryness.

Above: It is taken for granted that soap is a part of daily hygiene. Mainly fatty dirt can be removed with soap.

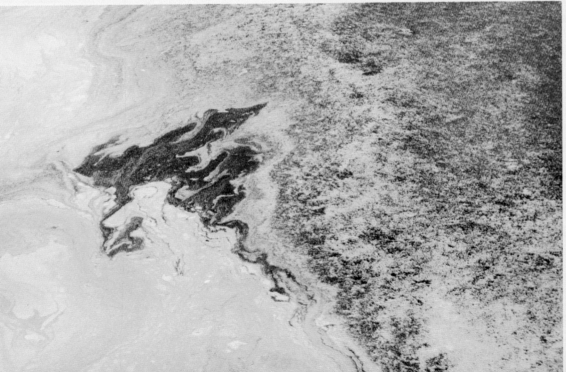

Left: If phosphates enter the environment by way of wastewater, as was formerly largely the case, watercourses can become so over-fertilized that algae blooms form. Other forms of life hardly stand a chance against so many algae.

WATER: A RATHER SPECIAL LIQUID

What is so special about water?

Water has properties that appear to contradict its molecular structure. Water is a very small molecule, made up of one oxygen atom and two hydrogen atoms. Chemically it is identified by the symbol H_2O. H stands for the hydrogen atoms, the subscript 2 signifies the quantity of hydrogen, and the O stands for oxygen. Despite being a small molecule, water is liquid at 32°F (0°C) and boils at 212°F (100°C) under normal atmospheric pressure. Hydrogen sulfide's structure is principally the same (H_2S) but it melts at −121.9°F (−85°C) and is already gaseous at −76.59°F (−60.33°C)! Sulfur is heavier than oxygen, but they stand in the same main group in the periodic table and so, from a chemical standpoint, are extremely similar. In actual fact, hydrogen sulfide ought to become liquid or gaseous later (i.e. at higher temperatures) than water or, in other words, water should not be liquid at room temperature!

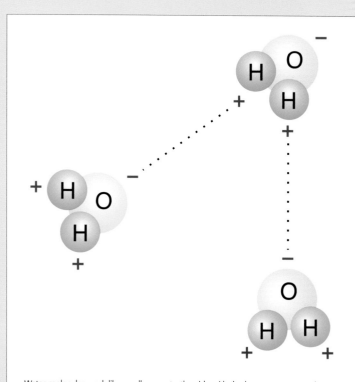

Water molecules work like small magnets; the side with the large oxygen atom is negatively charged, the two smaller hydrogen atoms are positively charged. The molecules thus attract one another through accurate alignment. The bond, here represented by the dotted line, is called a hydrogen bridge bond.

Water freezes at temperatures below 32°F (0°C) to a solid—it forms ice. The structures in the ice of this frozen lake were produced by the motion of the water during freezing.

Why does water freeze in winter?

This question can also be asked in relation to water as a liquid: why is water a liquid and not a gas at room temperature? The reason lies in one small detail: both hydrogen atoms are arranged to one side of the oxygen atom. The molecule looks a little like the head of Mickey Mouse. As the oxygen atom attracts the hydrogen's electrons very powerfully to it—more powerfully than the sulfur does in hydrogen sulfide—the side with the oxygen atom is negatively charged and the other side is positively charged. Water molecules thus behave like a bunch of tiny magnets, which attract one another through accurate alignment. Chemists say that water molecules are "polar." This attractive force holds the water molecules so well together that they form a very stable lattice—ice—that only cracks at 32°F (0°C) when the water becomes liquid. In flowing water, the forces between the molecules are also effective but are not sufficient to keep the water stiff. The hold between water molecules is referred to as the hydrogen bridge bond and is responsible for the special properties of water.

How do water drops form?

At rest, water concentrates to form small drops and does not simply flow apart. Hydrogen bridge bonds are also responsible for this. On the inside of the liquid the molecules attract one another from every direction. On the surface exposed to the air they can only be bonded sideways and beneath. Molecules on the inside of the liquid are thus more firmly bonded than those on the surface. Therefore, in terms of energy, the most efficient form the water drops can take is spherical, since in this form they have the smallest surface area per volume and thus minimize the number of molecules that are only partially bonded. Blobs of water thus concentrate to form small spheres, which on falling get broken up by air friction into the drop form that we recognize. If the bridge bonds are disturbed, for example by the introduction of washing-up liquid or heat, this surface tension of water decreases severely.

Interesting facts

• Water has its highest density at exactly 39.2°F (4°C) and not, as might be expected, at 32°F (0°C). This is because of the hydrogen bridge bonds. Glacial streams and the oceans' deep waters thus often have a temperature of exactly 39.2°F (4°C).

• Hydrogen sulfide forms in rotten eggs and accounts for their smell. Just a few molecules are enough to really irritate the nose.

• Hydrogen sulfide is extremely poisonous because it attacks hemoglobin. In low concentrations, however, dissolved in water, it can act as a cure for skin diseases.

The surface tension of water causes water drops to form. Without this adhesive force, the water, which is liquid, would disperse as a fine film on the surface of this feather.

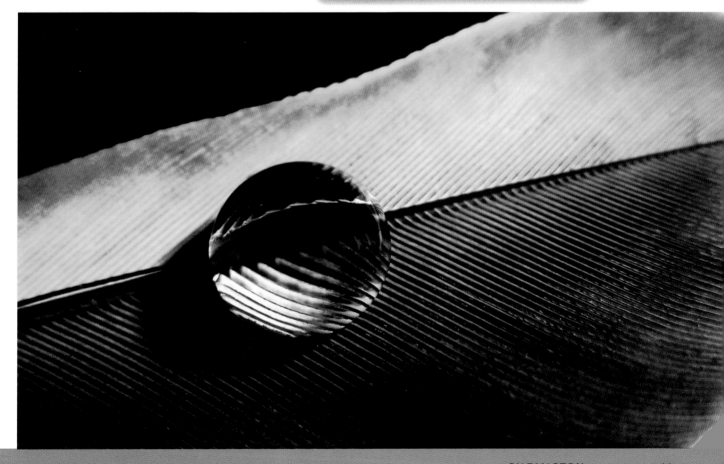

MINERALS AND ROCKS

Model of a crystal lattice—in this case a diamond. Each black ball represents a carbon atom that is bonded (except for the atoms at the edge) with four neighboring atoms at a time.

What is a mineral?

Minerals are solid substances that have a consistent chemical uniform structure, i.e. they have a homogenous basic structure, so that no matter what part of the mineral you examine, the same systematic arrangement of its atoms or molecules will be found throughout. If the atoms are regular and completely identically arranged, then they are pure crystals. If the composition is principally the same but the order is not always exactly the same, this is also a crystal but with imperfections.

These imperfections influence a mineral's color. A mineral is said to be amorphous if the structure throughout is generally the same but the molecules or atoms do not form crystals and are instead randomly arranged.

Are minerals stones?

It is true that rare minerals that look especially lovely are called precious stones (and less rare minerals are called semi-precious stones), but nevertheless, in the chemical sense they are not stones. A stone is rather a conglomeration of different minerals. It is thus made up of different small crystals, which together form the stone. Granite, for instance, is made up of three minerals: feldspar, quartz, and mica. If you

look at granite under a magnifying glass you can distinguish all three.

Why is marble so precious?

Limestone (stone made from calcium carbonate) is anything but rare. Marble is also a limestone but has been refined by nature. If limestone comes into contact with magma (the liquid stone from under the Earth's surface) in the Earth's crust, it will be extremely heated. If great pressure is also applied, the limestone is melted and at the same time compacted. Afterwards, if it cools slowly, it contains only tiny pores and is therefore very frost resistant.

Water can scarcely penetrate it. This compact stone can be highly polished and so was used in ancient times for magnificent building works. Furthermore, inclusions (impurities) during the melting process result in beautiful finely chased patterns within the marble. Apart from limestone, dolomite (a compound of calcium carbonate and magnesium) can also be changed into marble by pressure and heat. The right conditions, i.e. limestone or dolomite coming into contact with magma at a suitable pressure and then finding ideal cooling conditions, arise too seldom for marble ever to become a mass product of the Earth's crust. Furthermore, the marble must form near to the surface or else be transported there so that it can be quarried and used. Good marble thus remains even today a precious building material.

Brilliants are specially cut diamonds and are expensive and very sought-after. As diamond is the hardest natural mineral, cutting it is costly.

The great marble staircase at the Palazzo Reale in Naples, Italy. Its strength and fine-grained quality make marble a popular but (due to the high demand) very expensive building material.

Interesting facts

• Hardness of minerals is measured on a scale of values from 1 to 10. A crucial factor in determining the hardness grade of a mineral is the question of which other minerals can be cut or scratched with it. Diamond is the hardest mineral (10) and talc is the softest (1).

• A diamond is nothing more than pure carbon. If lead (graphite) were compacted under great heat, diamonds could be synthetically produced from it.

• We can use minerals to streak rough surfaces with color. The color comes from the abrasion of the mineral and can differ from the color of the mineral's complete crystals. Thus, iron pyrite (fool's gold), for example, is shiny golden yellow but the color of the streak it leaves is black.

• Ice is also a mineral, but because water exists only in liquid form at normal temperatures, we do not associate it with minerals.

• Quartz and glass are chemically alike, but quartz is crystalline and glass is amorphous (see page 104).

ACCUMULATORS AND BATTERIES: EN-ROUTE FUEL

How does a battery work?

A battery converts chemical energy into electric current. In the course of this, the property of what is known as redox reactions (see page 76) is utilized, i.e. losing and accepting charges in the form of electrons.

The first functional battery was developed by the Italian physicist Alessandro Volta (1745–1827). It was based on a discovery by the naturalist Luigi Galvani (1737–1798). Galvani was examining the musculature of frogs and noticed that the use of different metals as clamps for fixing the muscle would cause it suddenly to twitch.

Volta used zinc and copper discs and connected these through an acid electrolyte solution. The zinc is oxidized by the acid solution and enters the solution as an ion, during which process it loses two electrons per atom to the electrode. The copper disc is oxidized on the surface by the air oxygen. If the zinc electrode is connected to the copper electrode, then the electrons given off from the zinc flow to the copper and facilitate the reduction of the copper oxide to pure copper. If the electrodes are bypassed, then the current flows from zinc to copper.

Today, batteries function principally in the same way even though the electrodes and the medium enable higher performance. Alkaline-manganese batteries, for example, generate almost three times the performance compared with old zinc-carbon batteries.

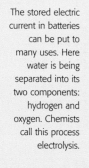

The stored electric current in batteries can be put to many uses. Here water is being separated into its two components: hydrogen and oxygen. Chemists call this process electrolysis.

Why do cars need batteries?

Strictly speaking, car batteries are accumulators (rechargeable batteries). To start a car, a spark must be produced to ignite the petrol in the engine. The spark is produced electrically, which is why the car will not start if the battery/accumulator is empty. Additionally, all the processes that require electrical current (e.g. light and radio) are fed by the car battery when a car has its engine switched off. During a journey, however, the accumulator is recharged via the generator, which uses the energy produced in the engine.

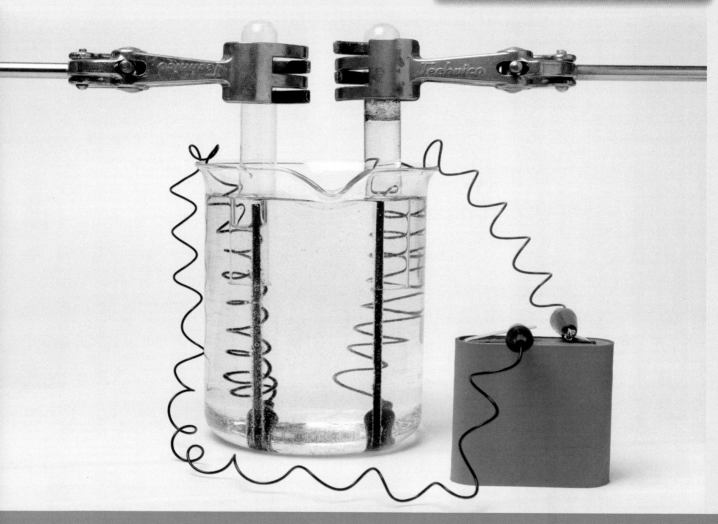

What is an accumulator?

An accumulator is a rechargeable battery. By applying voltage, the chemical redox process is reversed and thus the chemical energy is restored to the battery. The process in an accumulator flows in both directions, while in normal batteries it is irreversible.

What is a fuel cell?

Fuel cells produce current, as do batteries and accumulators, but they do not store energy; they are purely energy converters. The energy is generated from an oxidation reaction (combustion), during which hydrogen (H_2) and oxygen (O_2) are normally bonded to form H_2O. Unlike in internal combustion engines, it is not the thermal energy generated by hydrogen oxidation that is used to generate current. Rather, current is generated by the transfer of charge that takes place during oxidation via two electrodes, as is also the case

Car batteries are actually accumulators (rechargeable batteries). If an accumulator is discharged it can be charged up again. This can often be done just by connecting it to another car's battery.

with batteries. A fuel cell does not go flat like a battery does, but its fuel container needs to be filled in order to keep a constant current flowing. This system is extremely efficient and produces pure steam as a waste gas.

Prototype of a miniature fuel cell. Methanol (an alcohol) is used here as fuel. The electrical current is generated by oxidation of the alcohol.

The simplest battery: a lemon

By simply sticking a copper wire and a zinc wire (or zinc nail) into a lemon and short-circuiting this via a small light bulb, we can produce a flow of current that will light up the bulb. The current is caused by an oxidation of the zinc (anode) and reduction of hydrogen at the copper (cathode) This simple "bio battery" was used by Joseph Beuys in 1985.

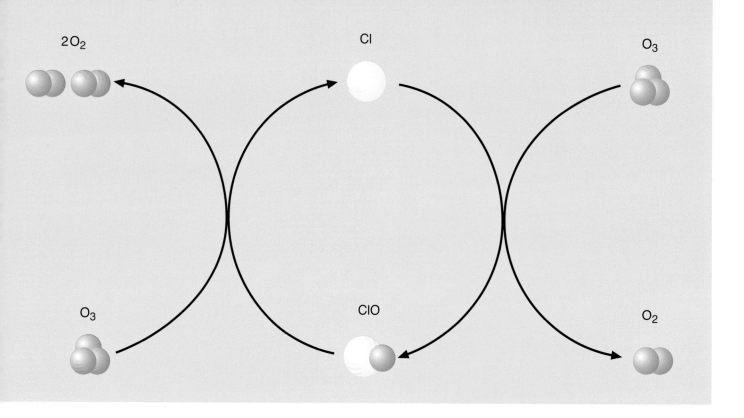

$2O_2$ Cl O_3

O_3 ClO O_2

OZONE: ABOVE GOOD, BELOW HARMFUL

The mechanism of ozone destruction by individual chlorine atoms. If a chlorine atom (Cl) strikes an ozone molecule (O_3), it grabs an oxygen atom (forming ClO, chlorine oxide) and the ozone becomes a normal oxygen molecule. If the ClO meets another ozone molecule, it loses the oxygen again. Two oxygen molecules (O_2) are formed from the ozone (O_3) and the oxygen (O). The chlorine atom attacks the ozone again and the cycle begins afresh.

What is ozone?

Ozone (O_3) is a molecule made up of three oxygen atoms in the form of a flat angle. At room temperature it is less stable than a normal oxygen molecule (O_2) and is therefore very powerfully oxidizing. It has, so to speak, an extra oxygen atom that is thus available for a reaction with other materials. In a pure ozone atmosphere, for example, wood would ignite spontaneously. Ozone also has an oxidizing effect on our nasal mucous membranes and has an unpleasant sharpness. It accounts, too, for the typical smell that comes from hot photocopiers. High concentrations of ozone in our environment near ground level are, due to ozone's aggressive nature, a strain on our airways and can cause headaches.

What is the ozone layer and why do we need it?

Due to extremely energy-rich cosmic radiation, ozone forms at high levels in the atmosphere (around 9–31 miles/15–50 km) from normal oxygen molecules. The total quantity of ozone is nevertheless very low. At normal atmospheric pressure the ozone layer would be compacted into

How is ozone created?

Ozone (O_3) forms when normal oxygen molecules break apart. The individual oxygen atoms are then highly reactive and join spontaneously with intact O_2 molecules. Ozone forms in two ways. Physically, energy-rich UV radiation (ultraviolet light in the atmosphere) or high voltages (e.g. laser printers, photocopiers, arc welders, and lightning strikes) can create ozone. Chemically ozone can be produced by electrolysis of water. Because ozone is so reactive it cannot be transported like other gasses but must be produced where it is to be used.

less than $^1/_8$ in (3 mm) thick. Ozone intercepts UV rays by absorbing them. In the process, every two ozone molecules are converted into three normal oxygen molecules. The majority of UV rays, which are dangerous for us, are intercepted in this way and do not reach the Earth's surface. Without the protective ozone layer it would be dangerous to remain in direct sunlight, since UV rays along with sunburn can cause skin cancer.

How was the hole in the ozone layer created?

The ozone layer is balanced delicately between the processes of ozone formation and ozone depletion by UV light. But there is another factor at work.

Waste gases caused by human use of certain substances, especially aerosol sprays and other chlorofluorocarbons (CFCs), disperse throughout the atmosphere. Usually, this is relatively harmless as the pollutants are greatly diluted. At higher air levels, however, the CFCs, likewise contingent on cosmic radiation, release individual chlorine atoms. These chlorine atoms have a catalytic effect and contribute to ozone depletion. As catalysts are not used up in a reaction, one chlorine atom can help to deplete the ozone almost indefinitely. The reaction is halted only when the chlorine atom meets another chlorine atom and Cl_2 is formed. Before this can happen, however, around 100,000 ozone molecules are usually depleted. The result is that the ozone layer has thinned out. The low temperatures at the poles—especially the South Pole—additionally intensify ozone depletion, so that the areas nearest the polar regions are particularly endangered by UV radiation.

The thickness of the ozone layer is measured with the aid of laser rays, whose light interacts with the ozone molecules. Here a laser developed for this purpose can be seen in the laboratory of the CNRS at the University of Paris, which is concerned with atmospheric research.

Does the hole in the ozone layer have anything to do with the greenhouse effect?

No, not directly. CFCs, on the other hand, which are known to be the main culprits responsible for the hole in the ozone layer, are powerful greenhouse gases (see page 219).

Cars without catalytic converters release nitric oxides in their exhaust fumes and play a big part in forming ozone at ground level, thereby poisoning the environment.

NITROGEN: PLANT FERTILIZER

What do plants live on?

They live on the sugar that they produce by photosynthesis in their leaves. In this process the carbon in the air, in the form of carbon dioxide, and water from the ground are converted into hydrocarbon. The carbon helps to increase biomass. Even so, plants need even more nutrients to be able to grow and thrive, although in much lower quantities than carbon. Proteins are made up of amino acids, i.e. acids with a nitrogen base. Without these, many important metabolic reactions in plants would stop, as enzymes, necessary for metabolism, could not be formed. Phosphorus (phosphate) and potassium are other important elements for plants. Nitrogen, in the form of N_2 molecules, is abundant in the Earth's atmosphere (comprising about 70 percent) but cannot be used by plants in this form. Plants need nitrate (NO_3^{2-}), which they take from the soil, usually with the aid of symbiotic fungi that inhabit their roots. A problem for large-scale agriculture is the associated exhaustion of the soil through nitrate depletion.

Why do plants not use the nitrogen in the atmosphere?

Because they cannot oxidize natural nitrogen (N_2) to nitrate. The only organisms that have developed enzymes capable of doing this are bacteria. Some plants, however, have developed a cunning way to get around the problem: they have absorbed the bacteria into their roots and hold them in small tubers. The plants supply the bacteria with air, from which the bacteria extract the nitrogen and gradually oxidize it to nitrate, which the plant in turn can utilize. It is mainly leguminous plants such as clover, alfalfa, beans, and peas that can do this.

What are fertilizers?

Fertilizers are natural or synthetic sources of nitrogen, phosphorus, and potassium. The simplest way to put nitrogen into soil is to spread it with liquid manure or sewage. Sewage is rich in urea and ammonia. Bacteria in the soil are important here as they convert the urea into ammonia and this in turn into nitrate, thus making the latter available for the plants to use. In agriculture,

Legumes can, with the aid of bacteria, store nitrogen that is in the soil. In this way they can self-fertilize the soil in which they grow.

the quantity of nitrogen used up by the plants is put back into the soil with the use of fertilizers in order to counteract soil exhaustion. Too much nitrogen content can, in its turn, have a harmful effect as it can damage the soil's flora and fauna, which can have a negative impact on crops.

Why does our drinking water frequently have too much nitrate in it?

Nitrate dissolves in water and is quickly washed out into the groundwater. In this way the soil is continually losing nitrogen. Normally, plants absorb the nitrate as soon as it is formed by the bacteria in the soil.

However, if the plants are given more fertilizers than they need (or if they are fertilized at the wrong time, for example in winter when they do not grow so quickly), the surplus will go straight into watercourses and eventually into deep groundwater layers. As all organisms use nitrate for the formation of proteins, the nitrate introduces unwanted growth of bacteria into the drinking water supply. The affected watercourses can then also develop algae blooms, and threaten to reach a "tipping point" (see page 89) if there is too much nitrate in the water. Some countries thus try to prevent farmers from spreading liquid manure on their fields in winter.

Above: Liquid manure is used in great quantities as fertilizer on fields. If the soil is over-fertilized, nitrates can seep into the groundwater (often drinking water) and lead to bacterial growth there.

Another consequence of too much fertilizer being used: algae bloom in a small stream. Very few animals and plant species can survive in such watercourses.

LIGHT BULBS, HALOGEN LAMPS, NEON TUBES: CHEMISTRY CREATES LIGHT

How does a light bulb work?

Electrical current flows through a thin filament, which heats up and begins to glow. For the lamp to shine with the brightest possible, almost white light, the filament must reach very high temperatures. For this reason, tungsten is usually used, which melts at about 6,152°F (3,400°C). In earlier times, filaments were made of osmium (with a melting temperature of around 5,972°F (3,300°C). At such high temperatures, the bulb could immediately ignite through a reaction with oxygen in the atmosphere. This is avoided, however, because a vacuum is created inside the bulb. But the low pressure in the bulb also has a disadvantage: at such high temperatures many of the atoms pass directly over to the gas phase, meaning that the filament gradually evaporates (this process is called sublimation) and disintegrates when it becomes too thin.

Modern bulbs therefore contain a protective gas that will not react chemically with the filament even at high temperatures, and it reduces the sublimation by its pressure. The most suitable gases for this are noble gases, as they are chemically inactive. Argon, xenon, or krypton are used, as the high weight of

A light bulb. A thin tungsten filament is heated to produce white light.

Neon advertising signs in Las Vegas. People can turn night into day thanks to artificial light.

their atomic nuclei reduces a rapid dissipation of the created heat, which would mean a loss of energy.

Low-priced bulbs contain a mixture of argon and nitrogen, as nitrogen molecules (N_2) are also relatively slow to react and do not have an oxidizing effect.

Why are halogen lamps so bright?

If halogens such as bromine or iodine are added to a bulb's protective gas, these will bond with the evaporating tungsten atoms. The resulting halogen tungsten gas decays at extreme temperatures into its component parts and gives off tungsten atoms, which condense again on the filament. In this way the filament continually repairs itself. At the same time, this process prevents deposits of tungsten from forming on the glass surface and the bulb socket. The bulb does not blacken and can be used at higher temperatures and hence produces a brighter light. Owing to the extreme heat, the bulbs are very small and compact and are made of thick quartz glass.

Why do neon tubes light?

Neon tubes use the effect of what is known as gas discharge. The application of a high voltage ionizes the gas, in this case the noble gas neon, allowing electrical current to flow through the gas. The energy of the current is absorbed by the electrons in the gas and given off again in the form of photons, and the gas begins to light up. As it takes a short time to build up a high voltage for ionization, it takes about a second for the tube to light after it is switched on. This high voltage is produced by a ballast.

Energy-saving bulbs contain gas instead of a filament. The gas is activated electrically.

Interesting facts

• The German brand Osram is well known for bulb manufacture. The name was formed from a combination of the two words osmium and wolfram (tungsten).

• Halogen bulbs should not be touched by bare hands, as fatty traces on the socket or glass would carbonize and overheat it. This could lead to the bulb bursting.

• Australia plans to ban the use of traditional light bulbs from 2010. They must all be replaced by energy-saving bulbs.

How do energy-saving bulbs work?

In principle they work in the same way as a neon tube, using gas discharge. However, in energy-saving bulbs an argon and mercury mixture is used as the gas. The electrical current evaporates the mercury after the bulb is turned on and thus increases the bulb's internal pressure. For this reason an energy-saving bulb takes some seconds to achieve its maximum brightness.

THE WORLD OF PLASTICS AND PLASTIC MATERIALS

Plastic materials are used every day in huge quantities. Recycling them is often difficult but can generally be achieved by precise grading according to the composition of the materials.

What is a plastic material?

Plastic materials, called plastics in everyday use, are synthetically manufactured solids made up of chain-shaped molecules on a carbon base. The chains are formed by the interlocking rows of small basic modules. The basic elements are called monomers (from the Greek *mono*, "single," and *merous*, "part"). The whole chain, which is made up of many monomers, is called polymer (from the Greek *poly*, "many").

Why does recycling plastic materials cause problems?

Numerous plastic materials can be melted down to form new products again. However, the molecules can become damaged by the effects of heat, which leads to a loss in quality of the material. The plastic materials also have to be sorted into their different types of polymers depending on which family they belong to, which is very time-consuming, especially as some plastic items may be composed of blends of plastic materials. This process is also either very labor-intensive or chemically so involved that what is known as the life cycle assessment or ecobalance turns out to be negative.

Is it dangerous to burn plastic?

It depends. At very high temperatures many plastic materials burn completely, without forming life-threatening emissions. However, only waste incineration plants can guarantee to reach the

The world of "P"s: PE, PP, PVC, PS, PUR, PET

Plastics are usually named on the basis of their chemical composition. PE means polyethylene, PP polypropylene, PVC polyvinyl chloride, PS polystyrene, PUR polyurethane, and PET polyethylene terephthalate. The abbreviations are easier to use than the full names and are more concise, which is why they have been implemented internationally. They are named after the monomers that make up the chains. These six materials form the basis of 90% of the global plastic materials produced.

temperatures required. Burning PVC is especially hazardous as highly dangerous dioxins (such as those released into the atmosphere in the Seveso disaster) escape from the chloride contained within it.

Why is rubber elastic?

If molecular chains are in irregular bundles, they can be hardened by the cross-linking of the individual chains but nevertheless maintain some elasticity. If the molecules are powerfully cross-linked, this increases firmness and the elasticity is reduced, forming what is known as hard rubber. If cross-linking is done with sulfur atoms, the process is called vulcanization. Modern rubber, for example in automobile tires, combines hardness and elasticity with good abrasion resistance and low rolling friction.

Flip-flops. They are popular plastic sandals, but some types contain health-damaging plasticizers, which can be absorbed through the skin.

Car tires are high-tech rubber products. The precision of the compound used and the degree to which the plastics molecules are linked produce the required firmness and, despite good road grip, low rolling friction.

SILICON: FROM GLASS VIA THE MICROCHIP TO IMPLANTS

How rare is silicon?

Silicon is not at all rare. On the contrary, after oxygen it is the second-most common element on Earth. Silicon makes up 25.8 percent of the weight of the Earth's crust and 15 percent of the entire Earth. Along with its calcium carbonate content (from ground mussel shells and coral skeletons), marine sand is made up mainly of silicon dioxide. Silicon dioxide, better known as quartz, is the raw material used in the production of glass and industrial silicon.

What is glass?

Glass is principally an extremely viscous fluid. Silicon dioxide melts at 3,133.4°F (1,723°C). If the molten material is cooled off before an ordered crystalline structure has time to form inside the mass, then the result is glass. Glass also occurs naturally. Silicate-rich lava forms a very dark, almost black glass called obsidian. And if quartz sand, for example, is melted by a lightning strike, small lumps of glass will form when it cools. Glass manufacture works in the same way, by melting and rapid cooling of silicon dioxide.

How is gel produced from silicon?

Richard Müller, a chemist from Dresden in Germany, manufactured synthetic silicon in 1941. Silicon is a chain made up of alternate silicon and oxygen atoms. In addition, hydrocarbons are bonded to the silicon atoms in order to complete the silicon's outermost electron shell. The chains can also be cross-linked and form meshes. The property of the silicon depends on the length of the chains and especially on the degree of the cross-linking. Pure chains are fluid and can be made into silicone gel. Moderate cross-linking, on the other hand, results in a rubber-like structure. With many cross-links, silicon becomes hard and resin-like. In this case, hydrocarbons control its solubility in solvents

Quartz sand under a magnifier. Every small grain of sand is a small quartz crystal. As quartz is pure oxidized silicon, sand is used as the raw material in the production of glass and industrial silicon.

The future: computer chips without silicon?

So-called quantum computers are a dream of the scientific world. These could make calculations and store information on the basis of their quantum mechanical effects. The first steps in this direction have already been taken. Less idealistic is the use of organic semiconductors. Through the addition of sodium atoms, carbon chains (polymers) become semiconductors. The advantages are the extremely thin film thickness and also the elasticity of the material. So the theoretical possibility exists that instead of printing on paper, chip-controlled thin films could be used as electronic books and magazines. The chip would also be flexible and very thin, enabling it to be integrated into the film. Such films could even produce animated pictures.

Silicon is omnipresent, whether in the form of expanses of windowpanes or as a chip in a cell phone. We live in the silicon age.

therefore be switched on and off as a conductor. The resistance in semiconductors can also be dependent on the direction of the current. For this reason, switching elements such as transistors have been produced for use in even microscopically small spaces, and this has led to the development of computer chips.

Below: Silicon wafers, an intermediate step in the manufacture of modern computer chips. The surface is smoothed to within a few millionths of a millimeter, i.e. almost perfectly flat.

so that the resin is first fluid and then hardened. As silicone is not poisonous for the human body it is used in plastic surgery, for example in gel breast implants inserted to augment breast size. However, it is mostly used in sealing compounds for its water-repellent properties and elasticity.

Why are computer chips made of silicon?

Pure silicon is a semiconductor. The conductivity of semiconductors depends on temperature. At low temperatures they are very good isolators. Thus, silicon is not conductive at room temperature. However, if it is heated, for example with an applied electric voltage, it becomes conductive. Silicon can

CERAMIC: FROM CROCKERY TO HEAT SHIELDS ON SPACECRAFT

Clay, from which this mug has been produced, is fired in a kiln and later cooled. The result is ceramic.

Porcelain vases were already being made in China in the 13th century. This vase is from the Yuan dynasty.

What is ceramic?

Ceramic is one of the earliest cultural and technical achievements of humankind. If clay is softened with water and then shaped, the end product after applying heat will be hard and stable. This opens up the possibility of producing vessels or other objects for everyday use. Clay consists of very fine grains of silicon and aluminum oxides. The size of the grain is usually below 0.00007874 in (2 (μm). The individual grains interfuse and bond with one another if they are heated at between 1,650°F and 2,190°F (900°C and 1,200°C). The ceramic becomes hard but is actually porous and permeable to water. The ceramic is glazed to make it watertight, a necessary property for crockery. To do this, a fine layer of ground glass is used. The glaze fuses with the ceramic body at 2,190°F–2,640°F (1,200°C–1,450°C) and seals it completely.

Why is ceramic heat-stable?

The components of ceramic have a very high melting point. When ceramics (except for porcelain) are fired, the individual components are not fused but linked by heating (sintering). Aluminum oxide (melting point around 3,720°F/2,050°C), boron nitride (melting point 4,890°F/2,700°C), or silicon carbide (sublimated at around 5,560°F/3,070°C), for example, are used as raw materials in heat-stable ceramics in modern technology.

Is ceramic used in technology?

Yes, ceramics are versatile and valuable components of modern technology. They appear as heat shields (in ovens, as heating elements, or for protection of the space shuttle on re-entry into the atmosphere), abrasion protection (in pumps), protection against wear (in engines), dental prostheses and replacement joints (where they offer stability and abrasion resistance), knives (ceramics can be harder than steel), insulators (e.g. for high-voltage wires or in spark plugs), and protection against corrosion.

How are high-voltage wires insulated?

Modern high-voltage wires are operated with voltages up to 420,000 V. The resistance of the insulators must be correspondingly high. At such high temperatures, glass or porcelain insulators are used and usually several individual insulators in the form of chains are combined. As the current

Who invented porcelain?

The oldest known porcelain comes from 7th-century China. Porcelain is made from a mixture of clay, feldspar, and quartz. Feldspar melts in the firing process, but does not form a uniform crystal lattice on cooling. It becomes more and more viscous and finally forms a sort of glass, which is what gives this type of ceramic its distinctive character.

at such high basic voltages can directly penetrate the atmosphere in the form of an electric arc, like that of a small lightning bolt, a sort of lightning conductor is installed to safeguard the insulator. This intercepts the energy and diverts it safely.

Why is good porcelain expensive?

The cost of porcelain production nowadays is no longer a relevant price determinant, even though there are differences even today with regard to the quality of fired porcelain. Prices are determined predominantly by design and the artistic production of fired patterns and colors in the glaze. At the Meissen porcelain factory, which was founded in 1710 and is the oldest European porcelain manufacturer, the famous "Onion" pattern is still done by hand today; only the main outlines are machine-made using a screen-printing technique.

The heat shield on the space shuttle is made up of many small ceramic plates. The air friction on re-entry into the Earth's atmosphere can rapidly heat the heat shield up to its limits, i.e. over 5,430°F (3,000°C).

SUGAR, FATS, CARBOHYDRATES: LIFE NEEDS ENERGY

What is sugar?

From a chemical point of view, sugars are carbohydrates, which means they consist only of carbon atoms and water molecules that are united into one molecule. Most sugars are made up of a simple basic structure: five or six carbon atoms form a chain, which is closed (or can be closed) with an oxygen atom to form a ring. Classic table sugar, sucrose, is made up of two rings, each with six carbon atoms. Glucose, on

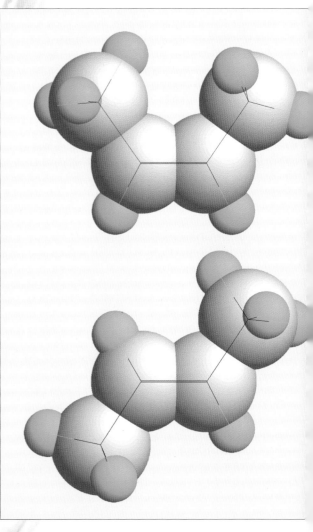

Above: Molecules with identical compositions can have a different outer form (the simple example shown here is butane gas). In the case of fatty acids, such a little thing can make the difference between healthy and unhealthy.

Left: Sugar (here cane sugar) is magnified three times. Its magnification reveals that it is made up of small crystals.

the other hand, is smaller and consists of just one single ring. It can thus be absorbed into the bloodstream more rapidly.

Is sugar always sweet?
No, most long-chain sugars, which are made up of the linking of many individual rings, do not taste sweet to us. Paper, for instance, consists of taste-neutral cellulose, an extremely long-chain sugar that is also contained in wood. Starch, another long-chain sugar (which is present in potatoes in large quantities), is broken down by enzymes into short-chain sugar. That is why bread tastes a bit sweet when it has been chewed for a while.

What are sweeteners?
Sweeteners are sweet-tasting on the tongue, usually even sweeter-tasting than normal sugar, but they have practically no calorific value. Sweeteners are important in diabetic food but are very controversial with regard to reducing calories, as they are considered to be appetite stimulants and are successfully added to animal feed to fatten them up. The effect of cutting down on calories is usually thus cancelled out by the increased urge to eat.

Are fats unhealthy?
No, on the contrary. Owing to their high energy content they are stored in the body, which can result in those undesirable rolls of fat. However, this happens only when the body is supplied with more energy than it needs for its metabolism and daily activities. Fats always have the same basic appearance: three fatty acids bond to a glycerol molecule and form a triglyceride. Saturated fatty acids are made up of long carbon chains to which the maximum possible number of hydrogen atoms is bonded. Unsaturated fatty acids also have long carbon chains, but with a lower amount of hydrogen atoms. As the human body itself does not produce unsaturated fatty acids, which are important for regulating many functions in the body (such as blood pressure and clotting, immune and inflammation response to infection), it needs to absorb them from food. Therefore fats can be not only healthy but also necessary.

Starch and acrylamide: are potato chips unhealthy?
Potato chips consist of virtually just starch and the fat in which they are fried. A diet of potato chips would be very boring and unhealthy, although the same could be said of a lot of foodstuffs. A bigger problem than the huge amount of calories is the acrylamide contained in potato chips. It forms when the starch is heated

How does a cell produce energy?
Sugar and fat are burned in the cell's mitochondrion (a sort of cellular power plant). The hydrocarbon chains are oxidized to carbon dioxide and water, whereby energy is released. We release the carbon dioxide into the environment on our breath.

and is said to be a mutagen and carcinogenic. The long-term consequences have so far not been sufficiently examined, but effects on animal DNA in experiments bear out this theory. The question is not so much whether acrylamide (and therefore the eating of potato chips) is unhealthy, but rather how unhealthy it is. Acrylamide is found not only in chips, but also in things such as crisp-breads, dark bread crusts, gingerbread, French fries, and coffee.

Potato chips, along with other highly heated foodstuffs, can contain large quantities of acrylamide, which is suspected of causing cancer.

SUGAR AND PETROLEUM: REALLY REFINED

What happens in refineries?
From a chemical point of view, the process of refining may be described as cleaning and improving. Refining is therefore a chemical operation that primarily removes impurities and optimizes the end product.

How is sugar refined?
Sugar is extracted either from sugar beet or from sugar cane. In both cases the raw sugar is a brown color and still contains secondary (non-sugar) plant substances. The sugar is dissolved in water many times, filtered, centrifuged, and crystallized, until it finally appears as white crystals in the form of pure sucrose. Sometimes the sugar is re-dyed brown. To do this, caramelized sugar in the form of syrup is added. Only 100 percent raw sugar is natural, unrefined sugar from sugar cane

An oil refinery in Scotland. The petroleum is cleaned and processed here for the production of fuel.

Paraffin, kerosene, diesel, fuel oil, gasoline... a bewildering variety

• Paraffin is made up of medium-length hydrocarbon chains, which all have a similar boiling point. Paraffin is not as flammable as gasoline, but it burns up almost completely and without soot, unlike diesel.

• Kerosene is principally the same as paraffin but it has additives for use in aircraft turbines. Diesel fuel is, like paraffin and kerosene, a blend of medium-length chains (10–22 carbon atoms) with different boiling points and burning properties. Kerosene and diesel fuel are both easy to produce but can tend to be sooty when burning if adequate oxygen is not present.

• Fuel oil for central heating systems is similar to diesel fuel, but it has more pollutants (such as sulfur), and it corrodes more rapidly. Fuel oil could be used as car fuel but has been ruled out on account of its exhaust emission levels, and because governments would be deprived of their customary tax revenue if fuel oil were used instead of gasoline.

• Aviation gasoline—as used for propeller-driven airplanes—is most similar to regular gasoline. It is often wrongly confused with kerosene.

Sugar cubes are pure white only as a result of the refining process. Brown sugar is also refined, but is subsequently dyed again by adding caramel.

and, like other sugar varieties except for sucrose, it also contains minerals, vitamins, and trace elements.

What is the difference between crude oil and gasoline?

Crude oil is a black, viscous blend of different hydrocarbons. More than 17,000 different compounds are contained in crude oil. Gasoline is refined from crude oil. In the process, long hydrocarbon chains are broken and converted into shorter chains with only five to eleven carbon atoms (what is known as the "cracking" process of crude oil). As a result, gasoline is lighter and evaporates quicker, but the calorific value increases significantly. Gasoline contains only around 100 different hydrocarbons and it has low viscosity and no color. Secondary substances are added to gasoline to enhance the quality.

Why does the use of petroleum lead to pressure on the Earth's climate?

The burning of hydrocarbons oxidizes carbon to carbon dioxide. Carbon dioxide is a greenhouse gas and therefore jointly responsible for the greenhouse effect (see page 219). Quantities of carbon that were converted over millions of years into hydrocarbons have been burned up by humankind in the course of just a few decades or centuries and returned into the atmosphere.

Jets are fueled with kerosene. This is simply a distillate of crude oil.

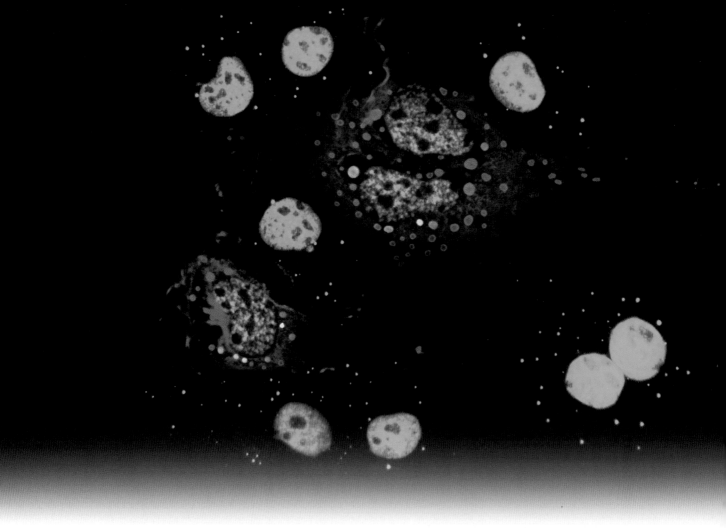

PRIONS: MOLECULES THAT CAN MAKE YOU ILL

Mutant proteins can damage cells severely or even kill them. This view, taken with a light microscope, shows two cells that have been attacked and ruptured by mutant prions.

Can molecules make you ill?

Yes, in many ways, for example by eating poisonous mushrooms. Many substances can interfere with metabolism or kill cells directly (e.g. by oxidation of cell membranes or influence of enzymes). As well as classic poisoning, molecules can cause complicated, long drawn-out diseases such as cancer, by chemically altering the genes, for instance, whereby affected cells (as in the case of cancer) react by growing in an uncontrolled way. Known examples of these are acrylamide (overheated starch, e.g. in potato chips), environmental poisons such as dioxins, and aflatoxins and ochratoxins in moldy food.

Are there molecular infectious diseases?

Yes, but the pathogen must succeed in multiplying or spreading its effect within the affected organism. That was thought to be impossible until prions were discovered by Stanley Prusiner. The American neurologist and biochemist received the Nobel Prize in 1997 for his discovery.

What are prions?

Prions are reactive protein molecules, i.e. proteins that mainly occur in the nervous system and brain on the surface of the nerve cells. Their function is to protect the cells from free radicals, copper ions, and oxidants such as hydrogen peroxide.

How does a prion make you ill?

Prions get their shape, as do all proteins, from the folding and collapsing of longer chains of amino acids. If a prion is not folded properly, its chemical properties can alter markedly. Defective prions turn the hydrophobic ends of the amino acid chains outwards—normally they would be tucked away on the inside—and make them water insoluble. That would be no problem in itself if another (deadly) effect did not arise simultaneously, namely that a defective prion transfers its folding structure to healthy prions when it is in direct contact with them. This means that the healthy prions change their folding structure and in turn become infectious. The pathogen (the defective prion) does not therefore multiply by duplication but by modification of the body's proteins. The nerve cells are badly injured by this and the organism reacts with disturbances in coordination and movement. When key bodily functions fail due to brain damage, fatality occurs. Diseases such as BSE (bovine spongiform encephalopathy or "mad cow disease"), CJD (Creutzfeldt-Jakob disease) in humans, and scrapie in sheep are caused by prions.

How do you become infected with prions?

Pathogenic prions can arise spontaneously from a genetic defect or a failure in the formation of normal prions in the body. Transmission is practically only possible by eating meat that is already infected. If the meat is heated sufficiently, the prions are destroyed. The outbreak of BSE disease in Europe could have been avoided, for cows are herbivores. However, for reasons of economy,

Despite its "mad" appearance this cow is perfectly healthy. As "mad cow disease" has such a long incubation period, the infection is only clearly recognizable in its latter stages.

Creutzfeldt-Jakob disease (CJD)

CJD could be regarded as the human form of BSE. It is normally triggered genetically and is very rare. During the BSE epidemic in Europe, a new version of CJD was identified. More than 150 people have died of it thus far. It is believed that in these cases BSE prions had been transmitted to humans. Owing to the long incubation period, which precludes early detection and containment of BSE, further cases of the deadly disease are expected in the future.

---

insufficiently heated cattle fodder, which among other things was manufactured from sheep that had scrapie, was fed to cows and the BSE epidemic was thus triggered. The possibility that other means of transmission could exist (e.g. via the cow giving milk to its calf or via saliva) is still a matter of hot debate.

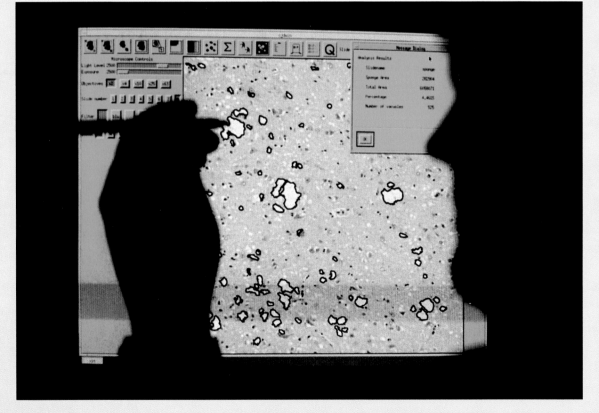

On this scan of a section of human brain tissue, a doctor marks the areas that are already badly damaged by CJD prions.

Genetic engineering

Evolution

Zoology

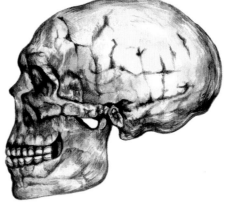

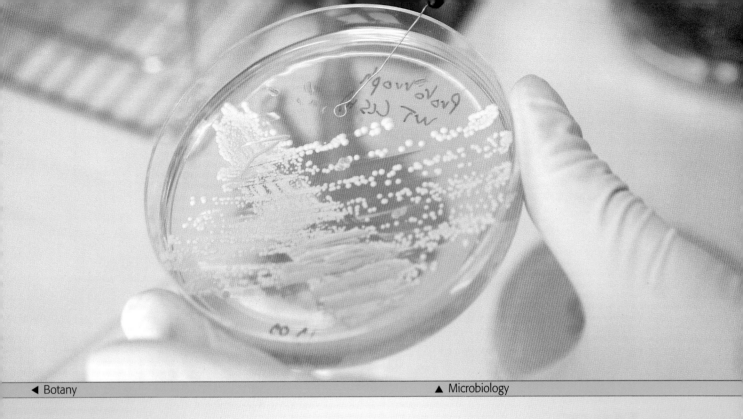

BIOLOGY

No other natural science explores the issues of life so comprehensively as biology. It is concerned with such diverse subjects as microorganisms, animals, plants, and fungi, and with the interaction of species with one another and their functions in their respective habitats. In practice there are cross-links to medicine, pharmaceutics, agricultural science, and food technology. The recording of consequences of environmental and climate change are also part of biology's remit.

Systematics

Genetics

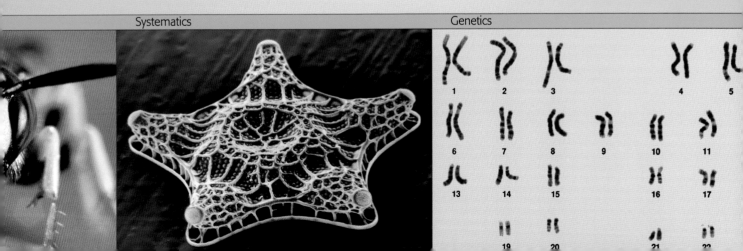

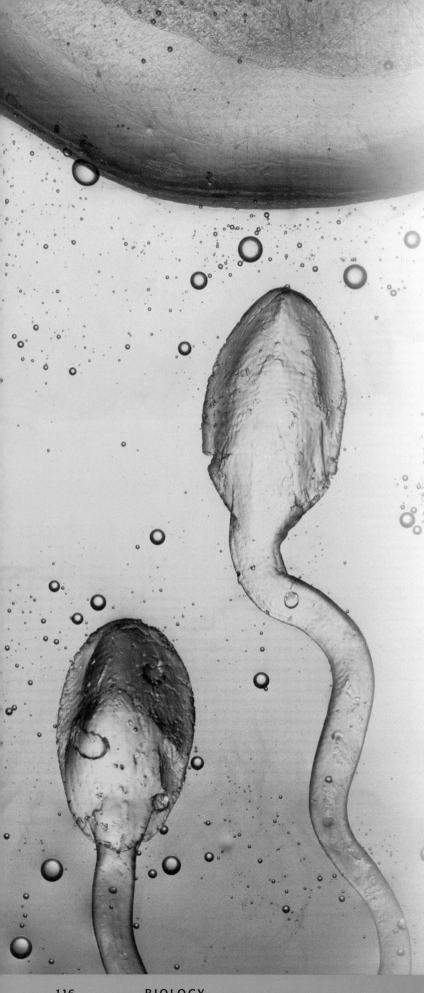

THE BIRTH OF LIFE: IN THE BEGINNING THERE WAS A CELL

When did life begin on Earth?

The question of whether life was created from nothing, whether God gave life to inanimate matter, or whether, as the Greek natural scientist Thales of Miletus (624–546 BC) believed, it came from water, neither philosophers nor natural scientists can answer for sure.

Around 4 billion years ago there was already water on Earth and an atmosphere. The first organisms were born into this dawn of the Earth's history, defined as the Archean eon, a geologic unit of time. More recent theories propose that simple organic compounds formed from inorganic molecules that were dissolved in water. Intense UV radiation, which could penetrate into the atmosphere unhindered by oxygen and ozone, supplied the energy needed for this process.

The 1953 Miller-Urey experiment conducted by two chemists, Harold C. Urey and Stanley Miller, showed that organic compounds such as simple amino acids and fatty acids can be created from components such as water, methane, ammonia, and hydrogen, if in the presence of an energy source (e.g. a flash of lightning).

What do fire and life have in common?

- Fire is varied in shape and form and can change (from a candle flame to a devastating forest fire).

- A kind of metabolism takes place in a fire (hydrocarbon compounds are oxidized to form carbon dioxide and water, in which energy in the form of heat is generated).

- Fire spreads, i.e. it grows and reproduces as long as it is "fed."

- Fire moves and reacts to outside influences (wind fans it, water extinguishes it).

- Fire is balanced between its "food intake" (fuel) and its emissions of end products (heat, soot, CO_2) through constant renewal of its own body matter (flames, embers).

Two sperm on their way to fertilize an egg cell. Cells are surrounded by a membrane.

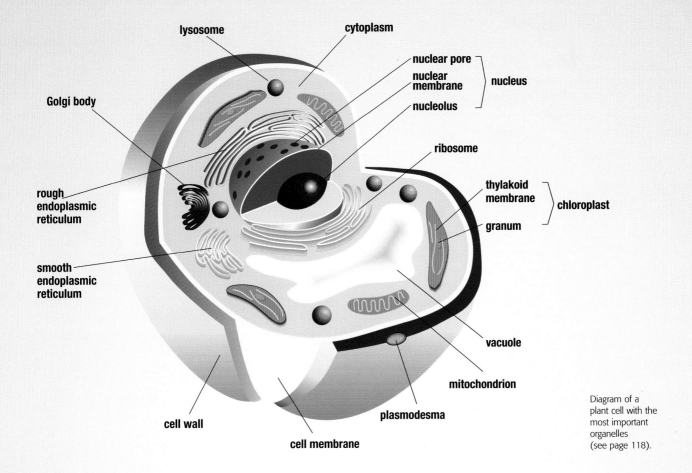

lysosome

cytoplasm

nuclear pore

nuclear membrane ⎤
nucleus

Golgi body

nucleolus

ribosome

thylakoid membrane ⎤
chloroplast

rough endoplasmic reticulum

granum

smooth endoplasmic reticulum

vacuole

mitochondrion

cell wall

plasmodesma

cell membrane

Diagram of a plant cell with the most important organelles (see page 118).

What distinguishes animate from inanimate nature?

Basically the following six characteristics:
- character and individuality
- metabolism and energy use
- growth
- movement and interaction with the environment
- reproduction and propagation
- evolution

What are creatures made of?

They are made of atoms, molecules, and cells. Atoms and molecules are the smallest modules which are needed for the creation of cell organelles (a specialized structure within a cell or unicellular organism) such as the nucleus and mitochondria. The cell (from the Latin *cellula*, meaning "small room") is the smallest viable unit. It is capable of absorbing nutrients, converting these into energy, reacting to stimuli (e.g. changes in temperature), moving and, above all, reproducing. Cells bind to form tissue (e.g. connective tissue) from which organs (e.g. skin and heart) are made. The organs in their turn form systems (e.g. the blood circuit) and finally the organism (human or animal), which comes into contact with its surroundings and lives in communities (biocenosis).

Are all cells the same?

No, the shape, size, and functions of cells can be very different. Besides the prokaryotes that have no cell nucleus, there are eukaryotes, organisms with a

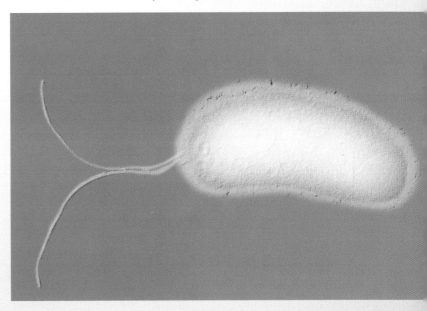

More than half of all people are infected with *Helicobacter pylori* bacteria. It is known to cause stomach ulcers and cancer of the stomach.

cell nucleus that are bound together to form a functional unit where independence is given up in favor of specialization. Thus, for example, skin, nerve, or muscle cells have different features. Eukaryotic animal cells are surrounded by a membrane, whereas eukaryotic plant and fungi cells have a cell wall in addition to a membrane.

What does the inside of a eukaryotic cell look like?

Every cell has a membrane that surrounds the cytoplasm with the cell organelles, and allows substances to be transferred (e.g. water and salts). The cell's organelles fulfill different tasks. Genetic information is stored in the nucleus, and the mitochondria—also known as the cell's power plants—generate adenosine triphosphate (the cell's main source of energy) by a process known as cellular respiration, which depends on oxygen being present. Proteins are sorted, converted, and stored in the Golgi body, the cell's "mail room." The endoplasmic reticulum's tasks range from protein production and transporting matter in the cells to storage functions. The chloroplasts in plant cells, which like the mitochondria have their own DNA, are used for photosynthesis.

What is the genetic data bank?

The software of life (to use a technical image) lies protected within the eukaryotic cell's nucleus.

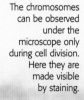

The chromosomes can be observed under the microscope only during cell division. Here they are made visible by staining.

The number of programs in which most genetic information (genes) is stored is distinctive for every species. Human cells, for instance, contain 46 chromosomes on which individual, personally different data is kept (see page 153). In mitotic cell division for cell renewal (e.g. blood or skin cells) or for cell growth (e.g. bone cells), the respective chromosome data file (to keep the same technical image) is copied and transferred to both daughter cells. If there is a copying failure (brought about by radioactive radiation, drugs, or mutagenic foodstuffs), the whole data file might possibly be affected. Uncontrolled cell growth—manifested in tumors— or infertility can be the result, but completely new characteristics may also emerge (see page 127).

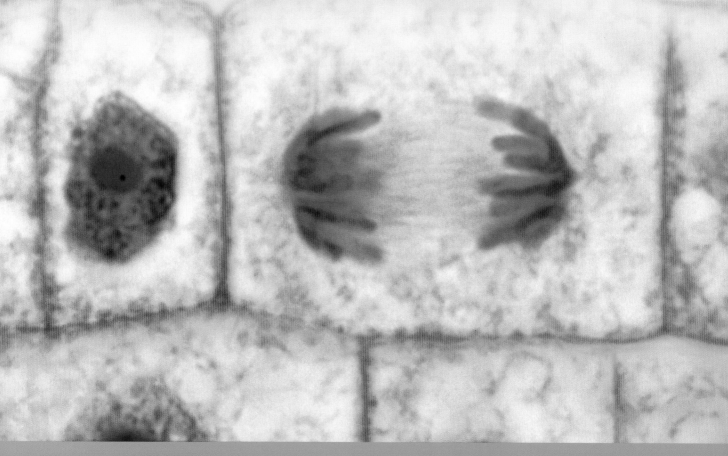

Microscopes: "seeing small things"

• The Romans and Greeks were already using convex-shaped lenses as magnifying glasses as early as 500 BC. Robert Hooke, one of the pioneers of microscopy, published a work entitled *Micrographia* in 1665, which contained numerous microscopic illustrations. Looking through the microscope soon became a popular pastime in the finest salons. Microscopy opens up a new world to anyone who becomes involved in it, whether they are viewing slides of animal or plant specimens, a diatom (microscopic unicellular alga) that is rich in structure and microscopically pretty, salt or sugar crystals, drops of water, or snowflakes.

• Micro artists like Johann Diedrich Möller (1844–1907) created patterns, images, words, and even scenes from diatoms, which were sold in slide form.

• The electron microscope gives a much more accurate image than purely optical systems can. The downside is the cost of the apparatus, the costly specimen preparation, and also the fact that living objects cannot be observed. The upside is the extremely high resolution, up to 0.1 nanometers (nm), whereas light microscopes can only identify objects up to 0.2 micrometers (μm).

The epidermis (skin) of plant leaves is punctuated by tiny stomas. Here, the underside of a camellia leaf is magnified 1,500 times.

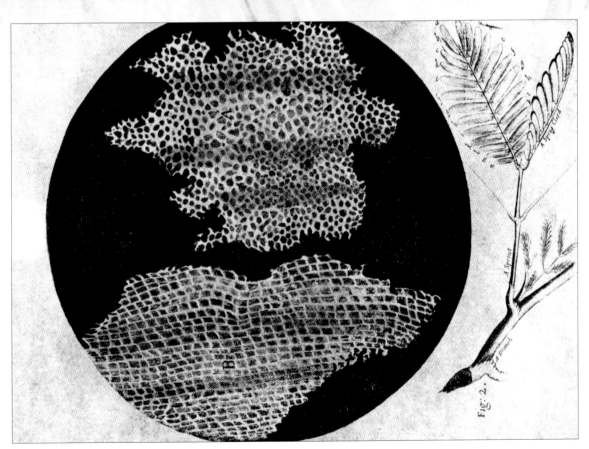

Robert Hooke (1635–1703) discovered the chambered structure of cork under the microscope and coined the expression "cell."

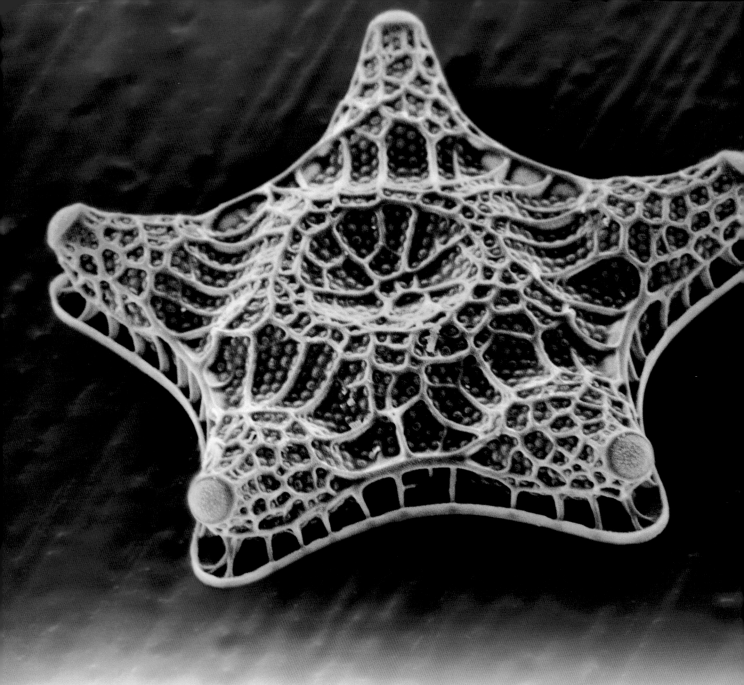

ORDER IN DIVERSITY

Many algae have a nucleus, therefore they are eukaryotes. This diatom species (magnified 1:3,000) resembles a starfish.

What is a kingdom?

Old school textbooks distinguish only between an animal and a plant kingdom. The zoologist Ernst Häckel (1834–1919) identified three kingdoms in 1884: animal (Animalia), plant (Plantae), and protist (Protista). The American botanist Robert Whittaker (1920–1980) proposed in 1959 the extension of biological taxonomy to include prokaryotes (Monera) and the kingdom Fungi. A sixth kingdom was added with the division of prokaryotes into Eubacteria and Archaebacteria by the biologist and evolutionist Carl R. Woese (born 1928). Genetic research prompted Woese to make a revolutionary new proposal in 1990: he suggested that in future only three domains should be distinguished, namely bacteria (Eubacteria), the archaea (primitive bacteria without a nucleus), and the eukaryotes (also called eucaryotes).

Which characteristics help us to distinguish between creatures?

Modern taxonomy groups creatures according to their characteristics. Prokaryotes (among them bacteria) have no proper cell nucleus (the DNA swims freely in the cytoplasm as a nucleoid, also known as the nuclear body or nuclear region), nor do they have membrane-bound organelles.

Bacteria live in the ground, in water, and in living and dead organisms. Archaea also have no proper cell nucleus, and they colonize extreme habitats (e.g. sulfur springs at over 176°F (80°C), or the Arctic and Antarctic ice regions) and tolerate extremely acid, salty, or alkaline environments. Up to now they are not known to be pathogens. In technology they are used, for instance, to produce biogas. And eukaryotes are creatures with a defined nucleus and include fungi, plants, animals, and unicellular and multicellular protists (algae, slime molds, amoebae, paramecium, and yeasts).

Are fungi animals without feet or plants without chlorophyll?

With more than 100,000 species worldwide (many of which are still waiting to be discovered), the fungi kingdom distinguishes itself from the plant kingdom by its lack of chlorophyll pigment and from the animal kingdom by the presence of a cell wall containing chitin. By means of photosynthesis, plants manufacture the organic substances vital for life. In doing so, they use exclusively carbon dioxide (CO_2) as a source of carbon, and produce oxygen. In contrast to plants, animals generate their energy not by photosynthesis but by feeding on other animal and plant organisms. Moreover, they need oxygen to breathe. Most animals are free to move from place to place and are equipped with sensory organs. Their cells are surrounded only by a membrane, so they do not have a cell wall like plants and fungi do.

Above: Trees, shrubs, and herbs as well as mosses and algae belong to the plant kingdom.

Right: Fungi have no chlorophyll. Many species feed on decomposing foliage and wood.

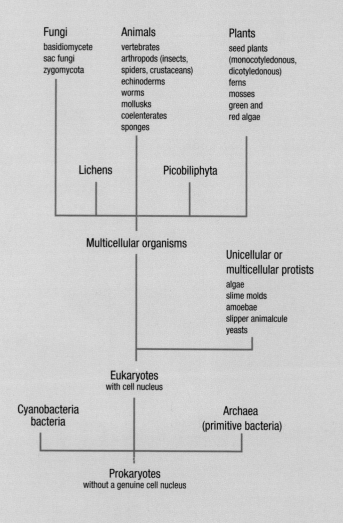

Fungi
basidiomycete
sac fungi
zygomycota

Animals
vertebrates
arthropods (insects,
spiders, crustaceans)
echinoderms
worms
mollusks
coelenterates
sponges

Plants
seed plants
(monocotyledonous,
dicotyledonous)
ferns
mosses
green and
red algae

Lichens   Picobiliphyta

Multicellular organisms

Unicellular or
multicellular protists
algae
slime molds
amoebae
slipper animalcule
yeasts

Eukaryotes
with cell nucleus

Cyanobacteria
bacteria   Archaea
                      (primitive bacteria)

Prokaryotes
without a genuine cell nucleus

The phylogenetic tree of life shows the evolutionary development of life forms, from unicellular to multicellular organisms.

What are lichens?

Lichens are a very successful combination of organisms. They are actually composed of two or three distinct species: green algae and/or cyanobacteria on the one hand, and fungi on the other. Indeed, lichens could be said to float between two kingdoms. The partnership enables both participants to survive even in extreme locations. The algae—capable of photosynthesis—supply the fungi with nutrients, whilst the fungi give the algae water and minerals and protect it from rapid drying out and from strong ultraviolet radiation. There are more than 20,000 species of lichen worldwide. They grow on bark, finished wood, old clapboard, acid peat soil, and on rocks in mountainous regions, but they also grow in smoggy inner-city areas. Some species are very sensitive and useful as bioindicators for long-term forecasting of atmospheric pollutants.

Which mountains consist of the remains of creatures?

The chalk cliffs on Rügen (an island in the Baltic Sea, just off the German coast) and the Jura mountain range (along the border between France and Switzerland) are formed from calcium carbonate shells of dead creatures such as foraminifers (small animal plankton) or deposits of diatoms and radiolarians that lived in the sea and either floated, swam, or crawled. Biologists, paleontologists, geologists, and climatologists can study and draw conclusions from these and other animals trapped in these strata (mussels, snails, fish, birds) about life on Earth in the distant past.

The portrait shows Carl von Linné, holding his favorite flower, the *Linnaea borealis* L., the Twinflower, which was named after him.

Why is Carl von Linné (Carl Linnaeus) called the father of taxonomy?

The popular, regional, and very different plant names (e.g. for dandelion we have "blow ball" and "pissenlit") are comparable to nicknames or pet names. In the same way that we have official registers of family names and first names, the Swedish naturalist Carl von Linné (1707–1788) introduced a system of binomial Latin names that allowed for the authoritative scientific names of all species. What is known as the Linnaean nomenclature consists of two Latin or Latinized words: first the genus is written (e.g. *Taraxacum* for dandelion), followed by the species (e.g. *officinale* for common). Plant and fungi genus and species names have to be different (e.g. opium poppy, *Papaver somniferum*), but animals' genus and species names may be identical (e.g. common toad, *Bufo bufo*).

Can there be confusion in the Linnaean nomenclature?

Yes, as the nomenclature normally applies to just one specific branch of science. It happens that from time to time botanists and zoologists may use the same names for entirely different organisms. For example, the zoologist understands *Prunella* to mean a small songbird, the dunnock or hedge sparrow, while a botanist calls a widely growing medicinal herb *Prunella*. And *Oxyporus* applies to a beetle genus as well as a fungi genus. An internationally uniform terminology is essential so that scientists from different countries can cooperate and communicate with one another, and, for each area of investigation (be it plants, animals, or even landscapes such as fens and moors, etc.), there are particular rules in place that govern definitions.

Where do scientific names come from?

The person who discovers a genus or a species generally names it. The name often refers to a special characteristic such as the color (white, *albus*), a surface structure such as hair covering (woolly, *lanuginosus*), a chemical or physical property (for example sleep inducing, *somniferous*), its time of appearance (spring, *vernalis*) or the place or country where it was first discovered (Sweden, *suecicus*). Dedicating a plant name to a deserving scientist is also a common practice (e.g. the camellia was named after the Jesuit father and naturalist Joseph Camel (1661–1706). The name of the first person to describe a plant (the author or authority) is added, usually in an abbreviated form, to the Latin name in the scientific literature (e.g. *Papaver somniferum L.*, whereby the "L" stands for Carl von Linné).

Chalk cliffs like the Seven Sisters at Cuckmere Haven in England consist of calcium carbonate from shells of dead animals.

THE ORIGIN OF BIODIVERSITY

How did the diversity of life develop on Earth?
We still do not know in exact detail the course of evolution—the development of simple forms to complex structured creatures and the alteration of species throughout Earth's history. However, paleontologists and biologists have compiled a wealth of information from fossil finds, comparative anatomical testing, and similarities in DNA. They have discovered, for example, that the ancestors of today's most important living animal and plant groups did not appear until the beginning of the Cambrian period 500 million years ago—very late considering the Earth's history. Guide fossils such as trilobites (from the Cambrian period) and ammonites (from the Devonian period, i.e. 416 million years ago, up to the end of the Cretaceous period 145.5 million years ago) enable the correlation of other finds. Tests on tree and herb pollens in soil, peat, and ice samples give information on climate, development of vegetation,

The crustacean *Aeger spinipes*, which lived in the Jura 200 million years ago. It is closely related to present-day prawns.

and human settlement (clearing and husbandry) in the last 10,000 years. Creatures with skin, hair, and even clothing can be preserved in dry desert climates, perpetual ice, and salt deposits as well as in wet, anaerobic peat bogs.

What are fossils?
The word fossil (from Latin *fossilis*, "dug up") is the term used for traces and remains of organisms that are more than around 10,000 years old. Impressions of plants (such as ferns) have been found, animals have left footprints, nests, or droppings, and under especially favorable climatic conditions pieces such as bones, teeth, snail shells, or scales have been preserved. Real fossils originate when the decomposed organic substance is replaced by calcium or silicic acid (as with mussel shells), or cavities are filled in (as with sea urchins). Stone copies are formed as the organism undergoes mineral replacement, i.e. becomes petrified. Alternatively, even fine structures of insects and plants trapped in liquid resin are preserved after the resin has hardened to form amber. Layers of rock with fossils can be dated by using the radiometric dating method.

These insects were trapped in amber (a once-liquid fossil resin) around 35 million years ago.

How is the age of fossils determined?

Layers of rock up to an age of 4.5 billion years are dated by the uranium-lead method, and up to 1.25 billion years by the potassium-argon method. Both types of radiometric dating are based on the fact that radioactive isotopes decay in a precise known time period. The half-life is described as a period after which only half of the original isotope is present. As no isotopes at all have reached the organism since it became embedded in the rock, it is possible in this way to determine the age of a fossil. For younger finds (for instance up to 50,000 years old) the radiocarbon method is used, in which drilled cores from perpetual ice and annual tree rings are used as a calibration. It is assumed that a creature (as long as it is alive) absorbs carbon in the form of ^{14}C isotopes. After death the supply of carbon ceases and decay begins—with a half-life of 5,730 years.

Who were the fathers of the Theory of Evolution?

In the 18th century, for the first time the idea was formulated that all creatures mutate and evolve. In 1809, the naturalist and philosopher Jean Baptiste de Lamarck (1744–1829) advanced the first theory of evolution. He concluded from his observations, among other things, that creatures bequeath to their offspring certain characteristics that they have acquired in their lifetime, and that every organism has the ability to adapt to the environment and has

The primitive bird Archaeopteryx lived around 150 million years ago. Its fossils were discovered near Eichstätt in southern Germany.

the urge to be perfect. He cited the giraffe's long neck as evidence for this theory: the giraffe that often stretched its neck to reach the leaves on tall trees would have given this ability to its offspring. However, Darwin's research and Mendel's rules (see page 150) refuted this theory.

What is Darwinism?

Charles Darwin (1809–1882), father of the Theory of Evolution, who gave his name to Darwinism, published his book *On the Origin of Species* in 1859. Motivated by observations he made while on an expedition on a survey ship in the Galapagos Islands and by the collections of finches and lizard species that he found there, he postulated the theory that species evolve by natural selection or die out. Fossil finds as well as the discovery of the Neanderthals in 1856 convinced him of his theories. It was only through the discovery of Mendel's rules (see page 150) that the mode of transmission of characteristics could be explained. However, Darwin's theory, one of the foundations of evolutionary biology, is still being debated, revised, and refined even today.

How do new species originate?

Changes to the genetic make-up by spontaneous and artificial mutations were and are the prerequisite for development of biodiversity. These developed characteristics must prove themselves in the fight for survival. Only then

Charles Darwin at the age of 69.

Darwin's key sentences:
- Animal and plant species did not originate by a unique act of creation.
- Species develop continuously with a tendency to increase in size. This leads to a constant struggle for survival among the members of the species.
- Similar organisms come from a common ancestor.
- Evolution proceeds slowly, not in leaps and bounds. It is advanced by natural selection of the fittest.

are they "selected," passed on from generation to generation.

In macroevolution (major changes in evolution, such as when a new species is formed), in the origin of mammals, for example, completely new structures developed over the course of time, namely hair, mammary glands, and the ability to regulate body temperature, all of which is still lacking in scaly, cold-blooded, non-suckling reptiles.

In microevolution (small genetic changes) there are changes of characteristics within a family within a comparatively short space of time, such as finch species in the different islands of the Galapagos archipelago that have different beak shapes or differently colored plumage.

If a mutation brings with it an advantage compared to fellow members of the species that have not changed, it will spread within the population (the group of organisms of the same

Left: This red-green marine iguana that lives on one of the Galapagos islands looks like a relic from the age of dinosaurs.

Below: The maned wolf, the largest wild dog in South America, has adapted itself to hunting in long grass during the course of evolution.

White skin and hair and red eyes are typical for albinos that (like this hedgehog) suffer from congenital lack of pigment.

genetic information that is stored in the DNA can be altered, passed on via egg and seed cells, and thus handed down from one generation to the next. Although only very few mutations bring advantages for the individual, they are very important for the dynamics of evolution.

In the 20th century, germs (seeds) were prompted by outside influences (mutagens) such as heat, powerful ionizing radiation, or chemical substances to spontaneously mutate. Artificial mutation techniques in plant cultivation made it possible to breed fruitful varieties from small and less fertile wild plants in economically viable amounts.

Mutations that affect just the somatic cells and not germ cells are not handed down. Mutagens such as environmental poisons or energy-rich radiation can, however, under certain conditions, alter the rate of division of normal cells so that uncontrolled growth of cancer cells emerges.

species in the same area). If a population is split up by outside influences (e.g. a rock fall or the formation of islands), the divided groups will evolve independently and adapt to their respective areas. If the former sections of the population are no longer capable of reproduction, new species emerge, as in the case of Darwin's finches. Selection gives evolution its direction; it determines whether an inherited characteristic can become established or whether it disappears again.

What are mutations?
Mutations are sudden, abrupt, usually insignificant changes in genetic make-up. By mutation, the

Red-green blindness is inherited via the x-chromosome. Around 8 percent of all males cannot distinguish the number 68 in this illustration.

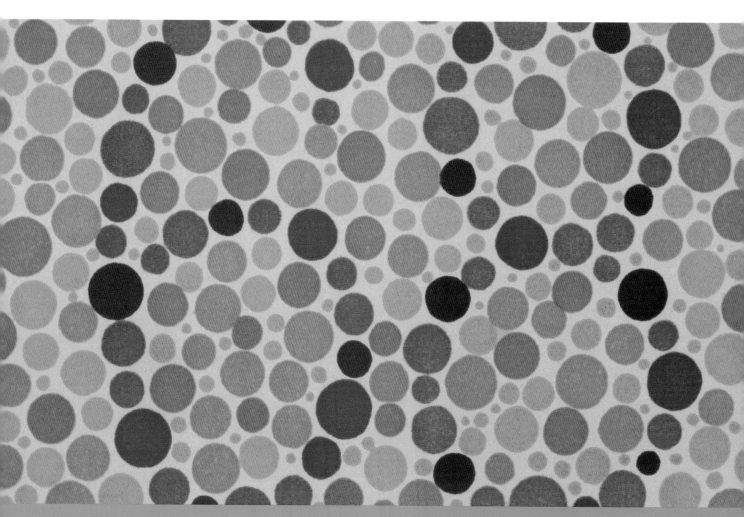

Good inventions take hold: homology and analogy

A similarity that results from a common ancestry is called homology. Bats' wings and elephants' feet, for example, look completely different but the bone structure is designed in principally the same way—upper arm, lower arm, carpals, metacarpals, and finger bones are from the same ancestry. The closer creatures are related, the more alike they are.

Similar conditions in different parts of the world demand similar solutions (convergent evolution). The American hummingbirds have their equivalents in the nectar-loving birds of Africa and Asia, the African elephant in the Indian elephant, the European wolf in the Tasmanian wolf (or thylacine, extinct since 1936), and the European beech in the Southern beech in the southern hemisphere. However, if different groups adapt independently of one another to a certain habitat or a certain way of living, then the problem-solving can be the same but the design will be different. Although pterosaurs, birds, and bats are vertebrates, they have developed completely different wing structures. In pterosaurs the wing skin is stretched by an extremely elongated finger. In birds the whole wing is feathered and the fingers are partially reduced and have grown together. In bats the skin is stretched between several fingers. Such analogies in development can also be seen in the streamlined form of penguins (birds), whales (mammals), marine reptiles, and fish, which were adapted for living and hunting in water. Likewise, dragonflies (insects), swallows (birds), and bats (mammals) are not related to each other although they fly and hunt insects and their wings fulfill a similar (analogous) function.

In the fight for survival does the strongest always win?

No, the ability of a population to survive depends mainly on the fertility of individuals. The more offspring are produced, the more diverse the outer appearance (phenotype) is, the better the genetic make-up (genotype) is mixed, and the quicker the favorable characteristics for survival can be passed on. That does not mean that the most beautiful, strongest, and biggest always have the advantage; what counts most is intelligence, adaptability, and the ability to cooperate.

Unbalanced selection can also end up in a dead end. If, for instance, the food supply dries up due to environmental reasons, then food specialists might be endangered. The Australian koala bear that only feeds off the leaves of certain eucalyptus trees, for example, would be sentenced to death if this tree species fell victim to climate change or pests. And if living conditions change, then what were once outsiders—those that are especially small or large, that are disease resistant or flexible in their eating habits—can occupy ecological niches and secure an advantage for themselves and their offspring to ensure survival.

In nature, competition for living space, light, water, mates, and food as well as the constant struggle against disease, predators, and the vicissitudes of climate see to it that no life form gains the upper hand. However, breeding (by artificial selection) assists those individuals that have characteristics desirable to reproduce.

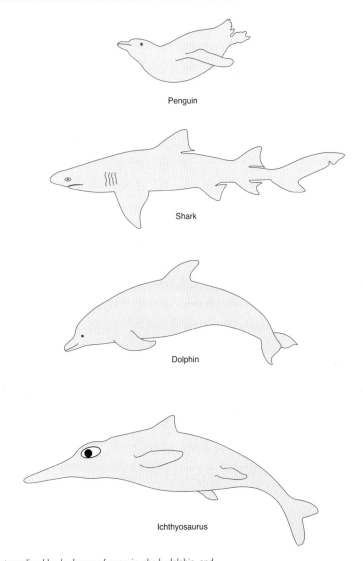

Penguin

Shark

Dolphin

Ichthyosaurus

The streamlined body shapes of penguin, shark, dolphin, and ichthyosaurus have evolved to adapt to their habitat.

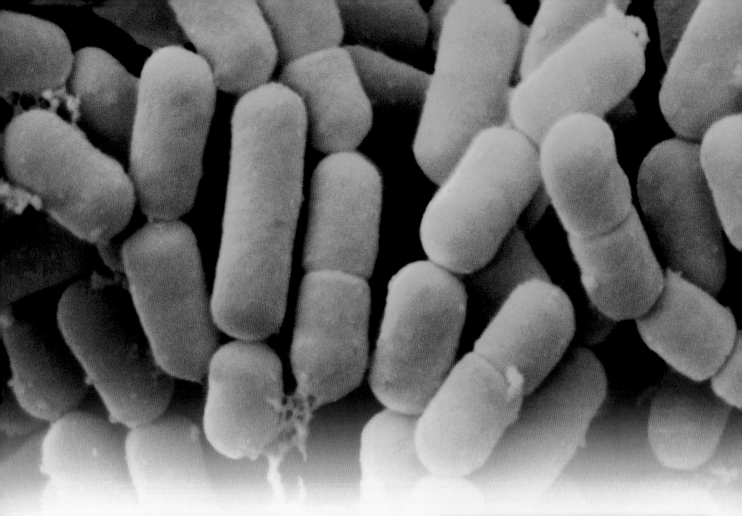

FROM THE BACTERIUM TO THE HUMAN

The lactic acid bacteria (*Lactobacillus*) are important aids in digestion.

What are bacteria?

Bacteria are microscopically small, usually unicellular, and do not have a proper cell nucleus. They belong to the prokaryotes. They have diverse shapes ranging from rods (bacillary), spheres (cocci), curves (vibriones), and spirals (spirilla), right up to screws (spirochetes). Bacteria can be found in the air, earth, and water, and in humans, animals, and plants. Many can survive drought, heat, cold, and lack of food, some of them for years as dormant bodies (spores or capsules). Rod-shaped bacteria are called bacillus, and they form heat-resistant spores.

Are bacteria pests or are they beneficial?

They can be either, as the task of bacteria (to break down organic substances) can be beneficial as well as harmful. Putrefactive bacteria, for instance, spoil meat, fish, bread, fruit, or drinks. The poisonous

Interesting facts about bacteria

- Bacteria were observed in water and human saliva by Antoni von Leeuwenhoek (1632–1723) in 1675 with the aid of a homemade microscope.

- Although around 6,000 species have already been identified, this is at most 5% of bacteria species existing on Earth.

- Around 30 billion bacteria are excreted in our daily bowel movement. Despite this, the intestinal flora that develops in the first days of life remains relatively stable for the whole of our lives. The intestinal bacterium *Methanobrevibacter smithii* improves conditions in the intestine by breaking down hydrogen and the end products of other bacteria so that food is utilized around 15% more efficiently.

- In 1999, the largest known bacterium was discovered. The sulfur bacterium—known as the sulfur pearl of Namibia (*Thiomargarita namibiensis*) and with a diameter of up to 0.03 in (0.75mm)—is visible with the naked eye.

- The ability of cyanobacteria to perform oxygenic photosynthesis 3.5 billion years ago is thought to have converted the atmosphere into an oxidizing one, which provoked an explosion of biodiversity through the development of oxygen-breathing organisms.

DR. KOCH IN SEARCH OF THE RINDERPEST MICROBE AT KIMBERLEY.
From a Photo by Frank Hancox, Kimberley.

Robert Koch (1843–1910) discovered anthrax (*Bacillus anthracis*) and tuberculosis (*Mycobacterium tuberculosis*).

- Do not leave leftovers lying around.
- Change hand towels, flannels, and clothes regularly.
- Store food in a cool place, especially in warm weather.
- Make sure your hands are clean after visiting the bathroom, tending to sick people, or touching animals.
- Use disinfectant when nursing the sick.

What is the difference between viruses and bacteria?

Viruses are so small (15–400 nm) that they can only be seen under an electron microscope. They do not have any of their own metabolic enzymes and are always parasitic. To reproduce they need the biological mechanisms of the host cell. Viruses consist of proteins and nucleic acid, either deoxyribonucleic acid (DNA) or ribonucleic acid (RNA). They are surrounded by a protein coat (capsid) and some have a lipid "envelope." Viruses are agents of infectious diseases in people (e.g. polio, measles, influenza, AIDS), in animals (rabies, foot and mouth disease), and in plants (tobacco mosaic virus). They often occur jointly

A microbiologist working with coliform bacteria and salmonella, which have been cultivated in Petri dishes.

substances (toxins) that result make food inedible or indigestible. On the other hand, bacteria are used in the production of cheese, yogurt, and sauerkraut. Equally, bacteria are used in medicines (antibiotics, hormones) and chemicals (butyric acid, lactic acid, butyl alcohol). Intestinal bacteria (there are 400–500 different species in the human intestines) are essential for our wellbeing. They split food into individual components so that they can be absorbed through the intestinal wall into the bloodstream and are then available for different metabolic processes.

Bacteria in the earth and water are also advantageous, as the carbon, nitrogen, sulfur, and phosphorus cycles are kept going by putrefactive and fermentation processes. Furthermore, bacteria are important for the biological phase in purification plants and in the decomposition of plant material, e.g. in compost heaps.

How can we protect ourselves from harmful bacteria?

Observing some rules of hygiene reduces the danger of infection and damage to health. Here are some simple rules to follow:
- Wash fruit and vegetables before eating.
- Store food securely away from vermin.
- Destroy any food that has been infested with vermin.

with fungal infections (e.g. the yeast fungus *Candida albicans*).

Can bacteria also cause dangerous diseases?

Yes, the pathogens of infectious diseases such as salmonellosis, tetanus, diphtheria, or typhus, for example. They are spread by transmission (e.g. airborne infection when coughing or sneezing) or through contact with an infected person or animal. The bacteria enter the bloodstream, and can destroy tissue or poison by toxins. A disease limited by time or to a specific area is called an epidemic (e.g. cholera and typhus). A global infection is a pandemic.

The avian flu virus represents a grave threat for poultry and humans.

Interesting facts

• Chickenpox and shingles are caused by the varicella-zoster virus (VZV), and herpes by its near neighbor, the herpes simplex virus (HSV). Antibiotics are ineffective against viruses.

• There are very few medicines that restrict the growth of viruses. In AIDS, for instance, zidovudine (azidothymidine, AZT) is used therapeutically.

• The genetic make-up of viruses (e.g. influenza) changes constantly so that new vaccines have to be developed again and again.

• Some viruses do not occur in specific hosts, i.e. they switch between birds, animals, and humans (e.g. avian flu and influenza).

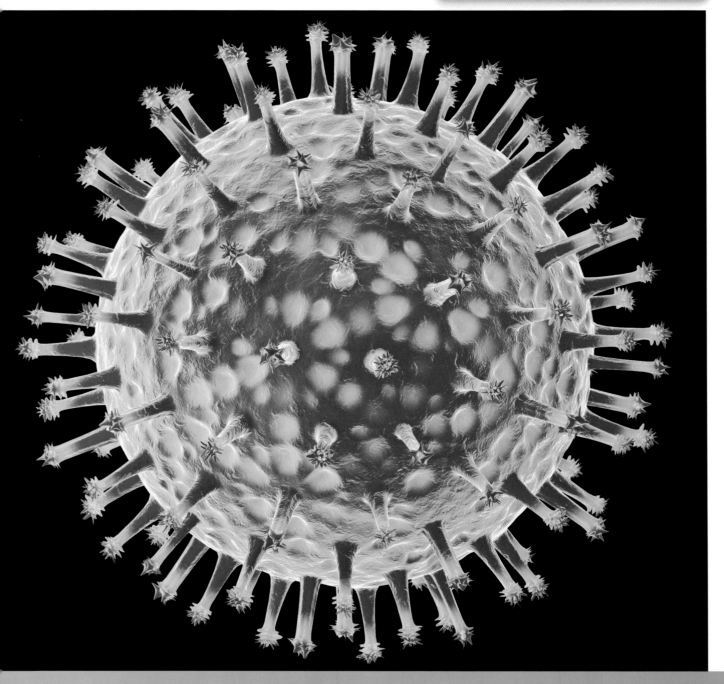

FROM ALGAE TO THE REDWOOD TREE

How are plants differentiated?

The plant kingdom is very broadly subdivided into fresh-water or salt-water algae and seed plants. Seed or flowering plants in turn are categorized as monocots or monocotyledons, i.e. containing one embryonic leaf or cotyledon (e.g. grasses and grains, orchids and lilies), and dicots or dicotyledons, i.e. containing two embryonic leaves (including single-furrow-pollen dicots such as *Magnoliopsida*, e.g. water lilies and magnolias, and three-furrow-pollen dicots such as *Rosopsida*, e.g. roses and carnations). All seed plants have a basic structure of roots, stalks, leaves, and flowers with an ovary containing one or more ovules.

Are all algae plants?

No, strictly speaking only green and red algae are plants as only they photosynthesize. The other algae species are unicellular creatures (protists) such as brown algae and diatoms. There are algae that live on tree trunks or rocks, on damp leaves or in damp soils, in the snow or predominantly in water (plankton). They can be unicellular or multicellular and live symbiotically with fungi or (like the zooxanthellae) with certain marine

Spirulina algae, which live in the strong alkaline water in Lake Natron in northern Tanzania, Africa, color the lake red.

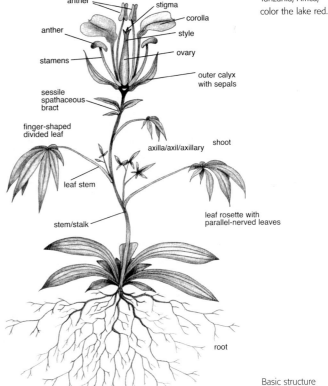

anther

stigma

corolla

anther

style

ovary

stamens

outer calyx with sepals

sessile spathaceous bract

finger-shaped divided leaf

axilla/axil/axillary

shoot

leaf stem

leaf rosette with parallel-nerved leaves

stem/stalk

root

root network

Basic structure of a plant.

animals. Laminaria kelp, which forms long stretches of seaweed in coastal areas, is especially striking.

How do plants feed?

If the glucose formed in the leaves is not needed for leaf, flower, or seed formation, the plant can lay down some food reserves. Plants, whose upper parts die off in winter, store deposits of food for hard times ahead—in roots (carrots), rhizomes (cassava or manioc), bulbs (tulips), or tubers (dahlias). In spring in some areas, the rising, sugar-filled sap (e.g. of maples and birches) is used for making syrup. The stems are like pipelines that transport sugar and many other substances. The plant makes use of a physics principle for transport: the leaves or needles have breathing holes called stomas, and these open in warm, dry air and give off water to the environment. A pull is created that draws up water absorbed by the roots together with the mineral salts dissolved in it. The suction power of trees' roots is so strong that they can pump water to a height of around 490 ft (150 m).

Why do some plants have such striking flowers?

The need to attract pollinators during the course of their evolution has led plants to create a huge diversity of shapes, colors, and strategies. Plants

This cross-section of a leaf shows the xylem (vascular tissue transporting water and minerals from the roots) and phloem (tissue that transports food and sugars from the leaves) and the spongy storage tissue (parenchyma).

What is rose fever?

Colds, irritable throat, running eyes, and sometimes also a high temperature, which occurred at the time of roses coming into bloom (June and July), were once regarded as symptoms of rose fever. Now we know that summer hay fever—more correctly known as seasonal allergic rhinitis—is predominantly caused by grass and grain pollen. Colds in January or February are frequently an allergic reaction to hazel or alder pollen. In August and September common ragweed (*Ambrosia artemisiifolia*), a native of North America that is spreading ever northward from eastern and southern Europe due to climate change, causes severe pollen and contact allergies.

that are fertilized by bees, beetles, butterflies, flies, hummingbirds, or bats have to attract their visitors either by their striking flowers (large, brightly colored petals, numerous flowers), an intoxicating scent (simulated sexual attractants, the smell of carrion), or by an offer of food (pollen, nectar). Just a few of the often very large male pollen are sufficient to guarantee fertilization and, with it, seed formation.

On the other hand, plants that rely on wind or water as a means of transportation do not need female, showy attractions.

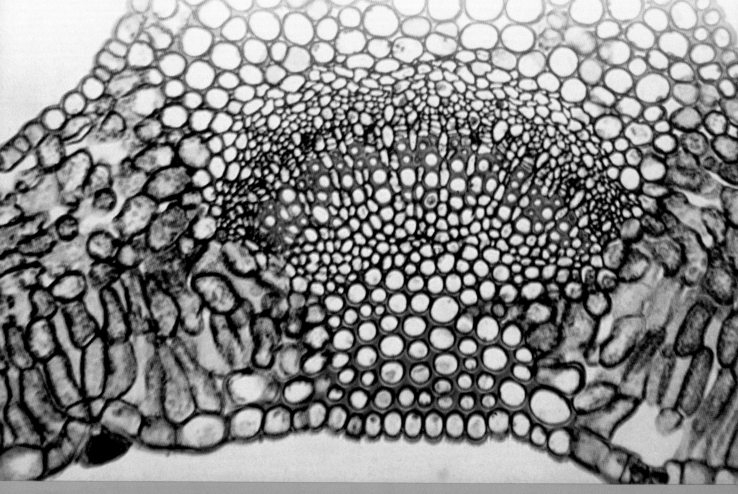

They produce immense quantities of small, lighter pollen, in swaying, hanging catkins that sprinkle pollen before the leaves open out, for example, or in the case of grasses (e.g. rye) in anthers on a long stem.

What happens in photosynthesis?

Photosynthesis is the process whereby carbon dioxide (CO_2), absorbed from the atmosphere, and water supplied by the roots use the Sun's energy to make glucose ($C_6H_{12}O_6$). Oxygen (O_2) is created as a "waste product." Glucose is both an energy supplier and also the base material for the synthesis of nutrients and reserves. The green pigment in plants (chlorophyll) absorbs light energy to facilitate photosynthesis. In the course of evolution, some plants have lost their chlorophyll and live as parasites on other plants (e.g. *Rafflesia* and the domestic broomrape *Orobanche*).

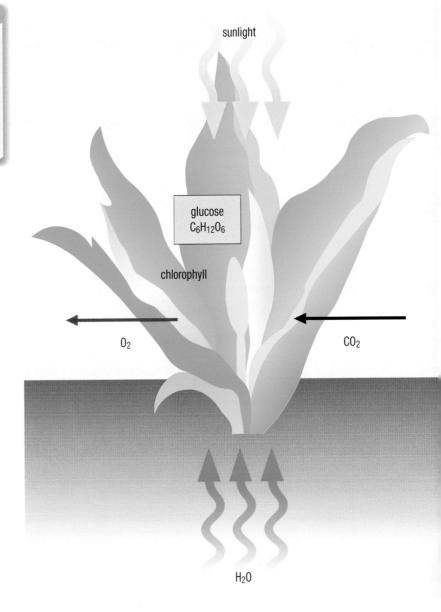

sunlight

glucose
$C_6H_{12}O_6$

chlorophyll

O_2

CO_2

H_2O

Above: This diagram represents a simplified version of the light reaction of photosynthesis.

Equation for light reaction

- Under the influence of sunlight, oxygen and glucose are created from carbon dioxide and water.
- The photosynthesis equation is:
  $$6\ CO_2 + 6\ H_2O + photons \rightarrow C_6H_{12}O_6 + 6\ O_2.$$
- From every six molecules of carbon dioxide and six molecules of water, one molecule of glucose and six molecules of oxygen are created.

Willow pollen sticks together with a putty-like substance and can be easily transported by bees seeking food.

FUNGI: THE UNKNOWN CREATURES

Do fungi photosynthesize?

No, fungi do not have the ability to photosynthesize. They live as destruents (an ecology term for decomposers), such as the wood-decomposing tinder fungus or the hoof fungus (*Fomes fomentarius*), or they live as parasites, such as the stinking parachute (*Marasmius perforans*), which lives in the mulch of coniferous forests. Ergot (*Claviceps purpurea*) lives parasitically on grasses, and the birch bolete (*Leccinum scabrum*) lives in symbiosis with the birch.

Is there a characteristic that makes a poisonous mushroom identifiable?

No, many edible mushrooms have poisonous or at least inedible look-alikes. Also, the blue color of the flesh when in contact with oxygen is not a reliable sign, as there are poisonous fungi such as the devil's bolete (*Boletus satanas*) which only show faintly blue, and edible mushrooms like the inkstain bolete (*Boletus pulverulentus*) which stain intense blue. The only safe method to protect you from poisoning is to have an intimate knowledge of the mushrooms that you want to eat. Good books on fungi can help, but you must read the text and not just look at the pictures!

Can you eat raw mushrooms?

No, with just a few exceptions (such as cultivated mushrooms, cèpes, and oyster mushrooms) edible mushrooms should not be eaten until they have been cooked for at least 15–20 minutes. Fungal poisons (such as in honey-colored agaric) are only destroyed by heat, and fungal protein is very difficult to digest.

What are magic mushrooms?

Magic mushrooms are fungi that bring on hallucinations. Apart from the fact that they are illegal, there is always the danger that they might be confused with poisonous look-alikes. The effect of hallucinogenic fungi is different from species to species and because of the variable concentration of the content, the effects are much more difficult to estimate than those of hashish. Personality changes and unforeseen reactions can occur even if they have been used only once.

Even the very desirable cèpes have a look-alike, the bad-tasting bitter boletus.

ANIMALS: CONQUERORS OF ALL HABITATS?

According to which characteristics are animals classifed?

The animal kingdom has numerous subgroups (e.g. coelenterates, insects, and vertebrates) whose species show a common structure. Thus, the coelenterates (*Coelenterata*) that live in the sea—among them jellyfish and sea anemones—have a radial symmetric body and a diffuse nervous system, but no skeleton and no blood circuit. Their bodies consist merely of two layers of cells with a gelatinous area between them. Insects (*Insecta*), which have mainly conquered the air and the ground, have a chitinous exoskeleton, a body with three sections, and highly developed sensory organs in common. The vertebrates (*Vertebrata*), to which fish, amphibians, reptiles, birds, and mammals belong, have an endoskeleton, a many-layered exterior skin with scales, feathers, or hair, a brain protected by a solid "capsule," eyes, ears, and olfactory organs, as well as a nervous system.

Why do some animals hibernate?

Some animals pass periods of cold and shortage of food supply by hibernating or entering periods of dormancy. During hibernation, the normal body temperature of mammals (e.g. marmots, edible dormice, hedgehogs) drops to values between 48.2°F (9°C) and 33.8°F (1°C). Breathing becomes

faint and the heartbeat slows. This together with fat reserves that have been built up during autumn feeding help them to survive. Badgers, raccoons, and squirrels wake from time to time from their winter dormancy in order to restock on food. Cold-blooded animals such as reptiles (snakes, tortoises, lizards) and amphibians (frogs, newts, salamanders), whose body temperature adapts to the temperature of their surroundings, can fall into a torpor that can last up to six months long. In hot regions there are animals that estivate (become dormant during hot or dry periods). Crocodiles and snakes belong to this group.

The marmot can stand upright thanks to its spinal column.

Are insects beneficial or harmful?

Both. In our environment, insects live on both useful plants and ornamental plants (e.g. bark beetles, potato beetles, leaf wasps, aphids), on timber (e.g. termites), on food stocks (e.g. moths,

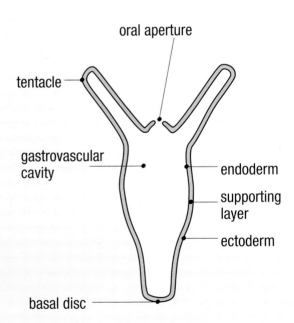

oral aperture

tentacle

gastrovascular cavity

endoderm

supporting layer

ectoderm

basal disc

Cross-section of a sea anemone. Coelenterates have neither an exoskeleton as insects do nor an endoskeleton as vertebrates do.

cockroaches), and as parasites (fleas) or pests (midges). Others are known to carry disease, such as the anopheles mosquito (malaria) and the tsetse fly (sleeping sickness).

On the other hand, around 500 insect species are a protein-rich food in many areas of Africa, Southeast Asia, and Central and South America. Furthermore, insects are used in the production of textile fibers (silkworms), dyes, varnishes, or waxes (e.g. the shellac of scale insects), and in the pharmaceutical industry (cantharides, a preparation made from the Spanish fly). Besides this, they are used as biological pest controllers in forestry and gardening (e.g. ichneumon wasps) and as laboratory animals (fruit flies, crickets, grasshoppers). Mainly, though, they serve to pollinate flowers (bees, bumble bees), as without them there would be no fruit or seed cultivation.

Fossilized insects from around 350 million years ago show that with over a million species, insects have conquered almost all habitats and regions of the Earth.

Are spiders insects?

No, the arachnids, to which ticks, harvestmen, and scorpions also belong, have four pairs of

Humpback whales (*Megaptera novaeangliae*), which often swim in coastal waters, can grow up to 50 ft (15 m) long.

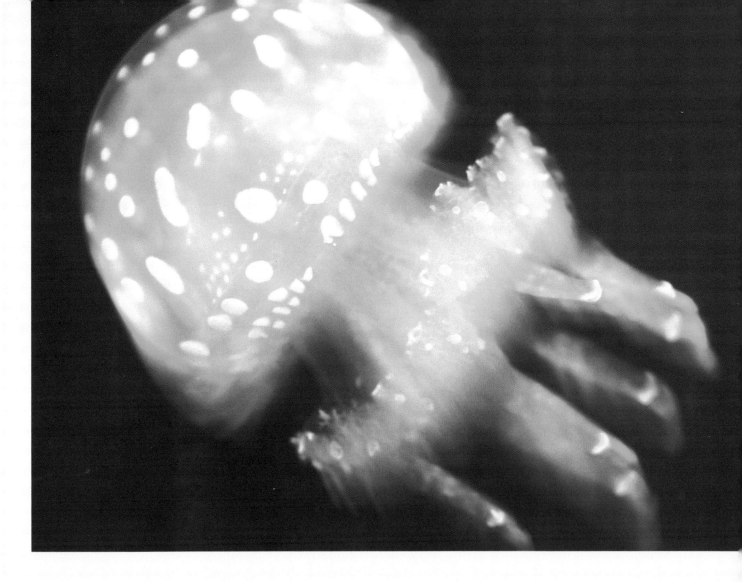

legs as opposed to the three pairs of an insect. Their body has two parts: the cephalothorax and the abdomen. Insects, on the other hand, have three parts: head, thorax, and abdomen. Spiders do not have compound eyes but usually eight simple eyes. These hunting animals are frequently equipped with poisonous claws, pincers, or sensory organs. Scorpions have a long tail with a poisonous sting.

What is bioluminescence?
Some animals, such as fireflies, but also different bacteria and fungi, produce by chemical reactions what is called cold light, i.e. no heat is created (unlike in a light bulb). Animals such as frogfish and butterfly fish, which live in the dark of the deep sea, produce light to attract prey or mates. The vampire squid (*Vampyrteuthis infernalis*), an octopus species, has light organs on its whole body that are used for hunting. Apart from this, it can emit clouds of light particles to confuse its enemies.

The spotted jellyfish (*Mastigias papua*) lives in the lagoons of the South Pacific. It feeds on animal plankton and owes its color to symbiotic algae.

Interesting facts

• Amphibians do not drink. They absorb water through their skin.
• Amphibious larvae breathe with gills. Adult frogs, newts, and salamanders, however, breathe with simple lungs and via the skin.
• Half of all vertebrates are fish, with about 27,000 species, while there are only about 9,800 species of birds. The oldest fish fossils to be found are 450 million years old.
• The skeletons of sharks and rays consist of cartilage and not bones as with other fish.
• All known bird species have a body temperature of around 107.6°F (42°C).
• The bone mass in birds makes up 8–9% of the body mass. In mammals, however, it constitutes up to 30%.
• Whales and dolphins are mammals and breathe with lungs.
• The cheetah is the fastest land animal.

HUMAN BEINGS:
THE PRIDE OF CREATION?

The fossils of *Homo habilis*, an ancestor of *Homo erectus*, were found in the Olduvai Gorge in northern Tanzania.

Where are the roots of humanity?
It is undisputed that Africa is the cradle of humanity. Around 4 million years ago, the *Australopithecus* species, the forerunner of modern humans, began to evolve. As with gorillas, the male was markedly bigger (5¼ ft/1.6 m) than the female (4⅓ ft/1.3 m). The *Hominid* "Lucy," found in 1974 and who lived 3.18 million years ago in what we know as Ethiopia today, already had an upright gait. Around 800,000 years ago in Africa, the advancement of *Homo erectus* began, which led to the emergence of the *Homo neanderthalensis* in Europe, and to the *Homo sapiens* (modern humans) in Africa around 120,000 years ago. From his African homeland, he conquered the whole world.

What has food to do with human development?
Around 2.5 million years ago, the upright-walking human (*Homo erectus*) was already producing stone tools. He cut up the meat that he had caught and began to roam through larger and larger territories to hunt his food. Feeding on flesh, which had higher calorific value than plants, led in the course of evolution to an increase in brain mass and at the same time to a decrease in the length of the gut. The modern human uses 20 percent of his entire energy production for his brain activity.

The skulls (left to right) show: *Homo neanderthalensis*, *Homo erectus*, *Homo sapiens*. In the course of human evolution, the volume of the brain increased and the facial skeleton shortened.

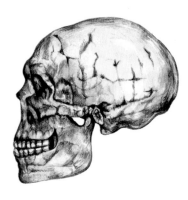
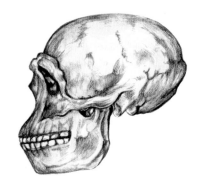
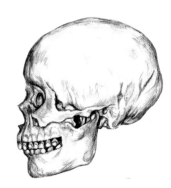

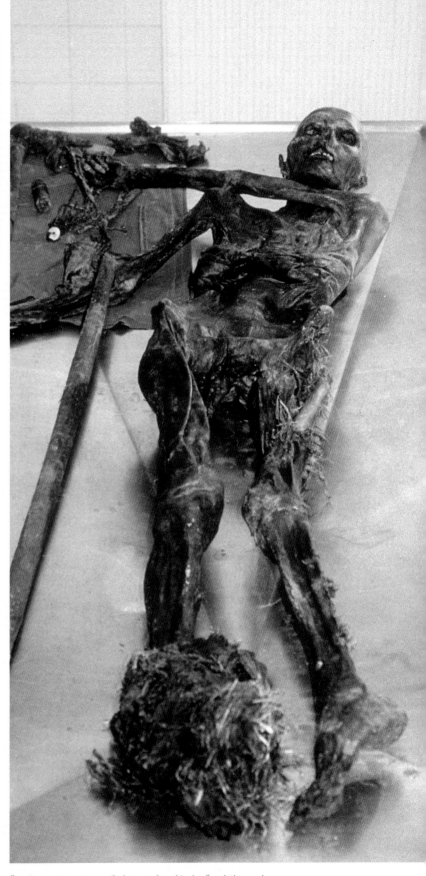

Ötzi the Iceman, a mummified corpse found in the Ötztal Alps on the border between Italy and Austria, sheds light on life toward the end of the Neolithic Age (around 5,300 years ago).

An ancestor of the modern *Homo sapiens* still lived in Indonesia 18,000 years ago. There in 2003 the remains of *Homo erectus floresiensis* were discovered; he was around 39 in (1 m) tall and weighed 55 lb (25 kg).

What distinguishes humans from apes?

Whereas apes move with a bent back supported by long arms, the double-S curve of the human spinal column enabled an upright gait and therefore the ability to "see the lie of the land." The teeth became weaker as evolution progressed and the cerebrum was freed for new tasks. The ape's grasp, which at best is suited for climbing, is not as skillful as the human grip.

Who was the Neanderthal man?

The Neanderthal man inhabited today's Europe for more than 100,000 years, and there are traces of him until around 27,000 years ago. After his discovery in the Neander Valley near Düsseldorf in 1856, he was long regarded as stupid, wild, and brutish. Now we know that the Neanderthals communicated, looked after their old and sick, and ritually buried their dead. They were successful hunters, slaying small animals such as squirrels, rabbits, and foxes, but also mammoths, giant stags, and cave lions. They knew how to make tools and decorative objects, they used fire, and had knowledge of the effects of medicinal herbs. Whether modern humans and the Neanderthals mated is still unclear, but it is proved that both populated the same area for some thousands of years. After the last great ice age (the Würm/Wisconsinan ice age in Europe), the Neanderthals died out. Modern humans, who had a higher life expectancy and more children, displaced them.

ECOLOGY: EVERYTHING UNDER ONE ROOF

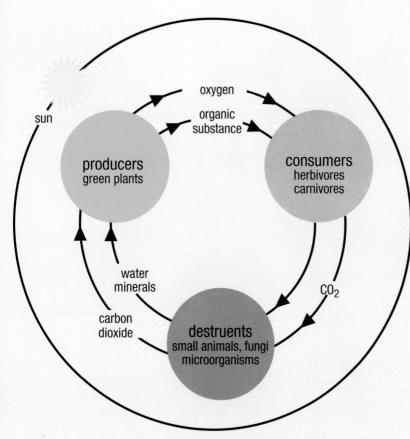

Producers—consumers—destruents. Each depends on the other. In nature's cycle nothing is lost.

What is understood by ecology?

Ecology (from the Greek *logos*, "study," and *oikos*, "house") means "the study of interrelationships of all organisms and their environment." The expression, coined by Ernst Haeckel (1834–1919), has also been used since the middle of the 20th century in the fields of social sciences and politics.

Success or failure in life: which factors make a difference?

We distinguish between outside influences (abiotic factors) such as light, warmth, oxygen, or soil quality, and influences of the animate environment (biotic factors). Species that share the same habitat (ecosystem) influence one another, whether competing for food, mates, or living space, whether as hunters or prey. Their relationships are in their turn controlled by abiotic factors such as long periods of frost or rain and the associated lack of food.

Which relationships exist in ecological systems?

The mutual dependencies in the animal kingdom, plant kingdom, and between species of different kingdoms are extraordinarily diverse and complex:

Symbiosis: by this we mean a freely entered relationship in which both sides benefit. Alternatively, some organisms have an obligatory symbiosis to both sides' advantage, e.g. sea anemones and clownfish, algae and fungi (lichens).

Parasitism: here any advantage is one-sided, benefiting the parasite, whilst the host suffers from it, e.g. fleas, lice, and ticks feed themselves and their offspring on the blood of dogs, cats, and humans.

Predator-prey relationship: this is profitable for the predator and, although deadly, not completely negative for the prey. The fox, for example, feeds (among other things) on mice. It is advantageous for the mouse species in that it eliminates the weak, sick, and slow animals.

Competition: this can be negative for both sides, especially when there is little food available and what little there is must be fought for, for example between scavengers (vultures and jackals).

The hummingbird sucks nectar from the flower of the bromeliad with its long beak and thus pollinates it. Both partners profit from the relationship.

Cooperation: as in herds of herbivores (zebras, antelopes, gnus). They are not competitors in areas rich with food, and they warn one another if there are predators, finding safety in numbers.

Neutralism: in which neither side is helped or harmed nor has any influence on the other.

Host-guest relationship: in which both parties make use of the meeting, e.g. a bee pollinates a flower as it collects nectar.

What is understood by the food chain?

It is the food relationship between organisms that are dependent on one another for nourishment. The chain goes from green plants (producers) via herbivores (primary consumers) like cows, up to carnivores (secondary consumers) such as lions. Decomposers such as bacteria, worms, insect larvae, and fungi (destruents), which feed on organic substances of other creatures, produce inorganic elements again. Without these saprobes the Earth's surface would have long ago been covered miles high with foliage, needles, wood, dead creatures, and excrement.

What do European alluvial forests have in common with tropical rain forests?

Alluvial forests affected by the dynamics of flowing streams and rivers are among the most species-rich and vital habitats in Europe. The soft woods of

The close living partnership (symbiosis) between anemone fish and sea anemones is well known.

The community offers zebras protection from predators such as lions and cheetahs.

What are biotopes and biocenoses?

Biotope (from the Greek *bios*, "life" and *topos*, "place") describes a location inhabited by a species but says nothing about its qualities. Significant for the evaluation of an actual ecological community (biocenosis) are indicators that give the experienced observer information about a location's conditions. Stinging nettles, for example, indicate that the soil is rich in nitrogen, while the presence of salamanders points to cool, damp locations.

Eat and be eaten—the frog that is just eating a dragonfly will itself be eaten by other animals.

alder, willow, and poplar are well adapted to the conditions that change with every flood. This habitat is also home to beavers, kingfishers, and early flowering plants such as daphne, snowdrops, and wood garlic.

In tropical rainforests—the most species-rich ecosystems on Earth—a good water supply ensures luxurious growth. In contrast to the constantly changing alluvial forest soils (thanks to their superimposed layers of gravel, sand, and fine sediments), many tropical soils are poor in nutrients. Metabolism happens almost exclusively in the higher levels of vegetation. Dead plants and animals are rapidly decomposed so that phosphorus, nitrogen, calcium, and trace elements quickly return to the materials cycle in the year-round almost unchanging tropical climate.

If, however, the rainforest is destroyed by slashing and burning, the nutrients present in the ash are only sufficient for one or two years for the cultivation of crops. What remains afterwards is more arid and red-colored (thanks to iron oxide) desert soil.

How do ecosystems react to new species?

New arrivals that have made their home in Europe in the last 500 years are called invasive animals (neozoes) or invasive plants (neophytes). Some species were introduced as zoological or botanical attractions (red-eared slider, ornamental jewelweed), others as game animals for hunting or for agricultural purposes (pheasant, fallow deer, maize, potato). Others were brought in inadvertently (potato beetles, ragweed). What is common to all newcomers is that they adapted to the ecological conditions of their new homelands very well and spread without the help of humans.

Few newcomers make a negative impression but some make the headlines. If the new species are superior to the natives in the rat race, for example, by being more fertile (wild rabbits), by having greater appetites (Aga toad), by producing seeds that survive for many years (giant hogweed), or by good cuttage (Japanese knotweed), then the native species will be pushed back to small strongholds or even eradicated. This is how literally hundreds of native species of cichlid died out after the introduction of the Nile perch to Lake Victoria.

The most varied communities can be found in tropical rainforests. Many animals and plants have adapted perfectly for life high above in the canopy.

BEHAVIOR: INNATE OR ACQUIRED?

What is behavioral research?
The subject matter of this research is the inborn or acquired behavior of animals and humans in their interactions with individuals of the same species and their environment. Findings are of interest to biologists, psychologists (in terms of behavioral therapy and advertising), sociologists and pedagogues (specifically regarding programmed learning).

Do animals behave like humans?
Up to the 19th century, animal behavior was often portrayed anthropomorphically, not least in the enormously popular works by the well-known zoologist and "father of the animals" Alfred Brehm. We also come across talking and thinking animals in fairy-tales, legends, and cartoons, their behavior revealing or caricaturing human characteristics. In reality these caricatures have little in common with animals—the brave lion, the sly fox, the wise owl, and the snake in the grass—and are basically misleading attributes. The question should rather be the other way round (when considering the human acquisition of food and choice of mate, to name but two examples): how much does human behavior unconsciously point to our "animal" past?

Konrad Lorenz, known as the "Father of the Greylag geese," in Altenberg near Vienna.

> **Konrad Lorenz: father of comparative behavioral research**
>
> Konrad Lorenz (1903–1989), one of the most important representatives of classical comparative behavioral research (ethology), received the 1973 Nobel Prize for Physiology or Medicine together with Karl von Frisch and Nikolaas Tinbergen for his discoveries concerning "organization and elicitation of individual and social behavior patterns" (the title of his publication). Lorenz placed less emphasis on experiments than on logging observed behavior. He recognized key stimuli, inborn trigger mechanisms, and in some animal species, such as ducks and geese, a demonstrable and genetically determined imprinting in the first hours after hatching.

Inborn or learned: how great is the influence of the environment?
Behavioral patterns that are important for the preservation of a species—such as swift flight in dangerous situations, the silent crouching of a fawn in a hollow, courtship behavior during the mating season, and the sucking reflex of a new-born—are often anchored in the genes and can be released by key stimuli. We used to use the expression "instinct" for this sort of innate behavior.

However, the difference between friend and foe, between edible and poisonous food, the differing tones of a bird's song, or successful hunting strategies must be learned from parents or others in the species or by trial and error. The ability of animals to learn has been researched and demonstrated in various experiments. Thus, ants in a maze, for example, find the quickest way to food after just a few attempts. The use of tools is not only known in chimpanzees and dolphins (which use a sponge as a sort of glove for their snouts when hunting for fish) but also in birds, which use twigs and leaves to ferret out tasty morsels from crevices.

Also the position in the group (hierarchy) is not inherited but must be fought over and defended again and again, in herds as well as in families. In the competition for mates and food (in humans known as jealousy), the hierarchy is noticeable: the highest-ranking animal and its offspring are entitled to the best scraps.

What is imprinting?

Within a very short, genetically determined time period, environmental stimuli are so permanently burned into the inner "hard drive" that certain behavior patterns appear as if inborn. The most well-known imprinting occurs in chicks that must first of all learn what their mother looks like. In the first hours after hatching, young goslings will

Above: Young lions learn to hunt successfully by practicing, observing, and copying the older animals.

A fledgling triggers the parents' feeding instinct by opening its beak wide.

What are precocial and nidicolous animals?

Precocial animals and birds, like reptiles, ostriches, and hoofed animals, leave their birthplace directly after hatching or after the birth and can follow their parents straight away. They are usually still fed and protected by their parents. Nidicolous animals and birds, such as storks, predators, rodents, and humans, come into the world relatively undeveloped and need intensive brood care due to their helplessness.

Пища, съедаемая собакой, не доходит до желудка и выпадает через отверстие в пищеводе. Но желудок — только под влиянием нервного возбуждения — выделяет желудочный сок.

approach any object that moves and utter regular sounds—whether it's a human, a football, or a cardboard model—and follow it unquestioningly anywhere. Konrad Lorenz demonstrated this spectacularly with greylag goslings that imprinted him. There is also sexual imprinting, which takes

Why does our mouth water?`

The secretion of saliva just by looking at or smelling food or by just imagining a tasty morsel is a reflex acquired by conditioning (learning) that can be observed in humans as well as in animals. Ivan Pavlov (1849–1936), a Russian physician, was awarded the Nobel Prize in Physiology or Medicine in 1904 for research pertaining to the digestive system. He established in experiments with his dogs that a repeated stimulus, such as the sound of a bell, that regularly preceded feeding could trigger secretions of saliva and other digestive juices in anticipation of receiving food.

Why do humans find small children and young animals cute?

At the sight of a small child or young animal most humans react with an involuntary urge to stroke, feed, and protect the young creature. A scheme of childlike characteristics of appropriate proportions (a large head in relation to the body with a high curved forehead, large round eyes, chubby round cheeks, short snub nose or snout, shorter arms and legs than in adults, and uncertain, rather clumsy movements) is the key stimulus for triggering caring behavior.

What has advertising learned from biology?

Manufacturers of dolls and stuffed animals, publicity strategists, and animated film producers who pay attention to the depiction of prototype children's faces in their products are taking advantage of the scheme of childlike characteristics. Politicians, salesmen, and managers attend seminars and training sessions where they are taught the importance of messages sent out using non-verbal communication—such as body language (e.g. puffing oneself up), facial expressions (e.g. smiles, frowns), gesticulations (e.g. a raised fist), and clothing. These messages are important for reaching target groups successfully. The food industry makes good use of the early imprinting on humans and animals of positive tastes and smells, as well as optical stimuli, and intensifies these in food design.

place in the sensitive and irreversible phase well before sexual maturity. Ducks that were reared by hens are known to have preferred hens as mates in the mating season. For animals that live in large social groups (e.g. in herds), the imprinting of the mother on her young immediately after birth is important for survival. She absorbs the individual smell by licking and sniffing so that she can find her offspring even in a large herd and will tolerate it when it is feeding from her teats. Young animals that have not been imprinted on her in the phase after the birth are warded off and prevented from drinking. Salmon recognize the taste of the water where they spent their first weeks of life and in which they will spawn as sexually mature fish.

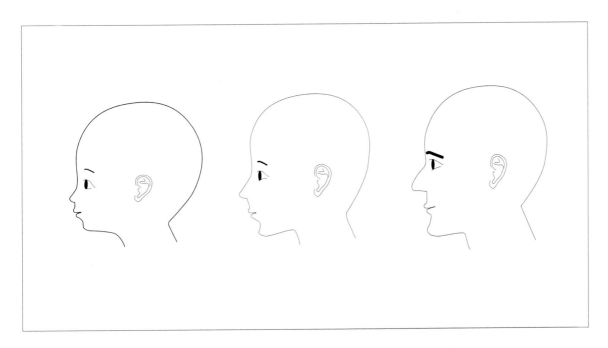

The round, childish proportions of forehead, eyes, chin, and nose (i.e. the scheme of childlike characteristics) trigger the protective instinct in adults. They alter in the course of development to become the more striking features of an adult.

Gregor Johann Mendel, the father of classic genetics.

GENETICS

What do we mean by Mendel's rules?

Mendel's rules were named after the Austrian Augustinian monk Gregor Johann Mendel (1822–1884). They were re-discovered 16 years after his death and today they form the basis of modern evolutionary biology and genetics. Mendel did numerous experiments on peas and discovered the principles according to which certain characteristics appear in the first, second,

What have Mendel's rules to do with counting peas?

Gregor Johann Mendel was often regarded as a bit of a nutty professor. He restricted his research on peas to clearly identifiable characteristics (seed shape, seed color, flower color, pod shape, pod color, flower axis, flower position) and he observed whole populations, not just a few individuals as his scientific predecessors had. He carried out 355 hybridizations and examined 12,980 products of these pea hybrid fertilizations. The publication of his findings in 1865 under the title *Experiments on plant hybrids* met with misunderstanding by his contemporaries but he is now often regarded as the father of classic genetics.

Below: Despite their different hair color, the similarity between these three brothers is unmistakable.

or third generation. On the basis of these findings, he was able to advance rules of heredity that are still valid today. Experiments with the fruit fly (*Drosophila melanogaster*), which has only four pairs of chromosomes and is the classic experimental animal in genetics, showed that chromosomes are the carriers of genes and that genetic information is stored in the DNA. The fruit fly's genetic material was successfully decoded in 2000, and human genetic material in 2005/6, since which time we know which gene lies on which of the 23 pairs of chromosomes in a human.

What are chromosomes?

• Chromosomes are thread-shaped structures in the cell nucleus, which consist of a single, very long DNA molecule. Each chromosome contains hundreds or thousands of genes, each taking up a specified region on the DNA molecule.

• Not all creatures have 46 chromosomes as humans do. The parasitic roundworm has just 2 chromosomes, the fruit fly has 8, the rat 42, the chicken 78, the mushroom 8, and the horsetail plant 216.

Why do children not look like their parents?

This question that frequently pops up in families can be answered with the help of Mendel's rules. If, for example, father and mother have blond hair, the children will also be blond (the principle of uniformity). However, if the father has black hair and the mother blond, the children can be black-, brown-, or blond-haired (the principle of segregation). If the black-haired father is very musical and the blond mother is very sporty, the offspring can be black-, blond-, or brown-haired and musical or sporty; they can have each hair color combination but also be musical and sporty (principle of independent assortment).

Mendel's rules are used in classic animal and plant breeding so that specific characteristics of the parents—certain color characteristics, an additional pair of ribs, good milk output or meat quality—will be passed on to the offspring. Desirable characteristics are then further developed while undesirable characteristics can be bred out by skillful selection. This work has been documented over decades in breeding books.

How does an embryo originate?

Humans, whether male or female, have a doubled (diploid) chromosome set, which means they possess 2×23 chromosomes, which differ between men and women only in the sex chromosome: the female

1.

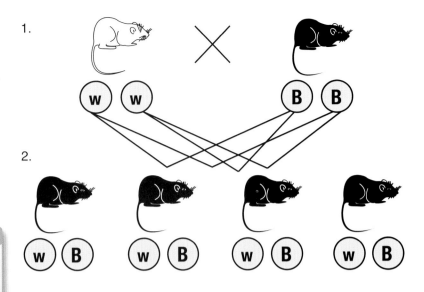

2.

3.

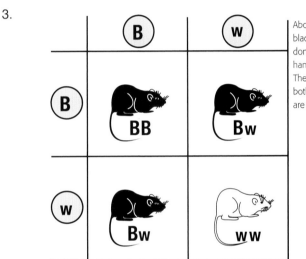

Above: The color black (BB) is dominantly handed down. The offspring of both mice (Bw) are therefore black.

In the next generation the characteristics split in two again. Homozygous mice (BB and ww) and heterozygous mice (Bw) emerge.

has an XX chromosome and the male has an XY chromosome. In cell division, which all body cells need for growth (mitosis), two daughter cells are created each with an identical diploid chromosome set.

It is different in the formation of egg and sperm cells. Here, what is known as reduction division (meiosis) must take place, so that only a simple (haploid) chromosome set remains. Thus, in the father, four sperm cells are created, each of which carries either a male Y or a female X chromosome in addition to the core 22 chromosomes, while the mother's egg cells, of which normally only one of the eggs ready for fertilization matures, only ever have an X chromosome in addition to the core 22 chromosomes. The parent's chromosome sets merge in fertilization, so that a diploid chromosome

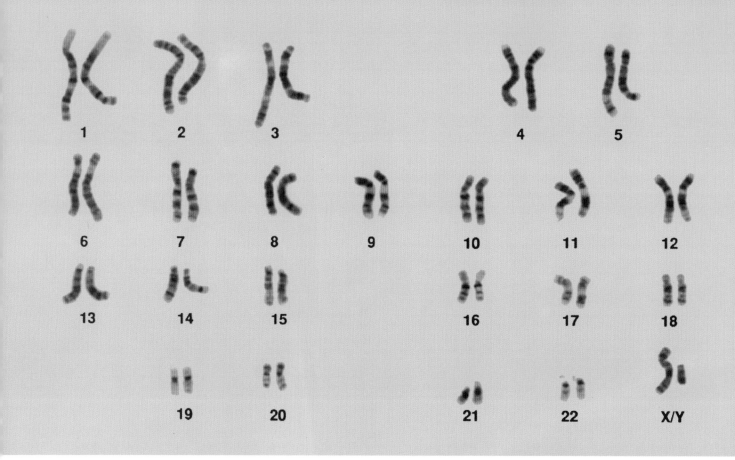

This microscopic picture shows the 2 × 23 chromosomes of a normal male karyotype. After dyeing the specimen, the chromosomes can be seen (1,000 times enlarged) as striped strands. The 23rd chromosome determines the gender (XY = male, XX = female).

set emerges, with a total of 46 chromosomes, which possesses in each DNA segment an alternative form (allele) from mother and father respectively. The genetic material is thus recombined.

Who determines gender?

The gender of the offspring, whether male (XY) or female (XX), is determined at fertilization by the father's sperm. If two egg cells are fertilized at the same time by two sperms, dizygotic (fraternal) twins are created, which accordingly also have different hereditary dispositions and can be different in gender. Monozygotic (identical) twins, which develop by division of a single egg cell, have the same genetic make-up and are of the same sex.

What is DNA?

DNA (Deoxyribonucleic acid) is the most important molecule for heredity in plant and animal organisms. Comparable to an architect, client, and building contractor in one person, DNA sets the structure for the cells but is also responsible for the implementation of the structure and the correct building materials.

DNA is made up of two long molecule chains that are wound spirally around a common (imaginary) axis in a double helix structure.

diploid chromosome set

Meiosis I

Meiosis I, reduction division, haploid cells with doubled chromosome set

Meiosis II

Meiosis II, equation division, four haploid daughter cells

In meiosis the four sperm cells with a haploid chromosome set emerge by reduction division and equation division.

Dr Alec Jeffreys' (born 1950) method of genetic fingerprinting has become very important, not just for proof of paternity, but also in criminalistics. A genetic profile of the culprit can be built up from the smallest samples at the scene of a crime. If it is thought that the culprit might come from a large suspect base (e.g. among the people living in a specific area), salivary tests can be taken, in which a swab is used to take some cells of the oral mucosa, which will be analyzed and compared with the DNA of the traces obtained at the scene of the crime.

If an offense is committed, the police may take only a real fingerprint (dactylogram); the taking of the genetic fingerprint must be sanctioned by a judge first, and is normally only done for the most serious crimes.

The possibility of creating national DNA databases to prevent crime remains a contentious debate.

The information on the DNA chains is coded by combination of the four bases: adenine "A," cytosine "C," guanine "G," and thymine "T," whereby the same bases always face each other—adenine and thymine, and guanine and cytosine respectively. The different combinations of these base pairs are responsible for the programming of the cell structure.

In DNA analysis, the hereditary predispositions (genome) on determined areas of chromosomes are examined. Thus, it is possible to draw conclusions about anomalies, predisposition to certain diseases, and external characteristics. Interestingly, the coded areas of DNA account for around 2 percent of the whole DNA. The other 98 percent is termed "junk

This illustration shows—from left to right in a clockwise direction—the formation of an embryo, in which the genetic material of mother and father is combined.

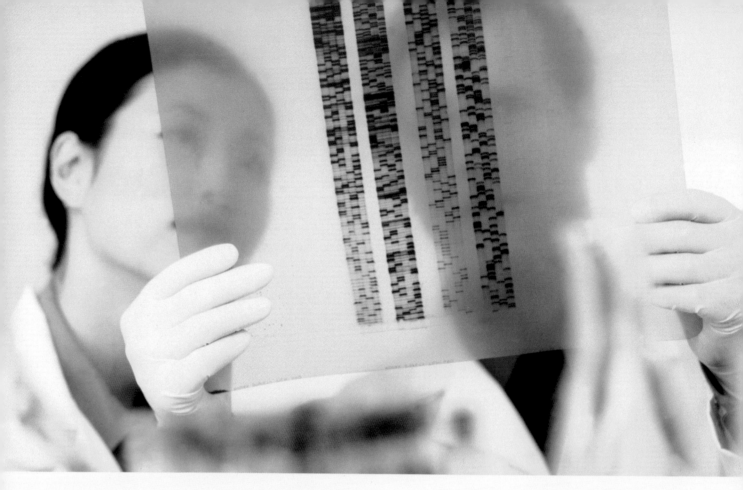

A comparison of the different lengths of DNA fragments of the parents with individual stripes (bands) of the child shows the family relationships.

DNA," a provisional label for the portions of the DNA sequence for which no function has yet been identified.

What is the genetic fingerprint?

The junk DNA characterizes the so-called genetic fingerprint, i.e. an individual pattern of base pairs for every creature. The smallest traces of blood, saliva, or sperm and specimens containing cells (e.g. hair roots or flaking skin) are sufficient for laboratory analysis.

As with a normal fingerprint, a genetic fingerprint will not reveal information about appearance, diseases, characteristics, or talents, but by additional examination of the X and/or Y chromosomes, information can be obtained about gender and anomalies (e.g. Downs syndrome).

How does a paternity test work?

For the analysis, several defined positions on the DNA are, as it were, cut out. From the amount and combination of the repeats of a defined letter sequence (A,C,G,T) in these gene locations (STR—short tandem repeats), an individual pattern results.

Due to the heredity of the number of repeats of the STR gene locations, it is possible to state the degree of relationship. The child carries the

mother's number of repeats and the father's number of repeats at every gene location. In the paternity test, the real father can be established

The characteristics of the fingerprint (dactylogram) are different in each person.

or paternity can be excluded by comparing the parental alleles (alternative forms of a gene). The probability of coincidental absolute conformity is less than 1:100,000,000,000. Family relationships can also be traced back over several generations.

How reliable are the results of genetic fingerprinting?

Every method is only as good as the people who use it. Sloppiness—contamination or mixing up specimens, improper use of equipment, or problems in data preparation—can contribute to errors.

Also, since identical twins have basically the same genetic code, a "positive" result of the genetic fingerprint at the scene of a crime could come from the twin of the actual wrongdoer. And according to a report in the *New Scientist*, it is also possible for the genetic fingerprint of a recipient of bone marrow donation to be adulterated.

Due to contaminated specimens there have been wrongful convictions made in the past, so repeat examinations are required in criminal proceedings.

Can genetics help to cure diseases?

Absolutely, and, with the aid of genetics in the future, doctors hope to be able to understand the molecular mechanisms of how cancer originates, and to be able to produce tailor-made medicines for individual patients that are free of side effects. Many diseases and characteristics can already be classified, more or less exactly, to certain segments within the chromosomes. Thus, for example, Alzheimer's disease lies on chromosome 14. Others are gender-specific. It is known, for example, that some diseases such as hemophilia and characteristics such as red-green blindness lie on the X chromosome. As men have only one X chromosome, they are more frequently affected than women, whose second "healthy" X chromosome can cancel out the defect.

It is known that chimpanzees, whose genotype at 98.4 percent closely resembles that of humans, are immune to malaria and AIDS. Scientists hope in the future, on the basis of those heredity dispositions, to be able to develop therapies for humans to protect them from these infections.

The genetic make-up of the dwarf chimpanzee (Bonobo) closely resembles that of the human (to 98.4 percent). Its habitat in the Congo is severely threatened by political and social unrest.

GENETIC ENGINEERING IN BIOLOGY

In many countries there is a requirement to label genetically modified products, e.g. soy.

What is meant by genetic engineering?

Genetic engineering is one of the most disputed topics in biology since the cloning of Dolly the sheep and the eruption of debates over genetically modified rice and maize.

Now that molecular biologists know about chromosomes, genes, and biochemical controls of creatures and certain viral genomes, they are able to interfere in the genetic make-up. DNA combinations beyond the species barrier open up research to far-reaching possibilities. The risks and ethical problems, however, will be with us for a long time to come.

What risks are associated with genetic engineering?

We know very little about the long-term effects of agricultural genetic engineering. Scientists warn, for example, of an increased tendency for allergies, alterations of the blood count, increased resistance to antibiotics, kidney damage, and miscarriages in humans and animals. There are already problems with uncontrolled contamination between cultivated and wild plants by genetically modified pollen. Neither the market nor the consumer will accept organically cultivated products

Italian scientists experiment with genetically modified mice in order to develop medicines for muscle degeneration caused by old age.

as organic, if they have been grown in the vicinity of genetically modified plants.

The danger of a rapid depletion of species diversity could also be underestimated, since it must be considered that new breeds might displace the wild species. In addition, there is a threat to farmers in that they could become economically dependent on companies that produce patented seeds and the specifically custom-made pesticides for those seeds.

What sorts of genetic engineering are there?

• Agriculture: the use of genetic engineering methods in plant breeding and the use of genetically modified plants in agriculture and the food sector.
• Medicine: the use of genetic engineering in the development and manufacture of medicines (e.g. manufactured human insulin using genetically modified bacteria) and in diagnostic and therapeutic procedures.
• Microbiology: the use of genetically modified microorganisms in environmental protection technology, and in industry for the manufacture of enzymes or fine chemicals.

What does "cloning" mean?

Cloning (from the Greek *klon*, "branch") is defined as the artificial production of two (or several) genetically identical cells or organisms.

The method of cell nucleus transfer (reproductive cloning) is today not only used for sheep, horses, laboratory mice and rats, but also for animal species threatened with extinction, such as the African wildcat, the white-tailed deer, the European moufflon, and the gaur.

The hope of some scientists is that in the future, tissue or even organs can be bred from the embryonic stem cells of a patient, which could later be available for therapeutic purposes such as skin, kidney, or heart transplants (therapeutic cloning). As the genetic material comes from the patient, the danger of immunological rejection does not arise. However, other risks—such as tumor growth and cancer—are not as yet assessable.

Stem cell research is also met with strong resistance in some countries for ethical reasons.

Who was Dolly?

Dolly originated from the udder cell of a six-year-old sheep (A), whose cell nucleus was implanted (in vitro) into the egg cell of another sheep (B), whose natural nucleus had been removed. The embryo, which carried only the genetic information of A, was implanted in another sheep (C), which gave birth to Dolly in 1997 in Edinburgh, Scotland. Dolly was a genetically identical copy of sheep A.

Dolly's life history highlights the problems with cloning. Already in 1999, Dolly's cells exhibited appearances of aging and wear and tear, which would not have been expected until after the tenth year of life. In 2003 Dolly had to be put down prematurely due to pneumonia.

Dolly, the cloned sheep, with her "spiritual father" Dr Ian Wilmut.

FOOD PRODUCTION

How do bacteria and fungi help in food production?

These days, most food is produced in industrial plants where bacteria such as *Escherichia coli* and *Lactobacillus*, fungi such as *Aspergillus*, and yeasts such as the brewers' yeast (*Saccharomyces cerevisiae*) are used on a large scale because they can be cultivated quickly and simply. The manufacture and preservation of cheese, yoghurt, sausage, jam, bread, lemonade, wine, and beer as well as a multiplicity of convenience products made with milk, cereals, meat, fruit, and vegetables would be inconceivable without the use of microorganisms.

The characteristic holes in Swiss cheese come from carbon dioxide that is produced by bacteria.

Where is lactic acid fermentation used?

The preservation of vegetables using lactic acid fermentation is a familiar process worldwide, whether it is sauerkraut in German, Russian, Greek, Roman, or Hungarian cuisine, *suan cai* in Chinese cooking, *tsukemono* in Japan, or *kimchi* in Korea. The chopped vegetable (white cabbage or Chinese cabbage) is mixed well with salt, placed in layers in earthenware crocks, and pressed down firmly so that the cell structures break open and the juice comes out. The cabbage is then stored in a cool place covered with a board or plate and weighed down with a stone. The board should prevent oxygen getting in so that no oxygen-loving bacteria are allowed to decay the vegetable. The anaerobic bacteria that are put into the pot with the cabbage can ferment the sugars in the cabbage (without any other ingredients) to form lactic acid, acetic acid, and carbon dioxide. Depending on the season and room temperature, the fermentation lasts between six days and three months.

Sauerkraut is low in calories, rich in vitamin C and B_{12}, and contains essential minerals and trace

elements such as calcium, potassium, sodium, phosphorus, and iron.

How does wine turn to vinegar?

Vinegar was produced in many ancient civilizations, by the Egyptians, Babylonians, Persians, Greeks, and Romans. It was used in medicines and cosmetics and as a condiment. Acetic acid bacteria (*Acetobacter*), discovered by Louis Pasteur (1822–1895), convert fluids containing alcohol, such as wine, beer, and cider but also grape and apple juice that contains sugar, into alcohol-free vinegar. The bacterium either locates itself (e.g. in apple juice or in wine left standing, which

Above: Sauerkraut, here shown before the beginning of the lactic acid fermentation process in an earthenware crock, is a German and eastern European specialty. It is made from fermented white cabbage, which is often improved with white wine.

How does cheese get its holes and blue veins?

In the manufacture of curd cheese from fresh milk, the lactic acid bacteria (*Lactobacillus*) cause the lactose to break down. The freed lactic acid allows the milk protein to curdle and prevents the growth of bacteria that ruin milk. Rennet, an enzyme from calves' stomachs, is produced organically with the aid of the mold *Mucor mihei* in fermenters, and allows the milk mass to coagulate. The solids are then separated from the whey, and placed into molds that will be used to press the curds and form blocks of cheese and, depending on the variety, flavored. Later they will be dipped in brine and stored in air-conditioned rooms to mature, or are injected with fungal cultures. *Propioni* bacteria produce carbon dioxide during the ripening process, which is responsible for the holes that are typical of Swiss cheese. The blue veins in gorgonzola and in Roquefort (cheese made with sheep's milk) are produced by a mold called *Penicillium roqueforti*. Different bacteria and yeast, mainly *Penicillium camemberti*, account for the white coating of camembert, its creamy consistency, and its great taste.

Right: Beer fermenting in copper kettles in the Budweiser brewery in the Czech Republic.

Alcohol and carbon dioxide—waste products as far as yeast is concerned—are immensely important in food production. While the alcohol is valuable for brewers and vintners, the carbon dioxide is needed for light baking dough.

In professional wine and fruit wine production, specially grown yeasts are added to the must, which contains sugar, to aid fermentation. Beer brewers feed the yeast with malt sugar from germinated barley or wheat and obtain the desired alcohol as a decomposition product.

Yeasts have a relatively high content of high-quality proteins and are thus used in the production of animal fodder. Cosmetic preparations containing brewers' yeast have also found a ready market.

Yeasts have recently been used to generate electricity in microbial fuel cells, and produce ethanol for the biofuel industry.

Does fast food make you fat and unhealthy?
Not always. However, the fats in fries, mayonnaise, small sausages, and cheese, and the sugar in Colas and ketchup, all of which are generally loved by children and often on offer in fast food outlets, have allowed obesity to become

Specialty oil and vinegars are produced with different herbs and spices.

is recognizable by the skin on the surface) or it is added by injection when being industrially produced. Unlike in wine fermentation, oxygen is necessary for this fermentation process, and heat accelerates the process.

How long have humans been using yeast?
Six thousand years ago in Mesopotamia, people were already using yeast fungi to brew beer. Without the yeast fungus *Saccharomyces cerevisiae*, there would be no wine or beer, and we would have to do without many varieties of bread and cakes. As the amount of yeast cells doubles around every 90 minutes in optimal temperature conditions and with sufficient food supply, it is easy to breed yeast fungi in great quantities.

What characteristics make yeast so valuable?
In anaerobic conditions (without oxygen), yeast converts sugar into alcohol and carbon dioxide, and uses the released energy for its own growth.

Cheeseburgers with fries are loved by many and can be found anywhere, but they are also very fattening foods.

a pandemic, which has grave medical and social consequences.

What is processed food?

In the recent past, an independent sector of industry has developed that extracts starch, protein, or fat substitutes from cheap raw materials and makes them into new, seemingly natural foods (so-called processed food). Vitamins, food coloring, and preservatives are added, and although some additives are permitted, which have to be declared by stating the E-numbers, customers are often duped into thinking they are buying healthy food.

However, not all processed foods should be dismissed out of hand. For instance, vegetables that have been deep-frozen immediately after the harvest often contain more vitamins than fresh goods that must be transported over long distances. This applies similarly to fish.

Is genetic engineering of food harmless?

It is advisable to mistrust genetically modified foods. We do not know enough about the side effects for people with allergies and other sicknesses, nor about the consequences for the food chain (e.g. the results of feeding livestock with genetically modified soy or maize). The fears of the traditional farming sector clash with the economic expectations of some major companies that have their eyes fixed firmly on the market for patented seeds and so-called custom-made herbicides and fertilizers.

Why are some adults milk intolerant?

Geneticists have established that humans were equipped with a genetically defined lactose tolerance that only lasted during childhood. Researchers propose that 8,000–10,000 years ago, a mutation must have occurred in the Caucasian area, which allowed lactose tolerance to extend to the entire lifespan. Thus, all the offspring of these humans (right up to the present day) show no health-damaging effects at all from consuming milk, unlike Asians or Africans, for instance, who generally cannot tolerate milk as adults and react to milk and milk products with diarrhea, flatulence, and cramps. These reactions are caused by the absence or lack of the enzyme lactase in the small intestine.

Modern methods of food technology are used in the industrial production of ready meals and convenience foods.

BIONICS: NATURE AS ROLE MODEL

Aircraft construction engineers copied the winglets on wing tips from nature.

What does bionics mean?

Bionics is an interdisciplinary field of knowledge that unites elements from biology, architecture, engineering, and design in order to echo concepts that are successful in the natural world (e.g. the flight of birds) and apply them technologically for practical human use. The term "bionics," introduced in 1960 by a major in the US Air Force, Jack E. Steele, was formed out of a combination of "biology" and "electronics."

What do airplanes and birds have in common?

Airplane construction has not only the streamlined body shape but also the design and arrangement of wing feathers in birds to thank for giving it valuable ideas. Birds, such as eagles and condors that seem to glide through the air for hours without any trouble, have long primary feathers on their pinions that can be fanned out to reduce aerodynamic resistance. In airplane construction, the wing tips are equipped with winglets, which fragment the air turbulence, reduce air resistance and therefore also energy use.

What do sharks have to do with kerosene consumption in airplanes?

The skin of rapidly swimming shark species is covered with densely packed scales. Very fine, stream-wise flowing grooves and ribs on their surface reduce friction resistance. Accordingly, the same principle is used in the design of riblets, which are stuck onto the outer skin of aircraft. They reduce the airflow resistance and can reduce the use of kerosene by around 6–8 percent.

Does architecture adopt nature's building principles?

Yes, in the construction of vaults, bridges, skyscrapers, and lighthouse towers many architects look to nature as a role model. The architecture of the Eiffel Tower, for instance, is similar to the structure of bone tissue. Telegraph poles are very economical on materials and wind resistant in the same way as blades of grass. When the architect and landscape gardener Joseph Paxton designed Crystal Palace for the Great Exhibition in London in 1851, which was burned down in 1936, he used the leaves of the tropical water lily, *Victoria amazonica*, as his model.

Left: The scales of the white shark were used as the model for the riblets that are stuck onto the exterior skin of aircraft.

Learning from animals and plants

Inventors and engineers are inspired by closely observing animals and plants.

• Leonardo da Vinci (1452–1519) analyzed the flight of birds and tried to transfer this knowledge to flying machines. His flying wings were constructed on the model of a bat's wing.

• The Karlsruhe structural designers of the running robots Lauron II (1996) and Lauron III (1999) were guided by the musculoskeletal system of the stick insect.

• The ultrasound that bats use for locating is applied in medical diagnostics.

• Flippers enabling divers to move more quickly are modeled on the webbed feet of frogs and waterfowl.

• The inventor of Velcro looked at the dispersion mechanism of a burr seed. These have barbed hooks that cling to an animal as it brushes past and in this way they spread to new habitats.

• Modern external house paint, window glass, awnings, and roof tiles mimic the so-called lotus effect. The leaf surface of the lotus flower is covered with a fine nap (a layer of fine fibers or hairs) and wax crystals. Dust and dirt particles (including fungal spores and bacteria) that are dissolved in water roll off them in droplets so that the leaf is always clean.

Crystal Palace in London was built using a revolutionary (for the time) new modular design of prefabricated iron sections and panes of glass.

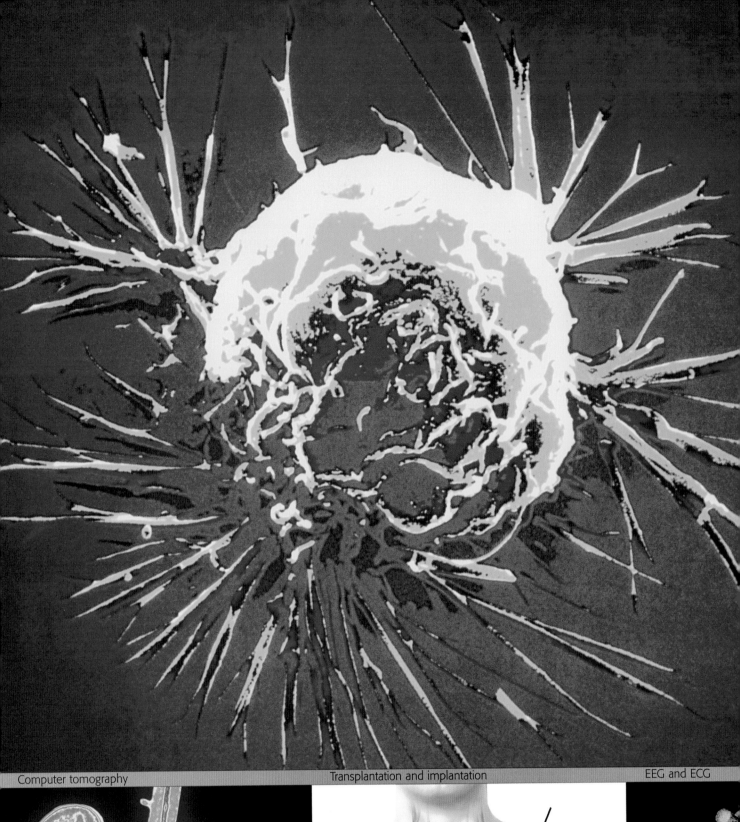

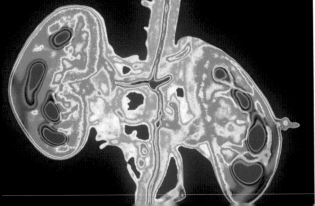
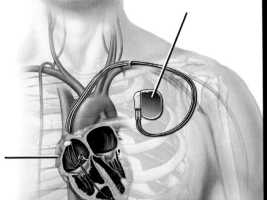

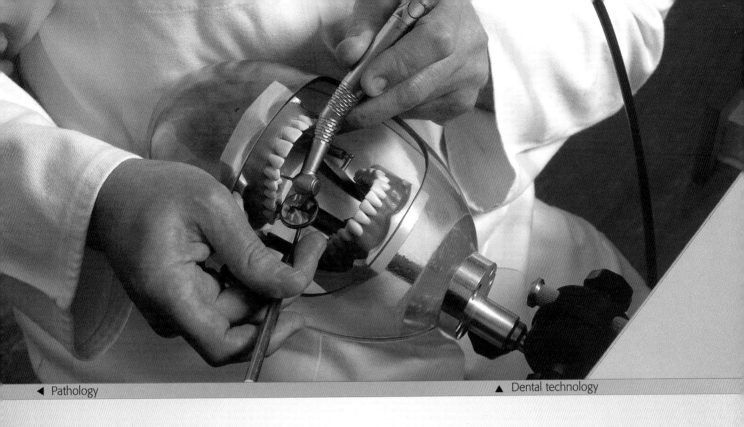

◀ Pathology

▲ Dental technology

MEDICAL TECHNOLOGY

Hardly any other science has made such great progress in the past decades as medicine. Rapid technical development has opened up research areas, and industry has made advances in expanding our foundational knowledge, which has also led to improvements in patient treatment. As a result, new procedures and technical aids in diagnostics and therapy have been established. Some of them are looked at in greater detail in the following chapter.

Technology in the operating theater

Microtechnology

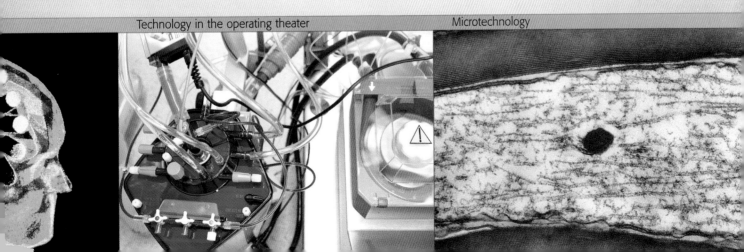

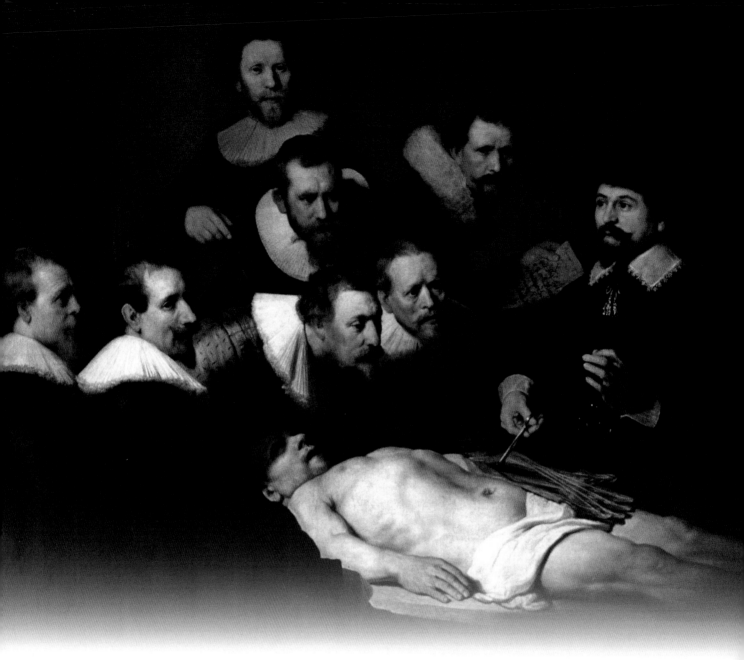

HISTORY OF MEDICAL TECHNOLOGY

Anatomical studies—as represented here in this 1632 painting by Rembrandt—were forbidden until around the beginning of the 16th century.

What is meant by medical technology?
Medical technology combines the scientific approach to problem-solving with the scope of medicine. With the optimal use of technology, doctors seek to improve the quality of life for individual patients. The task of medical technology is to constantly improve not only the existing technical state of affairs but also the medical standard of knowledge, so that optimal diagnostic and therapy procedures are available for both doctor and patient. This encompasses not only research

and development but also the establishment of new methods in medical practice.

When did medical technology originate?
The principles of medical technology are, strictly speaking, older than humanity, as in the animal and plant world it can be observed that creatures make use of certain aids when they can no longer cope on their own. The first humans were also able to recognize diseases and to take simple countermeasures against them. At the same time, they could pass on this knowledge to other people and thus establish a basis for development. Down the centuries, medical aids became more and more sophisticated and human curiosity led to research into the causes of medical conditions (in the form of scientific examinations), the checking of existing theories, and the documentation of knowledge

obstetrics and dentistry emerging as disciplines in their own right.

How did modern medical technology develop?

Sir Joseph Lister (1827–1912), with his observations on wound sepsis, markedly improved hygienic conditions for patients undergoing examinations by doctors. In 1895, Wilhelm Röntgen discovered that X-rays could penetrate the human body. Sir Alexander Fleming (1881–1965) discovered the antibiotic penicillin in 1928. In the 20th century, completely new forms of technology were developed, which further accelerated research: empirical data were collected on a hitherto unknown scale, and the computer made its entry into medicine. The digital age allowed a new orientation in research towards the microcosmos, and genetics and microtechnology now belong to the medical disciplines. At the beginning of the 21st century, the opportunities for medicine have never been greater—and further developments show no signs of slowing down.

New knowledge meant that many changes were made to surgical instruments within a short time frame. This illustration shows a table from J. M. Bourgery's authoritative 19th-century anatomy atlas.

In his writings, Hippocrates (around 460–370 BC) laid the foundations for many later methods of treatment.

gained. In this way, medical technology developed rapidly. It may have taken several thousand years until the Stone Age crutch was replaced by a prosthesis to aid walking—in Egypt prostheses from 2000 BC have been found—but no more than 60 years passed from the first industrially manufactured prosthesis to the high-tech products in use today (e.g. prostheses controlled by microprocessors).

Where did medical technology originate?

The Greek physician Hippocrates (around 460–370 BC) took the first verifiable step towards medicine and research. In his writings, he distinguished between disease and symptoms, and also between healing and pain relief. In the following centuries, further development in medicine was rather slow until Paracelsus (1493–1541), who laid the foundations for modern pharmacy, and Andreas Vesalius (1514–1564), whose studies led to him being recognized as the founding father of anatomy and surgery. In the course of the dissociation of chemistry and physics from alchemy, the first scientifically developed drugs and anesthetics emerged. The English physician William Harvey (1578–1657) was the first person to describe blood circulation. During the 18th-century Age of Enlightenment, sciences developed further, with

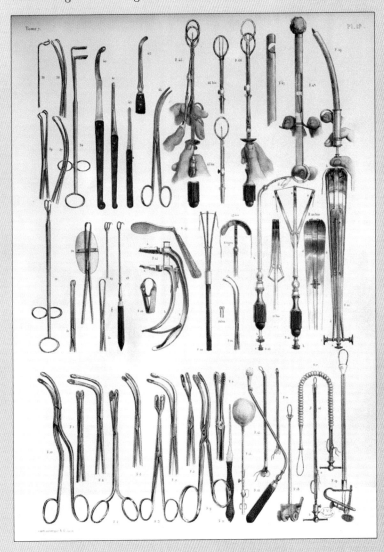

PHARMACY: THE SEARCH FOR DRUGS

How do we find drugs to cure illnesses?

First of all, the disease and its symptoms must be properly examined. If a pathogen is found, the search begins for an agent that influences the trigger in a defined way, i.e. a drug. The possible drug and the trigger for the disease are brought together and the reactions are reviewed afterwards, usually under laboratory conditions.

Comparisons with other pathogens already researched or clinical pictures are useful in this context.

If the drug shows the desired effect, further tests are carried out until it is proven to be effective and safe to be commercialized.

Molecular biological examination can also be used to discover the properties of a disease trigger.

How are medicines tested?

First of all, in the laboratory a series of different, purely chemical or purely physical tests are carried out so that right at the beginning any undesired effects that the medicine might trigger in the human organism can be recognized and prevented. Following this, the agents are tested in pre-clinical trials on cell cultures or on animals, the effects are documented, and, from them, possible effects on the human organism are deduced. Once satisfactory results have been obtained, the medicines are tested in four clinical trial phases. First, the agent is administered to healthy volunteers in small doses, to check whether the deductions derived from the first test series were correct. In phase two, the drug is used in hospitals in the treatment of, typically, 100–500 volunteer patients to test whether and how the intended effect works. In the third phase, the results are compared with the effect of other drugs. Phase four follows after approval of the drug, when long-term studies are conducted.

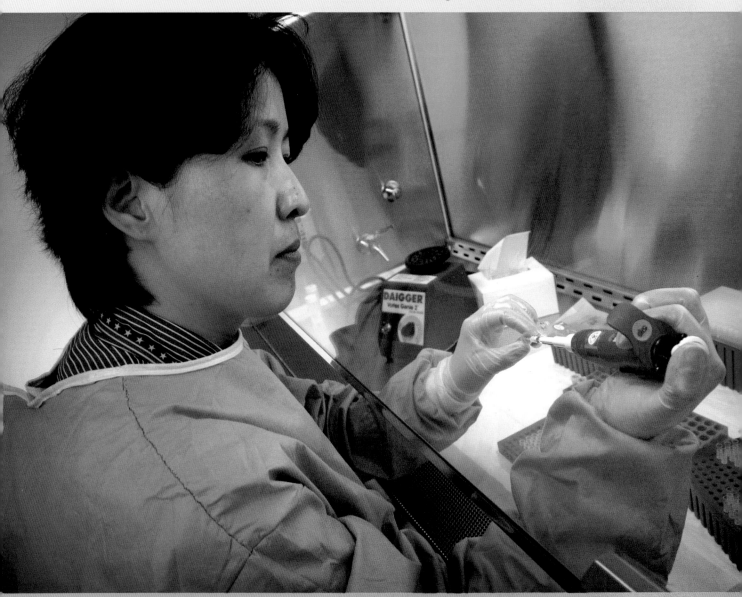

Which agents are healthier—those produced from plants or those synthetically produced?

The difference lies only in the manufacture of the active ingredients. Whereas in one case the completely natural active ingredient has to be extracted from the plant, in the other case it is produced in the laboratory by chemical reactions. In the latter instance, "synthetic" or "nature-identical" active pharmaceutical ingredients are created. The production of synthetic substances is normally a quicker and safer process than the production of natural ones, though there are differing views on the health advantages and disadvantages of particular medicines.

How are drugs manufactured?

A drug is principally made up of two parts: an active ingredient and a so-called "transport

Paracelsus presumed that every disease had a cause and that unless this cause was known therapy would fail.

medium." Hence, active ingredients that are for internal use are incorporated into water or alcohol, for example, to make drops or mixtures. If the ingredients are to be used externally, they are mixed with oils or an ointment base. Starch has also proved to be a good carrier substance for dried active ingredients.

In the manufacture of drugs, it is most important to realize that the carrier substance can have a diluting effect. This, in turn, should be taken into account in dosages, so that the active ingredient achieves the desired effect.

Besides the raw materials of medicine, Christian symbols could also be found in the first apothecaries of the modern age. In the view of Paracelsus, medicine could not work without faith.

appear white on the X-ray picture. As a rule, therefore, these images show the shape of the bones and foreign bodies.

If a contrast medium has been introduced into the body, then other parts of the body will also be made visible, just as they will by variations in the wavelength of the X-rays. The smaller the wavelengths, the better the X-rays penetrate the material, and vice versa: the bigger the wavelength, the clearer and richer in detail the X-ray picture is going to be.

The development of X-rays

The German physicist Wilhelm Conrad Röntgen (1845–1923) discovered the effect of the rays by chance in 1895 while working with a cathode ray tube. However, he was not the first person to create these sorts of rays in the laboratory. In 1887 and 1892, experiments were documented in which X-rays were created, but the X-ray effect was not commented on in treatises. Röntgen did not patent his discovery, so his invention spread extremely rapidly.

Why are X-rays harmful?

X-rays have an ionizing effect, i.e. they alter matter at an atomic level. As a result, they can break up atomic compounds, i.e. chemical structures such as molecules. In most cases, after short exposure to the X-ray, tissue reverts back to its original state. However, the possibility of permanent changes to chemical structures cannot be ruled out, particularly following prolonged or repeated exposure. Symptoms of radiation injury are nausea, exhaustion, dizziness, or headaches, and in serious cases there can be impairment of the genetic make-up, disturbance of organ function, tissue necrosis, or cancer.

What is CT (computerized tomography)?

Computerized tomography is basically the same as an X-ray in terms of the procedure. It actually consists of numerous X-rays, which are taken of different angles of the body based on digital geometry processing (a method using applied mathematics, computer science, and engineering to deal with 3-D models). In this way, a three-dimensional picture of the inside of the body can be built up with the aid of a computer. The advantage of the CT is that it can separate anatomical parts at different levels in the body,

X-RAYS AND CT: RAYS THAT GET UNDER YOUR SKIN

W. C. Röntgen's discovery of the rays (named after him in German) represented a milestone in the development of medical diagnostic procedures. He received the first Nobel Prize for Physics in 1901.

What makes X-rays visible?

X-rays penetrate the body where they can be absorbed by some materials, depending on their thickness and density. Bones, for example, with their high calcium content, can absorb a higher proportion of X-rays than soft-tissue organs or muscles.

In the X-ray procedure, the rays that have filtered through the body strike a film and color it black. The places where the rays were absorbed

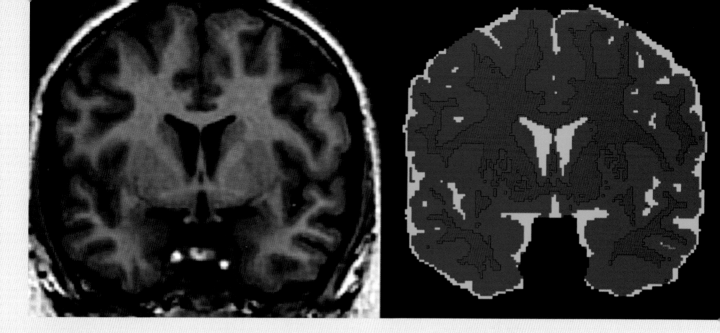

It is possible with the aid of a computer to process recorded data so that the different layers appear in color.

so that the CT can show sections of the body that, because of their physical position, would be hard to detect in an X-ray.

Why are X-rays and CT scans so useful in diagnosis?
The pictures produced by X-rays and CT scans supply knowledge about the condition of the inside of the body, especially the skeleton. Bone injuries, dislocated joints, but also foreign bodies can be

detected before treatment begins. Furthermore, they make possible sources of danger (e.g. injury) visible, for instance bone splinters that might be lying in close proximity to other organs. More than that, a CT offers the possibility of examining three-dimensionally the spinal column, internal organs, and the brain, and thus diagnosing other diseases.

As Röntgen did not patent his invention, other researchers, including D. Hurmuzescu and L. Benoist, rapidly furthered development using their own apparatus.

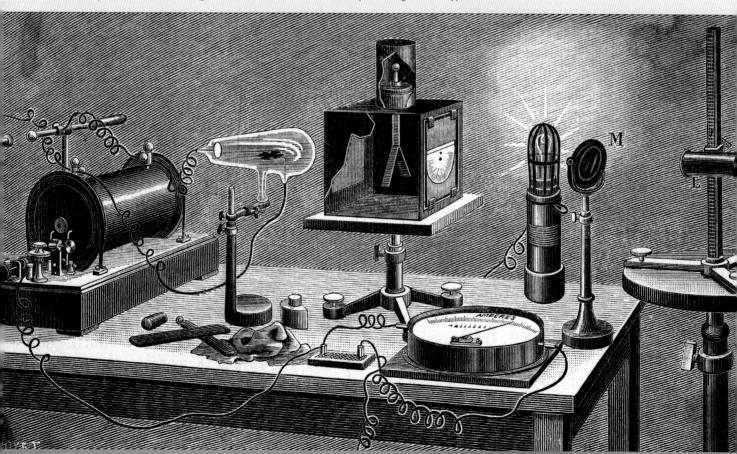

Can X-rays be used for healing?

Yes, since the 1970s X-rays have been used in radiation therapy (radiotherapy). This is where the ionizing effect of rays is utilized. With healthy cells, there is a high probability that any cell injury caused by radiation on the atomic level can be repaired, whilst cancerous cells normally would not be able to regenerate and would thus be destroyed. The body must have a sufficient period of recuperation between the individual radiotherapy sessions. There is also a possibility that the patient might not be able to tolerate the radiotherapy, depending on the sensitivity of the part of the body that is being treated. In this case, radiation injuries (described on page 170) can occur.

Are other rays used in the healing process?

Yes, light rays, for example, are frequently used for therapeutic purposes. Ultraviolet light is successfully used to treat skin diseases such as psoriasis and neurodermatitis. Infrared light, on the other hand, is used in thermotherapy,

In an MRI scanner the body is screened using radio waves and magnetic fields.

for back pain, arthritis, sprains, sports injuries, stress, or insomnia. Magnetic rays or magnetic fields have also proved to have a healing effect. These improve blood flow, stimulate metabolism, and boost resistance.

What is nuclear resonance scanning?

Nuclear resonance scanning or, more accurately, magnetic resonance imaging (MRI) is a procedure

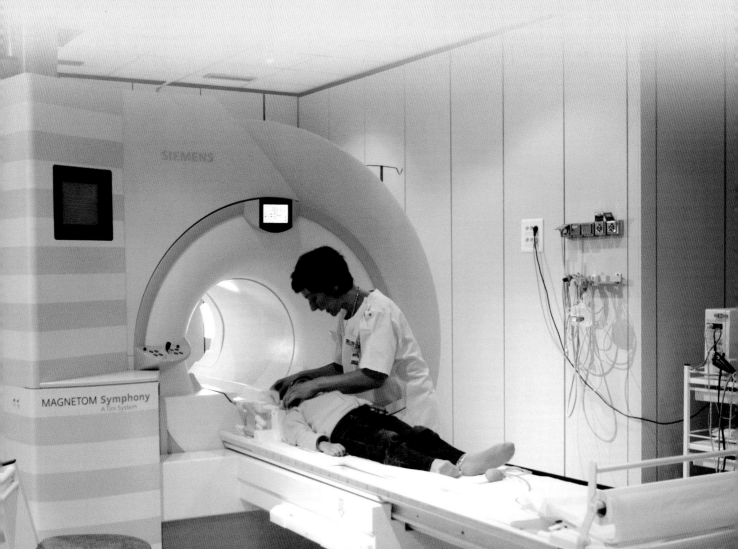

Pictures taken with an MRI scanner can provide information on the type of disease and further therapy options.

for locating magnetic fields in the body. In this procedure, the body is exposed to a magnetic field and radio waves set to a certain frequency. The atomic nuclei, specifically the hydrogen atoms in our bodies, behave like tiny magnetic spinning tops.

During the scan, a strong magnetic field is applied that alters the direction of this spin. Then pulses of radio waves are sent through the body, as a result of which the atomic nuclei again have enough energy to break away from it. When the radio waves are turned off, the atoms release this kinetic energy again. The frequency of the field is calculated based on the particular tissue being examined (fat, bone, or muscle). At the same time, signals are emitted that are clearly different from one another and a computer can put them together to form an image.

An MRI does not use damaging X-rays but it is not recommended for patients with metal parts in their bodies (metal prostheses, heart pacemakers, etc.) as these are heated due to the interactions between the high-frequency impulses and magnetic fields. In addition, the metal reacts to the magnetic fields and can cause injuries.

What happens in skeletal scintigraphy?

Skeletal scintigraphy (also known as bone scintigraphy or bone scan) offers the opportunity to examine bone metabolism. In this procedure, the patient is given an intravenous injection of radioactive substance and its carrier substance makes it travel through the body and collect in the bones. After a short waiting period, a detector is used, which can locate the markings in the body. The resulting pictures can detect any bone injuries already in the early stages of disease. With skeletal scintigraphy, it is possible to identify bone marrow disease, bone cancers, and bone metabolism disturbances such as osteoporosis.

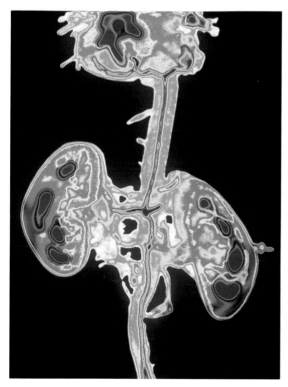

Computer tomography does not just show the organs but also gives information about other structures.

EEG AND ECG: BRAIN AND HEART

What does an EEG measure?

An EEG measures a faint electrical current flowing within the living brain, which allows the brain cells to constantly change their electrical state so that they can process data.

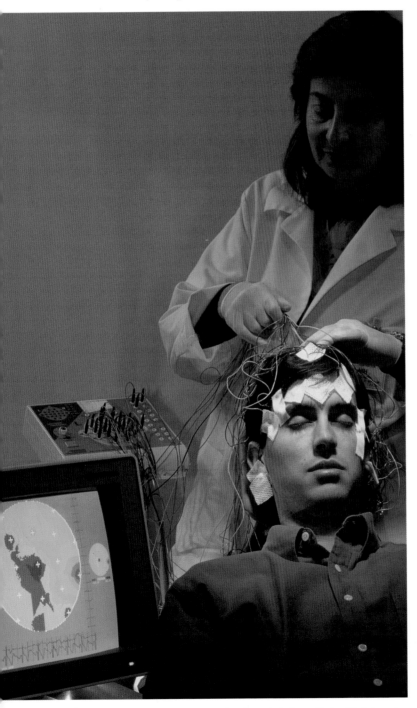

The examination of the brain's activity is done with the aid of electrodes that are placed on the scalp.

As they do this, fluctuations occur, which can be transmitted through the cerebral cortex to the scalp. If an examination is to be performed by EEG (electroencephalogram), normally 21 electrodes are placed on the scalp, forming an electrical network. Following this, if an electrical impulse is sent through the brain, there will be fluctuations in the network, which are then registered on a recording device. The result—the encephalogram—records the activity of the regions of the brain that are busy with the processing of information.

What does EEG data show?

As a rule, the brain processes all kinds of information and controls all the body's functions. Even if a person is asked to rest completely in the dark, the EEG will still reflect processes in the brainwaves such as breathing or digestion, as a sort of basic rhythm.

Obviously, the brain is more active when the senses are stimulated or when it is performing mental tasks. Therefore, the EEG readings change, i.e. the voltage fluctuations become stronger and rise above the basic rhythm.

If the voltage fluctuations fall below the basic rhythm despite increased brain activity being expected, this can be a sign of brain impairment.

The EEG is used to provide information about epilepsy, strokes, brain tumors, or inflammation within the brain.

What happens in an ECG?

The pumping action of the heart is due to a faint electrical stimulus that originates in the right atrium. The ECG measures this current and its effects through up to 12 electrodes that are put on certain places on the skin and record the signals.

This data supplies information about the frequency of the heartbeat and an accurate picture of the regularity of the heart rhythm as well as the electrical activity within the heart and the atria.

An ECG provides information on the general condition of the heart.

What are stress ECGs and long-term ECGs?

An ECG is normally performed when a patient is resting, i.e. the patient is lying down when the test is carried out.

Some heart conditions, however, cannot be detected in this way as heart trouble often occurs when the body is under great stress, or a condition

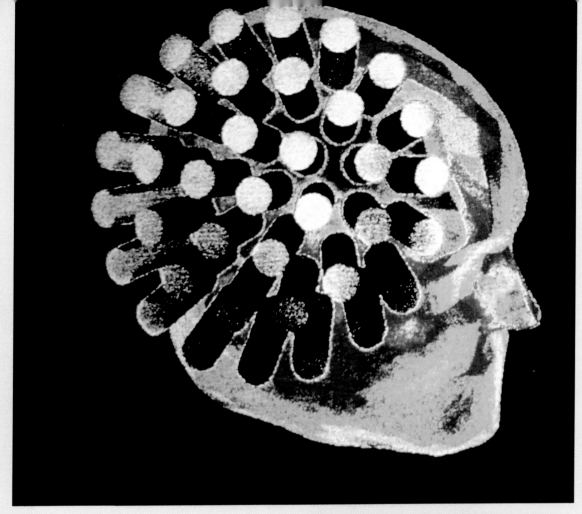

Left: The individual
areas of tension,
which occur on
the surface
of the scalp, alter
depending on the
brain's activity.

may occur only sporadically. A patient experiences greater physical stress and therefore an increased heart rate if they are asked to exercise, for example on a stationary bicycle, while the test is carried out. In principle, the test is the same as a resting ECG in that up to 12 electrodes are used. If the heart problem is sporadic, on the other hand, the patient may be asked to wear a device for several hours or days.

The data for the long-term ECG are stored on the device. In this test only between two and six electrodes are attached to the ECG recorder. The diagnosis is thus not so accurate, but using this method (and after further consultation with the patient), frequency and possible external causes of the heart problem, such as a certain medicine or a certain activity, can be established.

The ECG curve

The electrical processes in the heart can be read by looking at the ECG curve, from the impulse formation in the atrium passing to the ventricles, to repolarization, which shows that the chambers of the heart are relaxing. An ECG curve can vary depending on the location of the electrodes recording it.

A resting ECG is often done first so that it can be compared later to how the heart behaves under stress.

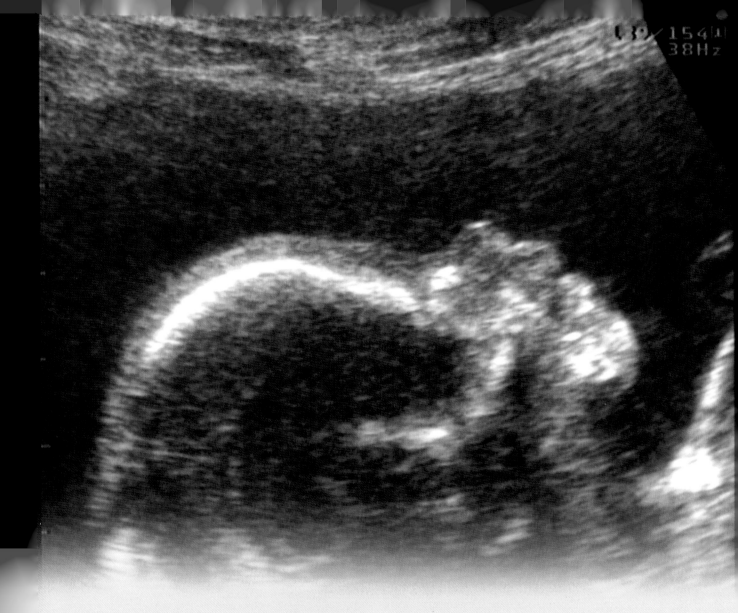

SOUND WAVES IN MEDICINE

Ultrasound waves bounce back as soon as they meet any degree of resistance. In this way they can detect outlines, as with this human fetus.

How does an ultrasound scanner work?

Basically, an ultrasound scanner consists of a transmitter and a receiver. Both are generally combined in the transducer. The transmitter emits high-frequency sound waves that are reflected as soon as they meet any resistance. The reflected waves are registered by the receiver and converted into electrical signals, which are represented on a screen. This principle is known in navigation as sonar or echo sounding. Medical ultrasound examinations (sonography) use this method to obtain an image of the condition of an internal organ. Cysts, tumors, vascular stenosis, any increase or decrease in the size of organs as well as calculi (kidney stones or gallbladder stones) can all be

diagnosed by ultrasound. Ultrasound scans are most frequently used in antenatal care. In some special cases, a contrast medium can be used to obtain a more accurate image. Ultrasound scanning is a low-risk diagnostic method but it has technical limits in the sonication of certain materials (e.g. bones), due to dispersal of the signals.

Can any organs be exposed to ultrasound?

Yes, on the condition that they are not hidden by bones. In those cases, other methods would be used (CT or MRI). Organs that can be examined by ultrasound without any problem are the heart (echocardiography), the thyroid gland, blood vessels, the abdominal cavity and its associated organs such as the liver, gallbladder, spleen, kidneys, and so on, as well as the womb and ovaries. Lungs and parts of the intestine and spinal column or joints do not lend themselves to being examined with ultrasound.

How are kidney stones removed?

Kidney stones are deposits that can form in the kidney itself or in the urinary tract. The ultrasound enables a diagnosis to be made and, as long as the kidney stone is not too large, a special form of the sound waves can treat it. (Larger kidney stones are usually removed operatively.) Lithotripsy uses high-intensity acoustic pulses or sound waves—rather like thunder that can cause a glass to vibrate or even to shatter—to break up kidney stones and gallbladder stones. There has also been some success in the treatment of myomas (or fibroids, lumps of fibrous tissue in the womb) with this method. Currently, experiments are being carried out to see if brain tumors might be treated in the same way. However, negative side effects (e.g. heating up of the areas that are to be treated) have so far excluded the introduction of the procedure into medical practice.

Can sound be used in other cases for healing?

Yes, sound therapy is used successfully in a number of fields, although in a different form and with different aims. Special sound mixtures or music compositions, for example, are used to calm people with psychiatric problems such as depression, anxiety, lack of self-esteem, poor concentration, or memory disturbance. These are also used as therapy for people with ear problems such as tinnitus (ringing in the ears), hearing loss, or sudden deafness. Furthermore, some dentists play soothing music during treatment instead of giving an injection.

Above: Kidney stones are destroyed by shock waves in a medical device called a lithotriptor.

Sound can have a calming effect: sound waves are used in some therapies where they are only perceived subconsciously.

ENDOSCOPY: OPTICAL EXAMINATION OF THE BODY

The laser endoscope is one of the latest developments in this field. It is used mainly for the examination of the mucosa in the stomach or intestine.

How does an endoscopy work?
Endoscopy is a procedure that enables the doctor to examine the inside of the body, or rather body cavities, using optical instruments such as mirrors, loupes (small magnifying glasses), optical sensors, or a camera. The examination is usually carried out by introducing the endoscope through a natural body orifice and feeding it to the part of the body that is to be examined. This is a relatively risk-free procedure for the patient.

What is an endoscope?
The classic endoscope is a tube-like instrument that has a light on the end. Inside there is a lens and mirror system, which the doctor looks through to see the areas to be examined. In some cases, special lenses can be used with a magnifying effect to enable more detailed examinations.

Modern endoscopes are flexible tubes containing flexible optic fibers that are combined with a light source and a camera. Pictures are taken and can be viewed on a monitor. Besides the flexibility of the endoscope, this system has the further advantage that, with the aid of images and video recordings, the clinical pictures and recovery processes can be documented and reviewed later.

Where is endoscopy used?
It can only be used in areas that are reachable via a natural body orifice or, sometimes, via a small incision. It is used in the gastrointestinal tract in the stomach (gastroscopy), the rectum (proctoscopy), or duodenum (duodenoscopy). The airways, urinary tract, abdominal cavity, womb, vagina, and joints can also all be examined using this method. The endoscopy examination procedure is not recommended if bones or other organs might be in the way.

There are also specialist devices that work on the same principle as endoscopes and are used in the examination of the throat, nose, and ear.

In which cases is endoscopy undertaken?
Due to the low risk for the patient, endoscopy is very useful for establishing diagnoses in the organs mentioned above. As well as that, an endoscopy is often carried out at short notice if the doctor suspects that an organ may be injured. And if the patient has had an accident, the endoscope is better than other methods of examination. On the one hand, the organ is still in an active state during the examination, and on the other, possible changes in color and structure of the tissue are visible (e.g. if there is bruising or swelling). In some operations, endoscopy is used to check the progress of the procedure

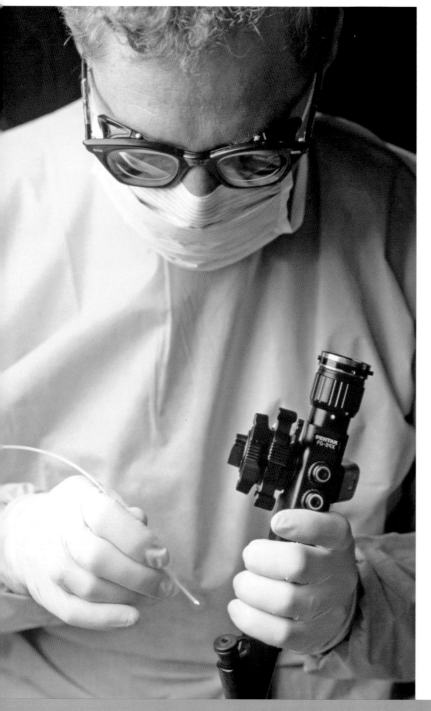

via the mirror or camera, and in microsurgery, the enlarged images of the organ to be operated on, along with its surrounding area, are absolutely vital.

Above: In many modern endoscopes, the camera system is placed into a special capsule.

Endoscopy outside medicine

The principle of endoscopy is used outside medicine, among other things in archeology, preservation of ancient monuments, the automobile industry, the aircraft and shipping industry, in the manufacture of musical instruments as well as in preservation of structures and industrial facilities. It is normally used to examine or inspect interior spaces that are difficult to access, or to monitor danger zones or dangerous terrain.

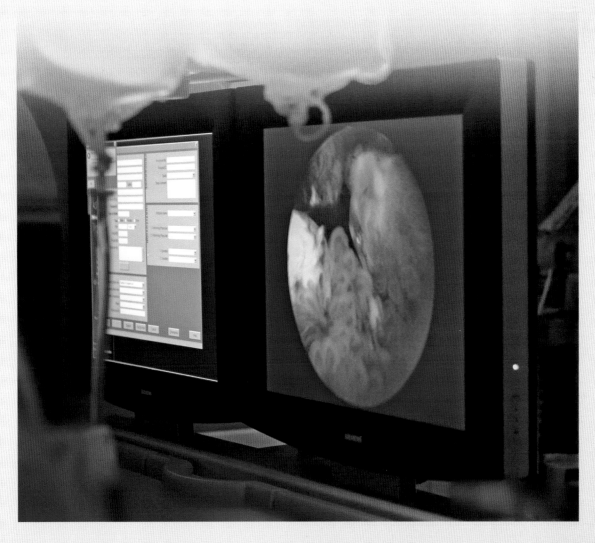

The images sent back by an endoscope—as here in a bypass operation—can supply prompt and vital information.

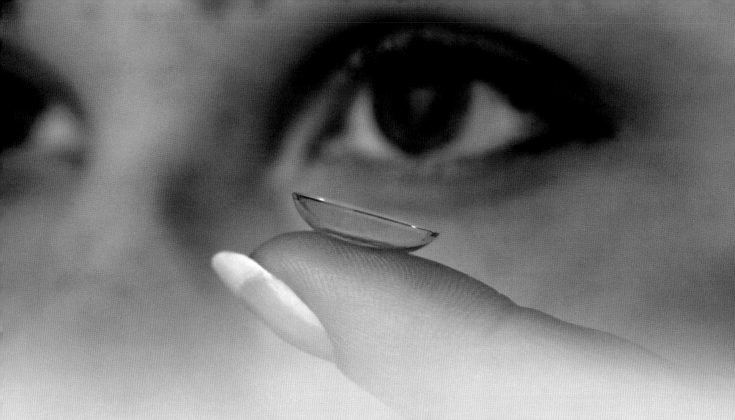

GLASSES, CONTACT LENSES AND LASER: TREATING THE EYES

What is the function of glasses and contact lenses?

They help to produce a sharp image on the retina when the eye cannot do this without support, perhaps because the muscles of the eye do not react sufficiently or the lens wrongly refracts light. A distortion in the vitreous body can also lead to the ideal point on the retina being out of alignment so that the light rays do not reach it optimally.

Glasses or contact lenses refract the light rays with the aid of a second lens before they enter the eye so that the light strikes the lens at a new angle. In this way, light hits the ideal point on the retina and a sharp image is created.

What is a contact lens?

Contact lenses are vision aids that lie directly on the eyeball and perform the same task as glasses. Contact lenses can be soft or hard. Soft lenses can form to the shape of the cornea, making them sit more firmly on the eye. They are more comfortable to wear but also pose a bigger risk for the eye, as deposits on the lens and lack of oxygen can lead to infections. Contact lenses can be used to correct nearsightedness and farsightedness and in principle they are cut in the same way as a glasses lens.

What happens in eye laser treatment?

The aim of laser treatment is to alter the shape of the cornea so that the eye no longer requires glasses or contact lenses in order to function properly.

The surface of the cornea is sliced with a knife and the resulting flap is folded to one side. The cornea that lies behind it is accurately shaped by the laser to form a curve that is comparable with the glasses or contact lenses that were being

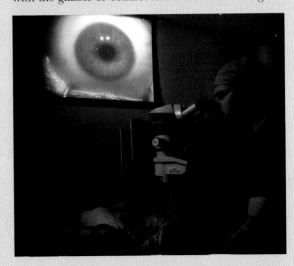

Laser treatment to the eyes normally takes just a few minutes and is these days relatively uncomplicated.

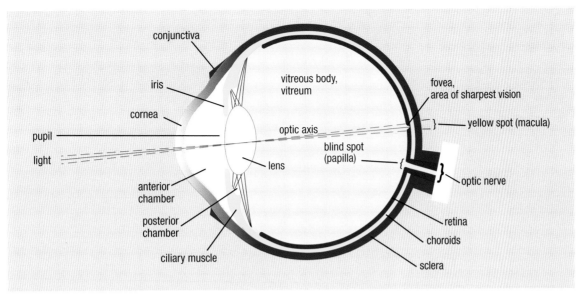

conjunctiva
iris
cornea
pupil
light
anterior chamber
posterior chamber
ciliary muscle
vitreous body, vitreum
optic axis
lens
blind spot (papilla)
fovea, area of sharpest vision
yellow spot (macula)
optic nerve
retina
choroids
sclera

The light rays are focused through the cornea and lens (pupil) so that the rays give an upside-down image on the area of sharpest vision at the back of the eye. The information is passed to the brain via the optic nerve.

Vision

The light that enters the eye is focused through the transparent cornea and the lens that lies behind it, so that an upside-down image is created on a focal point on the retina. In this process, the lens must focus the light rays so that they are bundled together at the point of highest visual acuity, i.e. at the focal point, otherwise a blurred image results as happens with short- and long-sightedness. The retina is made up of sight cells (receptors), which facilitate the recognition of contrast between light and dark, and between colors. The information is then sent via the optic nerve to the brain, where it is interpreted as a complete picture.

macular degeneration, blood vessels, which grow into the visual cortex triggering degeneration, are obliterated to prevent further ingrowth.

With some eye diseases, the appropriate treatment is to inject a substance, such as cortisone, directly into the vitreous body.

used. Following this, the flap is replaced. Due to the new refracted angle of the light through the cornea, a sharp image is once more created on the retina.

Laser eye treatment does not take long and is usually performed under local anesthetic.

How are eye diseases treated?

Technology and medicine offer numerous methods for treating eye diseases. Even dreaded eye diseases such as glaucoma, the loss of visual nerves, or macular degeneration (when the retinal cells die) can be treated these days. Laser treatment is also very important in combating these diseases.

The cause of glaucoma (increased pressure within the eye), for example, can be treated with a laser procedure in which the natural drainage channel is enlarged or laid open. In the case of

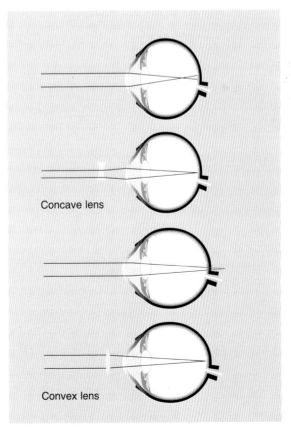

Concave lens

Convex lens

In nearsightedness the light rays are refracted through the eye's lens so that the image is focused on an area in front of the retina. In this case, a concave lens ensures that the angle of the light rays is adjusted before they enter the eye so that the point of focus lies on the retina. In farsightedness the light rays are focused on a point behind the retina. A convex lens provides the appropriate remedy here.

EVERYDAY AIDS TO COMMUNICATION

Can you speak without a voice?

If the larynx is destroyed by disease or in an accident, normal vocalization is no longer possible. In such cases, an electronic speaking device can be used that produces sound and takes over the functions of the larynx.

The sound is transmitted via the surface of the throat into the vocal tract of the pharyngeal space. The sufferer can articulate new sounds by using mouth and tongue movements that are comparable to those used in natural voice training.

A certain amount of practice is needed to use this device and the resulting speech that is created sounds extremely artificial, mainly because the device cannot alter the pitch to give the speech any melody, tone, or emotion.

Can hearing loss be cured?

Hearing loss and deafness can have several causes, some of which can be treated so that natural ability to hear is restored. Conventional hearing aids can only amplify incoming sound waves, which means that unwanted sounds (e.g. background noise) are also amplified. For this reason, the latest models are increasingly turning to digital technology, which is able to adjust the level of amplification automatically and adapt it to the surroundings within split seconds. A further advantage with the digital hearing aids is that it is possible to locate the sound source using several microphones and thus control the incoming sound more effectively. This is not possible with analog hearing aids.

Modern hearing aids are miniature devices that can be programmed so that they meet the requirements of the wearer.

How are blind people able to read?

A computer can make it easier for visually impaired people to read. Printed works are scanned into the computer and a special program is able to change individual parts of the text on the monitor (e.g. by increasing the contrast or enlarging it) so that people who are not completely blind can still detect something. Another aid that is not dependent on a computer—a screen reading device—works on the same principle. However, these days it is hardly ever used—at most in a transportable form as an electric magnifier.

A different computer program changes the texts displayed on the monitor into data format and enables the contents of the screen to be read aloud via voice output software.

More frequent, however, is the use of a different software program to convert the text into Braille, which can then be accessed by a Braille display connected to the computer, enabling the reader to read the contents of the screen by touch. Apart from the traditional Braille keyboard, there are also keyboards for specialized use, which can deal with specialist material such as shorthand and music notation.

Are there any improved communication devices in the pipeline?

To some extent, yes. There are ongoing experiments with artificial voice boxes, for example. Although no model has reached production stage, most recent developments show a marked improvement in quality.

There has also been progress with digital hearing aids in the last few years. Digital processing of acoustic signals is much more rapid, and sounds can also be filtered so that it is possible to cut out background noise.

Up to now it has not been possible to produce an artificial eye, but tests have been done for a vision prosthesis that sends image signals to the brain via the optic nerve.

High-tech wheelchairs

Diseases or accidents can leave people reliant on wheelchairs that must provide for more than just mobility. Over recent years, there have been a number of individual motorized wheelchair models equipped with computers that aid communication. Professor Stephen Hawking, for example, communicates with the aid of such a computer, which is controlled by the user's eye movements and through which he can project his synthesized voice.

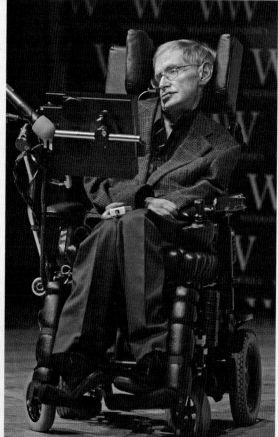

Above: The additional Braille bar on the keyboard enables blind people to read the screen contents by touch.

At the beginning of his illness, Professor Stephen Hawking was dependent on an assistant with pencil and paper for communication.

DENTAL TECHNOLOGY: CHECK IT OUT

Dental technicians manufacture tooth implants as well as all the tooth replacement parts such as bridges, crowns, and prostheses.

Why are teeth replaced?

A gap in the teeth, apart from the aesthetic issue, has a host of disadvantages. The jaw no longer has any pressure on it where there is a tooth missing and this can lead to it deteriorating. If only the opposite side of the mouth is used for chewing because of the gap, then the problem is intensified. When chewing, the pressure is normally distributed across adjoining teeth, so that if there is a gap, the surrounding teeth will experience greater stress and can become loose. In addition, the teeth and gums around the gap offer a greater surface area for bacteria and other pathogens to gain a foothold. This increases the risk that more teeth could be lost.

Thus, early replacement with a dental prosthesis is considered essential.

What's so bad about amalgam?

Amalgam that is used in dentistry is a mixture of substances, normally of metals such as silver, zinc, or copper, but it also contains mercury, which is poisonous. It is suspected that mercury can be released from this compound through the heat created by friction when chewing, for example, or by certain drinks. Although up to now there is no scientific evidence to prove this, amalgam has been controversial for some decades. It is still used today for fillings mainly due to its durability, ease of preparation, and low cost.

How is tooth implantation carried out?

These days, tooth implantation has increasingly become the preferred method of replacing a tooth. In this method, the diseased tooth is extracted and under local anesthetic an implantation bed is surgically placed under the gum in the jawbone and the implant is screwed into it.

In principle, the implant is an artificial tooth root made of titanium with a suitable crown set on top of it.

This method has many advantages over a bridge: the adjacent teeth are not altered as with a bridge, an implant has greater durability, and it can take stresses just as a natural tooth can. There is also an additional risk with a bridge that it may loosen, an unlikely thing to happen with an implant under normal conditions.

What advantages and disadvantages are there in laser treatment?

A laser very quickly treats a precisely defined area, blasting it with a very high-energy light. Dentistry uses the effect of this energy in a variety of ways. In tooth implantation, for example, it is used mainly to fix a crown or bridge onto the implanted artificial root, as due to the heat the crown material can be softened for a short time. Similarly, periodontitis (inflammation of tissue around a tooth) can be treated effectively with laser because the tooth enamel is not affected by brief radiation but the bacteria causing the periodontitis are. Gum treatments such as removal of growths can also be carried out by laser as modern dental lasers are equipped with sensors to detect any diseased tissue. Thus, the laser can pinpoint and treat just the diseased areas. If laser rays are used properly, there should be no side effects.

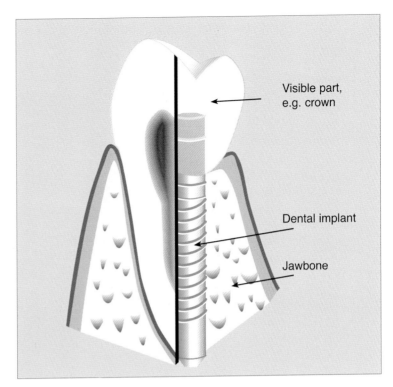

The implant (right half) is built up in the same way as the natural tooth (left half). The post remains in the implantation bed and assumes the role of the tooth's root. The post is topped off with a crown and looks like a natural tooth.

Despite modern developments, there is no real alternative to the drill for treating damaged teeth.

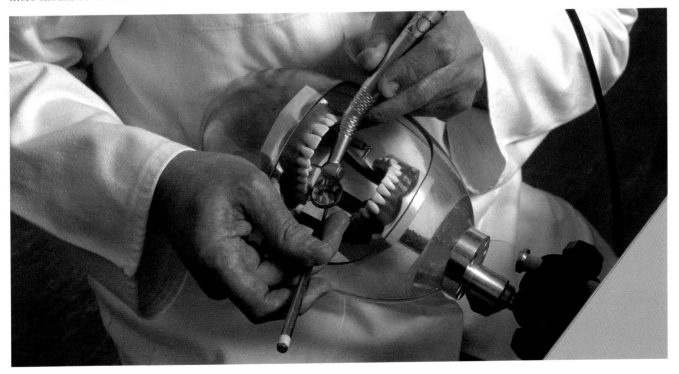

Modern prostheses are made so that they can withstand even extreme stresses, such as certain sporting activities.

TRANSPLANTATION AND IMPLANTATION: SUPPORT FOR THE BODY

How can the body's functions and body parts be supported?

There are many reasons why the body might need support: wear and tear, disease, or after an accident. In each case, the patient should be aware that no aid can completely replace the potential of a healthy body part; it can merely fulfil a supportive function. Support can be achieved by implants, i.e. by the implantation of an artificial aid, or by transplantation, i.e. by the transplantation of your own or someone else's body part. There are also many external aids that are used to support the body's functions without having to resort to surgery, among other things crutches, spectacles, and hearing aids.

What is a prosthesis?

Some parts of the body, generally joints or limbs, can be replaced by prostheses. In some cases, this is done by implantations or endoprostheses (Greek *endo*, "internal"), as in artificial hip or knee replacements. These types of prostheses remain in the body for long periods (usually several years) before they must be replaced. Other prostheses, exoprostheses (Greek *exo*, "external"), are used on the outside of the body, normally in the form of artificial arms or legs. In recent years, prostheses have become truly high-tech products. These days, with the incorporation of microprocessors, nerve signals can be picked up and converted into movements. In this way, the wearer of the prosthesis can even take up sporting activities again.

What disadvantages do these aids have?

There is always a risk with implants and transplants that the body might develop defense cells and reject the foreign body, i.e. attack and destroy it. For this reason, transplant recipients must take medication for the rest of their lives to prevent rejection occurring. Normally, the danger of rejection is a lot less if the patient has an autologous transplant (where their own tissue is used). Another problem arises from the medicines that are given to prevent rejection flare-ups. As these have a tendency to stop the reaction of the body's own immune system (so that it does not react to foreign bodies), the body can become incapable of fighting against other pathogens.

In joint transplants, there is generally the danger of fractures, swelling, tissue or nerve damage, and stress injuries. The risk of these sorts of injuries occurring in the early postoperative period is greater if the patient expects too much of the new joint, and the body has still not grown used to the transplant.

Does an artificial joint function differently from a natural one?

An artificial joint in structure and functionality is designed as nearly as possible to a natural joint. However, the actual functionality depends on the complexity of the implant.

In some cases, such as a complete replacement of the knee joint, the artificial joint assumes more functions than the natural one, as, for example, the cruciate ligaments, whose function is to provide additional support to the knee, have also been removed.

In partial replacements, as much as possible of the original joint is kept, as long as it is considered that no complications would arise as a result of joining together the bone with the implant. Otherwise, fractures, swelling, or injury to the blood vessels can occur.

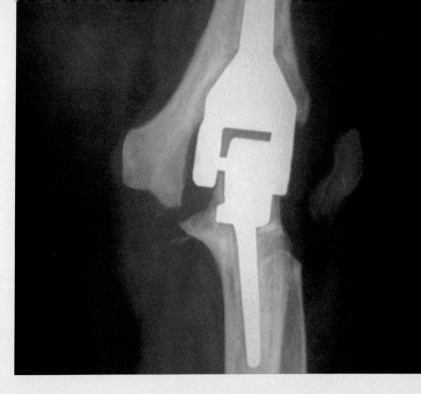

In damaged joints—here an elbow—the surgeon will normally try to preserve as much of the surrounding bone as possible.

Tests are already taking place with visually impaired people who, with the aid of an implanted camera system, are enabled to see, if only indistinctly. Here the optical system is being fine-tuned by computer.

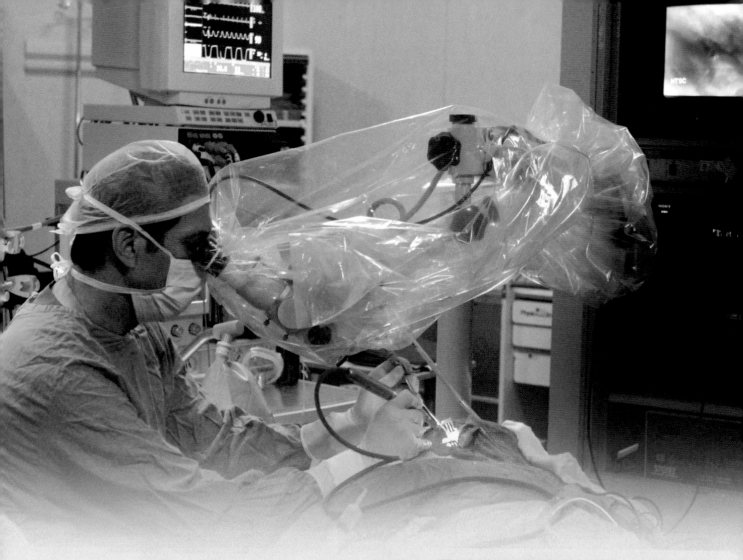

Microtechnology has opened up completely new possibilities in surgery, such as cochlear implants.

Can any part of the body be replaced?

No. With regard to the skeleton, for instance, medicine has reached its limits with the spinal column. Up to now, there is no prosthesis that would allow paraplegics to regain complete control over their bodies. Damage to the spinal column or spinal cord cannot be remedied technically even though there has been a great deal of research in this area over many years.

The same is true in other fields. Brain and skin organs cannot currently be replaced (or only very inadequately), since here—in the same way as with the spinal column—the necessary information flow can still not be completely safeguarded by an implant or a transplant, neither in the brain cells nor in the skin's nerve cells.

What criteria are used to determine whether to use an implant or a transplant?

Frequently, the limits of technology are the deciding factor, although generally implants are the preferred option because, among other things, the patient is not dependent on a donor. However, up to now

Autologous transplant

If the body's own tissue is transplanted to another area of the body, this is known as an autologous transplant. This transplant procedure is frequently performed on tissue, and more rarely on limbs, above all in the specialist field of tissue engineering (see page 205).

there is often no adequate artificial alternative for many transplants.

In heart disease, for example, the patient currently still has to hope that a donor organ will become available. Artificial hearts do exist, but they are hardly suitable for normal life; most models are more comparable to a pacemaker than to an independent organ. Generally speaking, whereas implants are usually used in bones and joints, transplants are resorted to in most cases where an organ has to be replaced.

Do artificial or foreign parts of the body last longer than one's own?

Artificial and foreign organs are more fragile than one's own; the risk of rejection is basically always present. A transplant can still be rejected even years after the operation. Statistics show that transplants last on average 13 years.

Artificial joints, on the other hand, have much greater durability even if their life expectancy is also limited. An artificial hip joint, for example, will currently last on average around 15 years, depending on its construction and the stresses placed on it.

Above: Robert Langer developed micro devices for the release of drugs by stimulus.

Right: The transplant patient is still dependent on donor organs, which must be transplanted within a short period after they have been removed.

KIDNEYS AND HEART: AIDS FOR INTERNAL ORGANS

What is dialysis?

Dialysis (Greek *dialusis*, "set free") describes a technical procedure to clean the blood of impurities, which is used in cases of acute or chronic renal failure. In a healthy person, waste products are filtered from the blood via the kidneys and liver and excreted via urine. If this function is no longer working properly, the kidneys may even become permanently poisoned. The patient must therefore undergo dialysis regularly, attending sessions that may last for several hours, when the blood will be cleaned by a dialysis machine that assumes the function of the kidneys and removes waste products from the blood and enriches the blood with additional substances.

A dialysis session may last for several hours and must be carried out several times a week.

Function of the kidneys

The kidneys could be said to be the human's waste treatment plant. Here toxins are removed from the blood and the water balance and acid content are regulated. The blood glucose levels and composition of the blood are also regulated. This is all done by repeated filtering of the blood and draining of superfluous substances via the urine.

In the case of permanent renal failure, a kidney transplant is inevitable. Dialysis in this case is regarded as a temporary solution.

What happens during dialysis?

The dialysis machine assumes the function of the kidneys in that harmful substances are filtered from the blood via a salt solution. This happens by the two fluids (blood and salt solution) flowing past one another in opposite directions. A semi-permeable membrane separates them from one another and only small molecules and ions can pass through it.

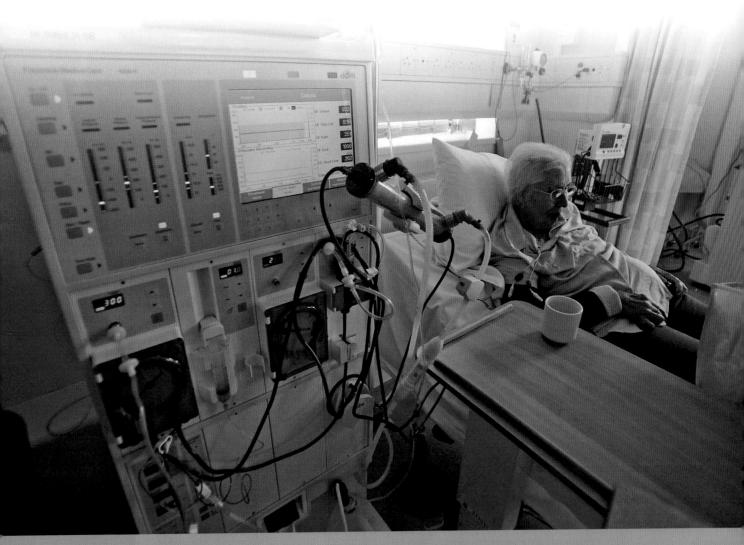

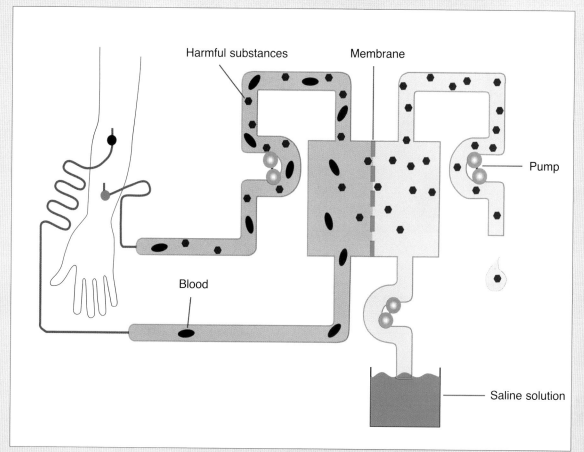

Harmful substances   Membrane

Pump

Blood

Saline solution

Left: The dialysis machine filters out noxious substances. The saline solution absorbs the noxious substances in the bloodstream through the semi-permeable membrane and thus the blood is cleansed.

The waste products are much smaller than the blood, so they are able to pass into the salt solution. Just before the blood returns to the patient's body, the blood is passed through an air trap so that air bubbles do not enter into the arteries, as this could trigger an embolism.

How does a defibrillator work?

Before every heartbeat, an electrical impulse is emitted from one of the atria, causing the heart muscles to contract. If this impulse is emitted too powerfully or too irregularly, it can result in ventricular fibrillation or arrhythmia. A defibrillator delivers an electric shock to make the heart's muscles contract violently for a split second. When the muscles then relax, the next natural impulse hopefully returns the heartbeat to normal.

A defibrillator should be used as soon as possible after the event, as during ventricular fibrillation the heart is not able to deliver oxygen to the body via the blood and lasting damage can occur even in a short space of time. These days there are also implantable cardioverter defibrillators (ICDs), which are used in patients with an increased risk of cardiac arrhythmia.

In some cases, this situation results in a vicious cycle that is difficult to break. This is because

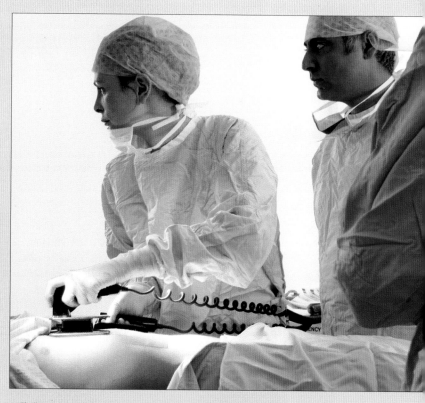

Defibrillators are not only used in the operating room. They are also available for use in certain public areas and can be used by laypeople to give emergency assistance.

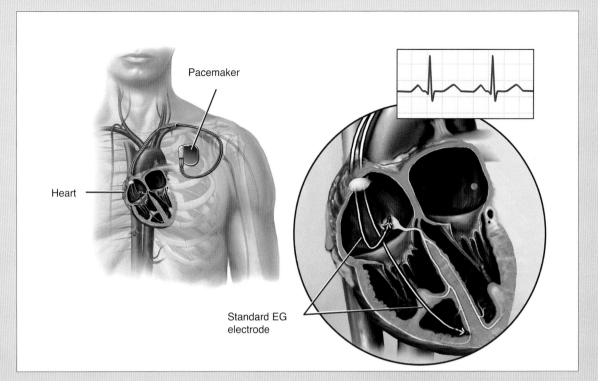

Pacemaker

Heart

Standard EG electrode

Cardiovascular system

The cardiovascular system's task is to supply the body with oxygen via the blood and to remove carbon dioxide from it. In this process the heart is center stage; in normal conditions it pumps the blood through the body at a speed of 10½–12½ pints (5–6 liters) per minute. Gaseous exchange takes place in the lungs—carbon dioxide is given off and oxygen is absorbed. On its circuit around the body, the blood supplies the individual organs with oxygen and other necessary substances before it returns to the heart. When more oxygen is required, the heart rate increases so that the blood is pumped more quickly through the arteries.

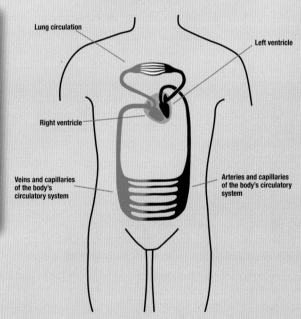

The oxygen supply of the body is controlled via the heart-lung circulation. The heart pumps the blood to the lungs where gaseous exchange takes place. The oxygen is transported in the arteries to the areas that require it. As the oxygen is used up, CO_2 is created, which is transported back to the heart via the veins.

while the defibrillator forces the heart to beat by applying an electric shock, it also causes the muscles to overexcite electrically so that for a few milliseconds there is interference with the next electrical impulse. While this short period is sufficient to break through the vicious cycle and give the heart the chance to find its own rhythm once more, there is always the danger that the ventricular fibrillation could begin again with one of the subsequent heartbeats.

What is a cardiac pacemaker?

A cardiac pacemaker is an artificial device that regulates the heartbeat by impulses. It is normally used if the natural impulses in the heart's atrium, which make the heart beat, are too slow or too

irregular. It assumes the function of the SA (sinoatrial) node and emits electrical impulses at regular intervals. The natural impulses are emitted as before, but they are normally ineffective as the stronger impulses of the cardiac pacemaker override them. Modern cardiac pacemakers are equipped with sensors so that the device only comes into use if the heart's rhythm becomes too slow.

Are there other types of pacemaker?

Yes, pacemakers can be used anywhere to reactivate organs when natural electrical impulses or shocks are failing to activate the vital reactions of an organ. Bladder pacemakers, for example, help paraplegics with bladder control. In some cases of paralysis, a respiratory pacemaker can take over the function of the diaphragm, and in severe or chronic cases of intestinal inertia, intestinal pacemakers help to stimulate intestinal activity. Brain pacemakers are used to stimulate certain regions of the brain with electrical impulses, which will then trigger certain reactions in the body or, alternatively, stop them. These brain pacemakers are used in cases of multiple sclerosis, dystonia (a movement disorder causing involuntary muscle contractions), or patients with Parkinson's disease.

What dangers are there for patients with pacemakers?

As with any implant, there is a risk of infection with pacemakers. Beyond that, pacemakers can also be susceptible to magnetic or electromagnetic waves, such as from metal detectors, security systems, or transformers. Modern models are made so that they work perfectly well within external electromagnetic fields, such as those from mobile telephones or loudspeakers. Programming is now also possible, so that the cardiac pacemaker can react to certain of the body's requirements. For instance, if there is a need for increased oxygen, as when the body is engaged in effort, the impulses are emitted more rapidly, which causes the heart to beat faster and the blood can transport oxygen more rapidly to the areas that require it.

What does a heart-lung machine do?

A heart-lung machine can take over the functions of the heart and lungs for a limited period. It is used mainly in heart or lung operations to maintain the circulation, respiration, and metabolic functions of the body. The machine is connected to the patient's blood circulation and the blood is pumped through the machine. Inside the machine, the blood is enriched with oxygen, filtered—to avoid foreign bodies or blood clots entering—and then fed back into the body. The heart-lung machine, as with the dialysis machine, is not a permanent solution, but can be used only for a short transitional period.

Heart-lung machines are mainly used in operations to ensure vital gaseous exchange.

TECHNOLOGY FOR HOSPITALS

The protective (green) clothing in the operating theater is primarily used to prevent the open wound from coming into contact with germs or foreign bodies such as hair.

What is the difference between disinfection and sterilization?

Disinfection denotes the process in which living and dead pathogens (viruses, bacteria, fungi, and so on) are rendered harmless, so that they can no longer cause infection. Sterilization takes this a step further, and destroys all traces of living microorganisms, including their spores. Complete sterilization is currently only possible under special laboratory conditions, as microorganisms are ever-present in our environment.

Why do major operations take place in sterile areas?

In order to keep the infection risk as low as possible for the patient. Major (i.e. long and complicated) operations, in particular, represent an extremely critical and very stressful situation for the body. Additionally, often the health of the patient is weakened before the operation and many natural protective mechanisms of the body are not functioning optimally. As a consequence, the body is very vulnerable to infection during an operation. Disinfected or sterile areas—in which the amount of pathogens is far less than is otherwise usual in the environment—lower the risk of infection.

How are instruments sterilized?

Operation instruments are normally sterilized by steam in an autoclave. This pressurized container is technically similar to a pressure cooker. In it the material to be sterilized is heated under pressure to obtain a higher temperature. In exceptional cases or outside the operating theater, other sterilization procedures are used, such as hot air sterilization, whereby the instruments are exposed to direct heat or antiseptics, in which chemicals or gases have a sterilizing effect.

Why are patients put on an artificial respirator when they are under general anesthetic?

To eliminate the risk that the patient's breathing could be compromised under the general anesthetic: artificially induced deep sleep also has an effect on the airways, and that could lead to an interruption in the breathing. Additionally, the air used in artificial respiration is usually mixed with a gaseous anesthetic to ensure that the patient stays asleep during the operation.

How are technical faults dealt with in a hospital?

A range of security systems is in place to deal with technical faults. A power failure, for example, could be a catastrophe for a hospital. For this reason, equipment that is dependent upon a continuous supply of electricity in order to function is equipped with a complete energy management system as standard. This system reacts very quickly to compensate for power fluctuations and failures. For cases when there may be problems or failures in technical control instruments and computer equipment in a hospital (e.g. program failures), a so-called watchdog is built into the system. Normally, this is concerned with system components, which receive signals at regular intervals from the installed software or the associated microcontroller. If these signals stop, countermeasures automatically begin. Depending on the system, an alarm can be triggered or parallel-installed software can be run.

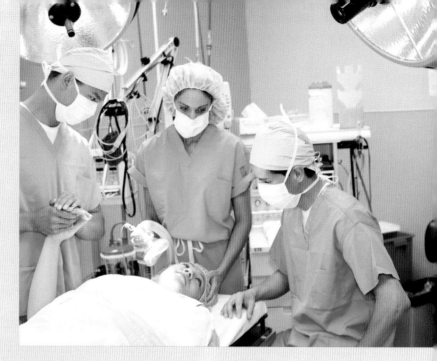

The patient must be prepared before the operation so that the risk of infection is kept as low as possible.

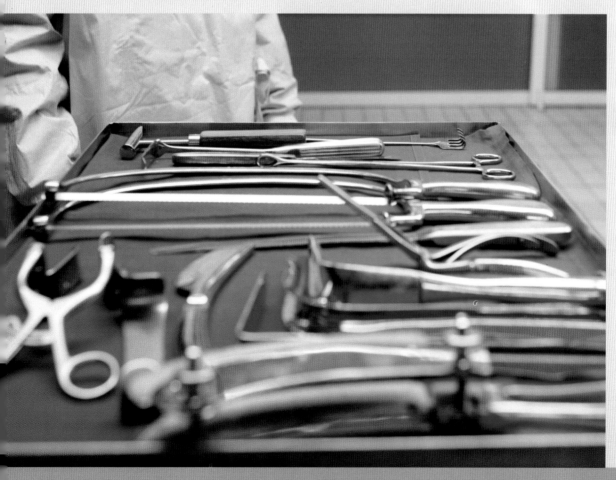

Sterilized instruments reduce the risk of infection markedly.

PLASTIC SURGERY: MUCH MORE THAN JUST A BEAUTY TREATMENT

What is plastic surgery?

Plastic surgery is a specialist field of surgery that includes operations that aim to restore impaired organic function due to congenital damage or damage caused by injury to the body. Its aims also include the removal of disfigurement or abnormal tissue. Reconstructive and aesthetic (cosmetic) surgery are important branches of plastic surgery. Cosmetic surgery is concerned mainly with operations such as facelifts (rhytidectomy) or liposuction (removal of surplus body fat).

What does reconstructive surgery achieve?

In reconstructive surgery, bodily functions or whole parts of the body are restored. They may have been lost due to illness, deformity, or accident. In this area of the specialty, fingers, toes, feet, and earlobes, among other things, can be replanted, and tumors, malformations, and misalignment of limbs can be removed or corrected.

What is meant by burns surgery?

Burns surgery is an important part of reconstructive surgery, which concentrates on the treatment of burn wounds. It includes care for minor burn wounds and removal of areas of dead skin, right up to skin grafts, which are necessary if the tissue swells due to the burn, as this can restrict blood flow. Additionally, severe burns lead frequently to scarring of the skin. With the help of plastic surgery, the damaged tissue can be saved or at least partly saved. Another focus in this area of plastic surgery is the treatment of nerves that have been burned. At the moment it is still not possible to reconstruct the finest nerve fibers, but burns surgery can, with prompt intervention, ensure that at least the larger bundles of nerves remain intact.

Why is ultrasound used in liposuction?

There are several techniques of performing liposuction. Ultrasound is only used in ultrasound-assisted liposuction (UAL) and has a similar function to its use in the removal of kidney stones (see page 176). The ultrasound is used first of all to emulsify the cells of the fatty tissue before the operation, so that subsequently, merely what is left of the fat—liquid and cell remains—needs to be sucked out.

Can plastic surgery heal?

Plastic surgery mainly sets the healing process in motion when it is used in the reconstructive sense (i.e. in burns or accidental injuries). In many cases

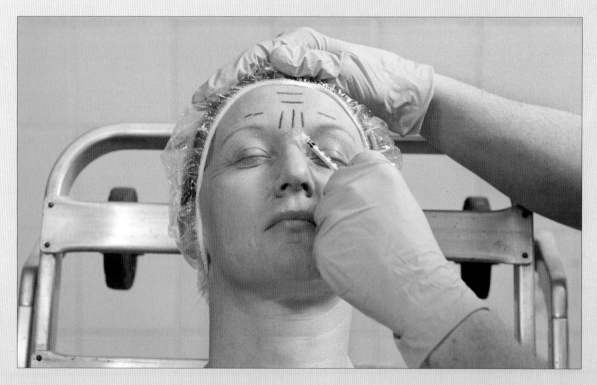

Anti-wrinkle treatment—often done by injecting specially treated fatty tissue to make the skin smooth—is classed as part of a plastic surgeon's work.

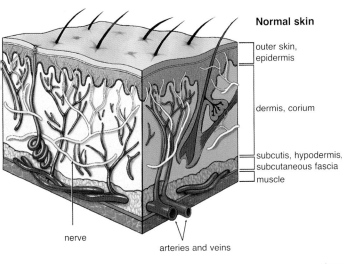

Normal skin

outer skin, epidermis

dermis, corium

subcutis, hypodermis, subcutaneous fascia

muscle

nerve

arteries and veins

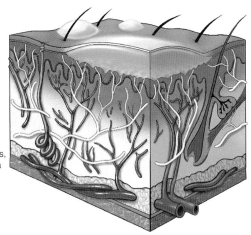

Second-degree burns

- Formation of blisters

- The outer skin is affected as well as parts of the dermis

- The entire dermis can be affected

Above: Due to the sensitivity of the skin, second-degree burns (caused by boiling water, for example) can cause great if not irreversible damage.

of cosmetic surgery, the potential healing effect of surgical intervention has been found to be more on the psychological level, as patients can gain self-confidence and new zest for life by altering their outward appearance cosmetically. However, the psychological effects of cosmetic operations depend very much on individual factors, over which the surgeon has no influence.

Hand surgery

Hand surgery (as with burns surgery) is, due to its complexity, another specialist area within reconstructive surgery, as in this field it is also possible to transplant limbs and plastic surgeons must undertake a further one-year-long fellowship to qualify. If a thumb is lost, for instance, and the original part cannot be sewn back onto the hand, a toe could be transplanted. This would maintain important functions of the hand (e.g. the grab and grip functions).

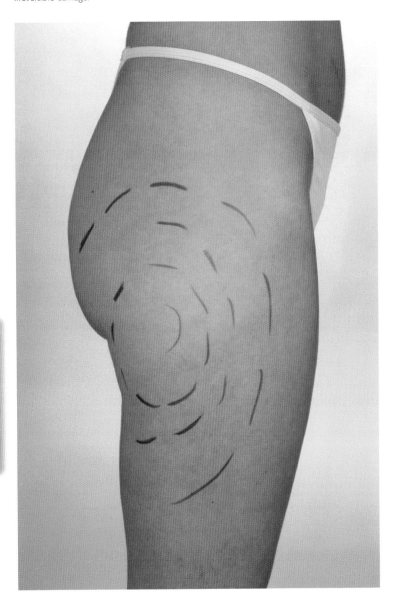

Exact planning in the run-up to an operation is essential, as most results are irreversible. The outside of the thighs, together with tummy, hips, and bottom, are all classic "problem areas" where liposuction is used for correction.

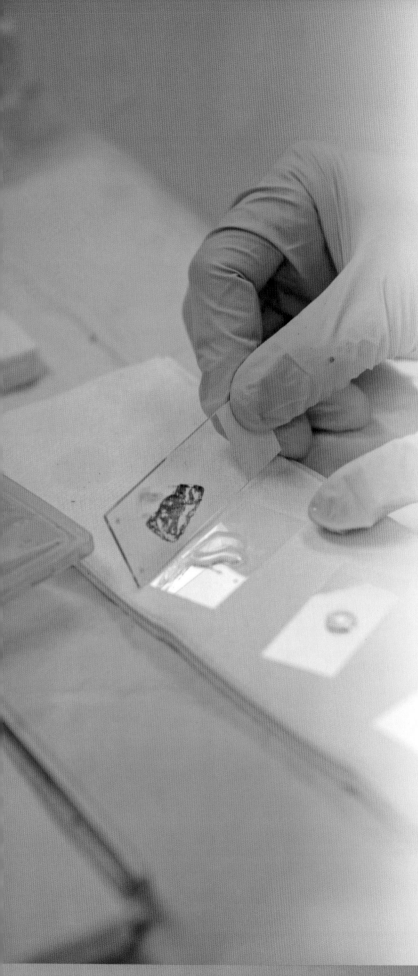

PATHOLOGY: THE EXAMINATION OF DEAD BODIES

What is pathology?

The science of pathology (disease research) examines clinical pictures and the courses of disease. The causes and effects of symptoms, malformations, and abnormal bodily functions are also studied in this medical field. Thus, infections, circulatory disturbances, and the examination of cancers, for example, are all core areas of pathology. Apart from that, pathology gathers together from the different areas of knowledge all the data that are connected with the diagnosis or course of diseases. The specialist field of social pathology developed from this area of pathology. It is concerned, among other things, with the examination of connections between disease and prevailing social conditions.

Which fields of medical knowledge does pathology cover?

Historically, pathology was not at first considered a science in its own right, but an area that was covered by other fields of medicine. For this reason, there are numerous subgroups of pathology that are established within current medical branches, such as molecular pathology, which belongs to molecular biology, or gynecopathology, which is a branch of gynecology. In time, pathology developed out of these different fields of knowledge until it was realized that there were parallels even between different disease processes. From there, pathology basically extended into all areas of biology, including medicine, chemistry, and physics.

What is the difference between pathology and forensic medicine?

Pathology's job is to investigate diseases or symptoms. In contrast, forensic medicine is geared first and foremost towards finding out as much useful information as possible. Pathologists primarily gather together knowledge about disease processes from numerous independent scientific fields—they are not concerned with clearing up possible crimes. Furthermore, forensic medicine has a different scientific focus from pathology. For instance, toxicology (the scientific study of

The preparation of specimens is done in different ways, depending on the kind of pathological examination to be carried out.

poisons), forensic molecular biology (examination of the genotype), and thanatology (the science of death with regard to its psychological and sociological aspects) belong to the field of research of forensic medicine just as traumatology (the science of injuries) or sexual medicine do.

What happens in an autopsy?

In forensic medicine, the expression "autopsy" primarily means an examination of a dead body (postmortem).

It is carried out to ascertain the cause of death or to reconstruct the course of death. The first thing that is done in an autopsy is to examine the external condition of the corpse in minute detail and to describe it. Then the internal examination is carried out. Visible changes are documented and specimens (of the organs, bodily fluids, etc.) are taken for further examination. All the information is written down in the autopsy report.

When is a pathological autopsy performed?

A pathological autopsy is carried out for different reasons. In some medical settings, the patient will be examined after death so that the doctors can obtain more information about the disease. In other cases, an examination is performed for reasons of medical quality assurance, for example to ascertain whether any mistakes were made

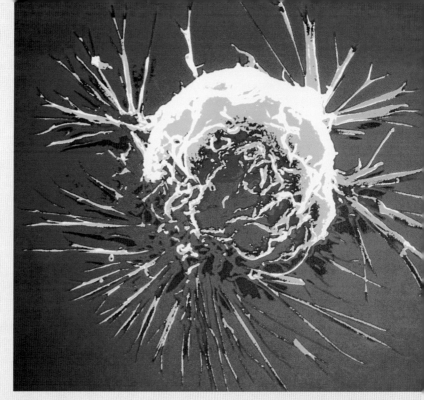

Pathology does valuable work in detecting cancer: breast cancer cells can be diagnosed with the aid of an electron microscope.

with diagnosis or treatment. Otherwise, postmortems are carried out mainly for educational and research reasons, for medical students as well as doctors.

Below: A pathological examination must be carried out in an extremely structured and careful way. Even the most minute traces can provide important information.

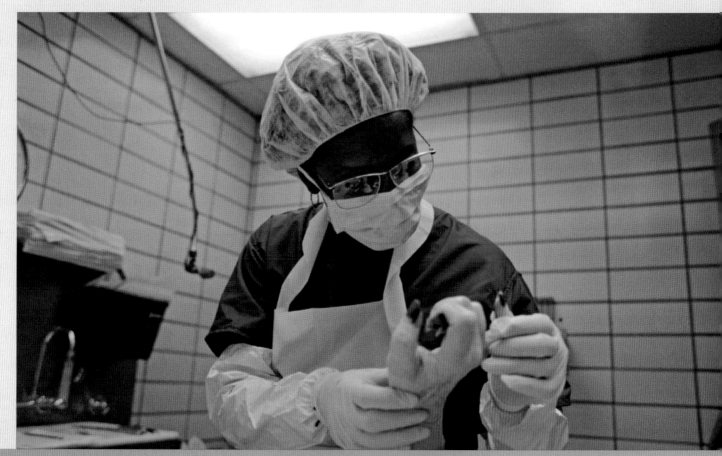

What technical devices are needed for pathological or forensic examinations?

Computers have become a very important tool in the work of the pathologist and forensic pathologist. As both fields fall back on knowledge and data from numerous other fields in the course of their work, the collection of information and checks with their own examination results has become a central part of pathology. For this reason, extensive data banks that hold written and illustrated findings have been in existence for years. This makes it easier to check results and supplies a basis for further research.

How can a forensic pathologist contribute to solving crimes?

The analysis of the specimens taken at an autopsy is dependent on the predetermined aim of the examination of the body and the information gained from it. If the cause of death is not clear, for example, then a toxicological examination of the specimens, i.e. a search for poisonous substances, will be prominent. As well as that, serological (antibody reactions) analysis can provide information on diseases that the person might have been suffering from at the time of death. In cases where a body has to be identified, the genotype can be determined by a molecular genetic process with the help of specimens, and

In forensic medicine, examination of the crime scene must also be undertaken, as this evidence will be used when the medical results are evaluated.

thus contribute to identification. For cases where the person has been dead for a long time or where there may be only a few bodily remains, forensic anthropology can help to reconstruct the appearance of a dead person.

How are samples examined?

Immunofluorescence is one way of examining samples, giving microscopic evidence of pathogens, for example. Dyed, labeled antibodies are used by the direct variant to reveal bacteria or proteins in the blood or tissue samples.

Enzyme histochemistry represents another way of dyeing certain substances. In this process the properties of proteins (enzymes) that can promote a

---

The development of pathology

In ancient times, examinations of dead bodies were performed mainly for anatomical studies. Modern pathology did not really develop until the 18th century, after the Italian researcher Giovanni B. Morgagni (1682–1772), now considered as the father of modern anatomical pathology, had published his first textbook, *On the seats and causes of disease*. The first prosector (a person who carries out dissections) was employed in the general hospital in Vienna in 1796. Jean-Frédéric Lobstein (1777–1835) occupied the first chair for pathology in 1819 in Strasbourg.

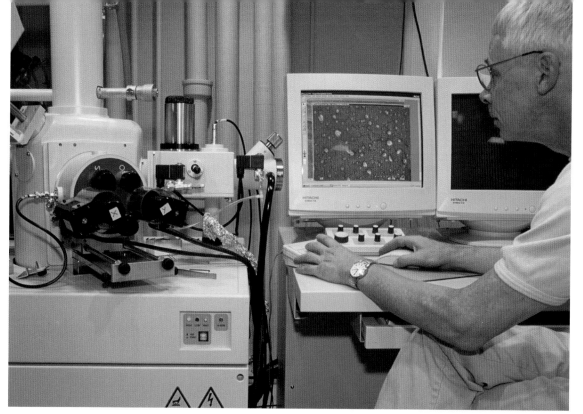

The results of an electron microscope examination are shown on the screen.

Below: Kathy Reichs is a forensic anthropologist as well as author of best-selling crime novels. Her specialist area of forensic medicine plays an important part in solving the cases in her novels.

chemical reaction are used. The tissue samples are first of all set with a colorless substrate. If the enzyme is present, it is converted through a chemical reaction into a pigment. This form of diagnosis plays an important role in the detection of cancers.

The electron microscope

Electron microscopes magnify to a much larger scale and to a higher resolution than traditional light microscopes. In the former, samples are bombarded with electrons in a vacuum. The negatively charged electron rays are deflected by the positively charged atomic nuclei of a specimen and/or reduced in their energy. These deflections and energy reductions are—depending on their type of construction—picked up by a fluorescent screen or detectors and converted into images. The electron microscope is not only used in pathology, but also for researching structures in other sciences.

GENE RESEARCH

What are genetic diseases?

Genetic diseases are diseases or symptoms that can be passed onto subsequent generations via the genes. This does not mean, however, that a carrier of such information will inevitably succumb to the disease. Numerous genetic diseases are manifested only under certain conditions. This can cause a genetic disease to skip a generation before it re-appears.

Can genetic diseases be treated?

Genetic diseases are congenital, but some, such as bodily deformities, can be treated quite well these days. For others, only the symptoms can currently be treated, as in the case of hemophilia, in which the blood does not clot, resulting in minor wounds leading to major loss of blood. Other diseases are untreatable within the limits of current research and development, such as color blindness (red-green color blindness) or albinism (genetic lack of the pigment melanin in eyes, skin, and hair). If a genetic defect results in the body not being able to form certain substances (e.g. hormones), the missing substances can sometimes be administered. In this way, dwarfism or anemia may be treated.

In which fields can genetic engineering be of help?

Genetic engineering has been used in forensic medicine for a long time. In this context, genetic examinations yield information that is invaluable for identifying bodies or the person responsible for a crime. In addition, so-called green genetic engineering is able to manipulate the genetic make-up of plants to give them new characteristics without the greater breeding costs. Thus, in the past it has been possible to increase resistance and yields in plants. However, some undesirable side effects are starting to appear, and some foreign characteristics could be transferred to creatures that feed on the plants. How this will affect human beings in the long term is still being examined.

What goals is stem cell research pursuing?

The cells of a complex organism are normally so differentiated that they can only perform certain tasks. Liver cells, for instance, are designed for completely different functions from nerve cells. However, with so-called stem cells, this is not the case. They are not differentiated but produce specialized daughter cells by division. The complex processes in stem cells are being researched at present, in order to be able to control certain processes in the body. By targeted use of stem cells, it could be possible in the future to heal damaged organs or even replace them. In addition, specially treated stem cells open up the possibility of using them for the dispersal of active ingredients within the body or even counteracting the effect of diseased body cells (such as in cancer).

What happens in artificial insemination?

Artificial insemination is used to produce a pregnancy and was first developed for the dairy cattle industry. There are several techniques. In the in vitro fertilization (IVF) process, the egg cells are fertilized by sperm cells outside the woman's body. The fertilized eggs are then reintroduced into the woman's uterus where their further development can take place. In intrauterine insemination (IUI), on the other hand, selected sperm cells are transferred directly into the uterine cavity. No hormone treatment is required before this procedure (unlike IVF), but it has a lower success rate.

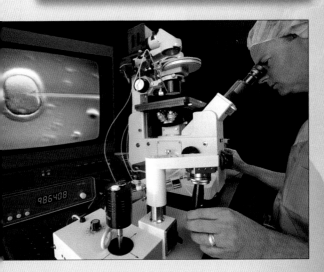

Above: Fertilization of the egg cells takes place by in vitro fertilization under the microscope.

Right: These stem cells from human bone marrow are responsible for the formation of blood cells.

THE FUTURE OF MEDICAL TECHNOLOGY

What can a Lab-on-a-Chip do?

The Lab-on-a-Chip (LOC) represents a new development in microtechnology or, to be more precise, microfluidics. This is an attempt to reduce a complete chemical laboratory for the examination of fluids to a microscopic size. Instead of having enormous quantities of test tubes in a laboratory complex, countless capillary vessels are brought together on a chip of just a few millimeters in size. Besides trouble-free transportability, it has a further advantage in that results are achieved more rapidly as multiple tests can be carried out at the same time. In the last years of the 20th century, the development of LOCs really took off. Of course the technology is not completely developed yet, but some LOCs are already being used in the framework of process controls in analytical fields of industry and in research and development. It is really

The finely structured composition of a nerve cell and its long, fine axon represent an enormous challenge to microsurgery.

just a question of time until they are used as a matter of course in the field of medicine.

Can nerves be replaced?

Damaged nerves can basically regenerate themselves, as long as the damage is not too great, as it would be for quadriplegics or victims of very bad burns. At the moment, researchers are in the initial stages of developing nerve prostheses to be

Even though robots and computers can already take on a large part of human work these days, operations are still carried out by people.

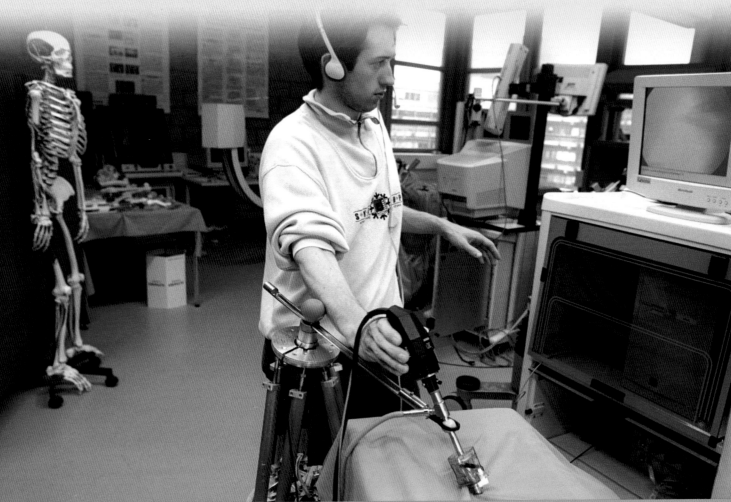

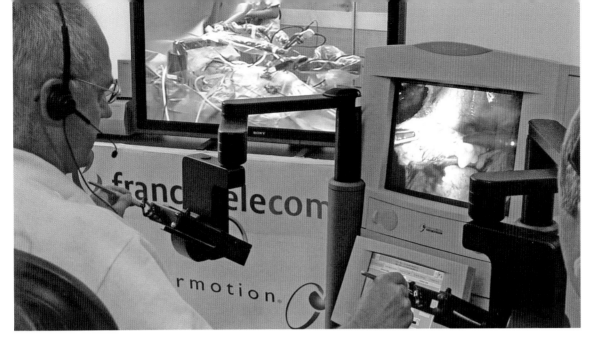

With the aid of cleverly designed technology, it is possible to control operations from a distance. This means that the surgeon can stay outside the operating theater during an operation.

able to restore nerves completely. Constructing microscopically fine fibers that can assume the function of an intact bundle of nerve fibers while also not being rejected by the body, however, is not an easy task.

Will machines perform operations in the future?

In the last 20 years, surgery has made enormous progress. Many operation theaters are already equipped with modern robots that are controlled by surgeons. Much more precise work can be done by using the finest instruments with the appropriate control than can be achieved by a hand with a scalpel. The surgeon does not even necessarily have to be present in the theater any longer: there have already been experiments in which operating theater robots have been controlled via the internet. However, it will be a long time until these experiments are translated into safe procedures that can be used in medical practice.

Diagnostics is a different matter, as many opportunities have opened up for distance diagnosis. Today it is quite normal to bring together experts via rapid communication links, such as the internet, to give their expert opinions on a diagnosis. However, giving a distance diagnosis directly to the patient is, for the time being, still unrealistic.

Could human organs be bred in the future?

The answer to this question depends on the development of stem cell research (see page 202). The theoretical basis for breeding organs already exists and the first successes in stem cell medicine have also been seen. However, at the moment these are restricted to stem cell transplantation, in which stem cells from a donor are transplanted into the bone marrow of a recipient. These must be compatible, i.e. the tissue characteristics must be identical in order to avoid rejection. Through research into the development of stem cells, scientists expect to be able to produce targeted differentiated daughter cells, i.e. to be able to breed whole organs.

Stem cell research is the subject of controversial debate worldwide and its results are met with extreme criticism—as discussion about the implied ethical and legal aspects shows whenever any new publication in this field appears. When and whether breeding of organs will ever be implemented cannot be forecast at the moment.

> **Tissue engineering**
>
> Though it still does not work with complete organs, it is already being done with tissue: in tissue engineering, tissue cells are extracted from fluid tissues such as blood and bred away from their hosts (i.e. outside a living organ) before being implanted back into the original tissue in order to accelerate the healing process.

Stem cells are stored in liquid nitrogen in special containers.

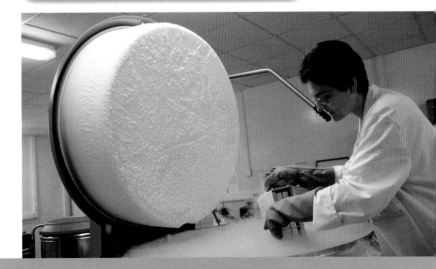

Mineral resources

Geography

Soil science

◄ Meteorology   ▲ Ecology

GEOSCIENCE

Geoscience embraces different disciplines that study the Earth
either as a whole or in its geospherical parts. Geology, geography, soil
science, meteorology, and ecology belong to geoscience. Research in
these disciplines has resulted in the piece-by-piece gathering of
knowledge about how the Earth's systems function. Researchers today
obviously know much more than they did 200 years ago about the
connections between the Earth's individual subsystems, but much
still remains unknown.

Climatology   Geology

HISTORY OF THE EARTH AND GEOLOGY: HOW THE EARTH CAME INTO BEING

How old is the Earth?

It is not possible to say exactly when the Earth originated. Geologists assume that around 4.6 billion years ago a "primitive Earth" was formed from matter from the solar nebula. It resembled a hot, molten, unformed lump and was frequently struck by meteorites. In this earliest phase, the Hadean eon (which lasted until about 3.8 billion years ago), the Earth became bigger, took shape, and slowly cooled. In the following Archaean eon (until around 2.5 billion years ago), temperatures dropped to under 212°F (100°C) and so a solid crust hardened on the surface. Our planet now had its form. Only then could life begin to develop, in the so-called Proterozoic eon.

How are rocks categorized?

The Earth's crust is made up of different rocks that are usually separated into four groups depending on the way in which they originated. All rocks that originated from cooled magma are called igneous rock (magmatite). To this group belongs granite,

which is cooled in the interior of the Earth, and basalt, formed in volcanic activity by cooled, solidified magma on the Earth's surface. The second group consists of sedimentary rocks. These are formed by layers of solid deposits (e.g. in the case of sandstone) or organic matter (e.g. in the case of limestone) that have been compressed and hardened over time. The rocks in the third group are called

A crater caused by a meteorite in the Arizona Desert, USA.

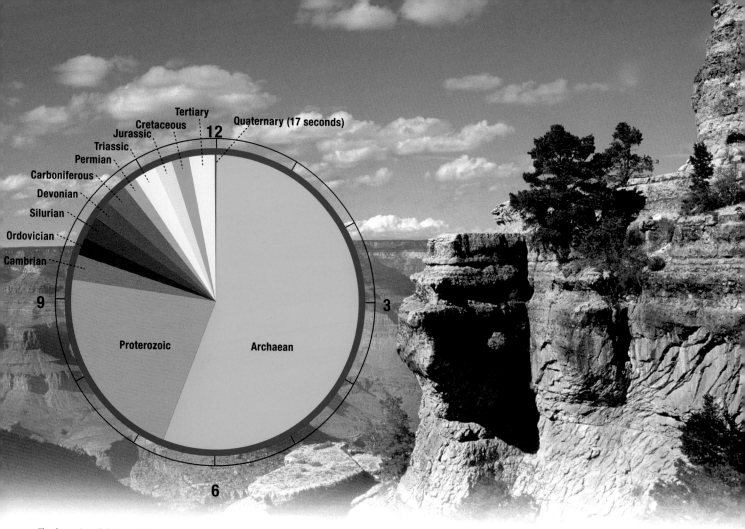

Tertiary
Cretaceous
Jurassic
Triassic
Permian
Carboniferous
Devonian
Silurian
Ordovician
Cambrian

Quaternary (17 seconds)

12

3

6

9

Proterozoic

Archaean

The formation of the Earth "in twelve hours." The age in which we live is the two-million-year-old Quaternary, which makes up just 17 seconds of those 12 hours.

In the Grand Canyon in Arizona, USA, millions of years of the Earth's history can be studied layer upon layer.

metamorphic rocks. These evolve from the other rocks. Thus, for example, sediments change under certain conditions into the metamorphic rock slate. Since high temperatures and high pressure are needed to change the original rock, metamorphic rocks are usually formed deep within the Earth. The fourth group is the very rare meteoric rock.

What does the inside of the Earth look like?

The inside of the Earth begins below the Earth's crust, which is just 25 miles (40 km) thick. It is divided into the Earth's mantle (25–1,802 miles/40–2,900 km thick) and the Earth's core (1,802–3,959 miles/2,900–6,371 km thick). The Earth's mantle is made up of solid rock, as is the Earth's crust. Although the temperature at the lower limit of the mantle can reach more than 6,332°F (3,500°C), due to the high pressure, the rock does not melt. Almost 80 percent of the Earth's core consists of iron and other metals, which are molten in the outer core.

In the inner core there is a hot ball of iron. Due to extreme pressure conditions, the metal here is solid, even though, at 12,092°F (6,700°C), it is hotter here than on the surface of the Sun.

How deep can you drill?

Currently, the deepest borehole ever to be drilled is on the Russian peninsula of Kola, situated between the White Sea and the Barents Sea. The drill head reached a depth of 7½ miles (12 km) in 1981. In relation to the scale of the Earth, this depth represents just the tiniest scratch. The German Continental Deep Drilling Program (KTB) planned to drill to the same depth, but managed only a depth of 5⅔ miles (9.1 km) in 1994. The main problems are the high temperatures at those depths (which prevents the drill head from being able to cool sufficiently) and the enormous pressure to which the bit is exposed. With technology as it stands today, it seems highly unlikely that drilling more than 8⅔ miles (14 km) would be possible.

THE ICE AGES: WHAT IMPRESSION HAVE THEY LEFT ON THE EARTH?

Gigantic glaciers once gouged out the Norwegian fjords. After they melted, the valleys filled up with sea water.

How do ice ages originate?

Science gives a variety of explanations for the significant decrease in temperature that would be required to trigger an ice age. There could possibly have been cooling as a result of huge meteorite strikes that sent clouds of dust into the atmosphere so that the Sun's rays could not reach the Earth. Fluctuations in the Sun's activity could also have led to the change between colder and warmer periods. Another theory suggests that continental drift might have influenced the ocean currents and thus had an effect on the climate. A shift of the angle of inclination of the Earth relative to the Sun or an altered orbit of the Earth around the Sun have also both been debated as other possible causes.

Is there still evidence of the ice ages today?

Yes, glaciers several miles high have planed down the Earth's surface, pushing piles of debris in front of them, and scouring out valleys and streams.

What ice ages were there?

The best-researched are the last four ice ages. These have different regional names; the European (named after the rivers to which the ice sheets extended) and North American names are as follows: the Wisconsinan ice age was the latest (lasting from 110,000 years ago to 12,000 years ago). Before that were the Illinoian ice age (200,000–130,000 years ago), the Kansan ice age (455,000–300,000 years ago), and the Nebraskan ice age (680,000–620,000 years ago).

The Norwegian fjords or the Great Lakes (e.g. Michigan or Erie) are impressive evidence of this, having been gouged out by ice. The Baltic and many lakes in the European Alps (Lake Como and Lake Constance, among others) are relics of the ice ages. Other distinctive remains are the ground, lateral, and terminal moraines. These are embankments of rocky debris, stones, and boulders that the ice pushed in front of it as it spread. After the ice melted they remained and can be seen today as smaller ranges of hills in many places.

How do glaciers originate and move?

For glaciers to form there must first be considerable precipitation at low temperatures. If this occurs over long periods of time, enormous amounts of snow and ice pile up and they exert pressure on the Earth's surface. Just like under skis or sled runners, the pressure leads to a film of water forming, on which the glaciers can "flow." The speed of flow depends on the mass of the ice and consequently on the precipitation that feeds the glacier. The greatest surge ever measured was that of the Kutiah glacier in the Himalayas, which in 1953 moved about 7½ miles (12 km) in just three months.

Could there ever be another ice age?

Yes, there could. Furthermore, it is not clear whether the ice epoch is currently at an end or whether we are in fact living in an intervening period, what is known as an "interglacial." Such warm periods as ours occurred again and again between the cold spells in the past. Even though at the moment all the talk is of man-made global warming, much of what we know points to the fact that we are still in the ice epoch. From 7,500 until 5,000 years ago, it was markedly warmer than it is today. Subsequently, it has become ever cooler on the long-term average, although always with fluctuations. In antiquity, for instance, Hannibal could only cross the Alps because they were largely ice-free. In the 17th century during the so-called "little ice age," average temperatures were well over 2°F (1°C) colder than they are today. Some researchers believe that in the long term,

How far did the ice masses spread?

During the biggest spread in the Pleistocene, around 32% of the land surface worldwide was covered with ice. Today it is still 10% covered, concentrated in the polar regions and in the high mountains. The ice was able to spread more in the northern hemisphere than in the southern hemisphere. Broad stretches of North America, northern Europe, reaching as far as England, the Netherlands, Germany, and Poland, as well as northern Asia and the areas around the high mountains (the Himalayas, Rocky Mountains, and Alps) were buried under glaciers that were miles thick in parts. In the southern hemisphere, it was mainly the Antarctic ice sheet that spread, along with glaciers in the Andes and Patagonia in South America as well as glaciers in New Zealand and Australia.

The map shows the global ice covering during the Riss/Illinoian glacial stage, well over 100,000 years ago. The sea level was markedly lower than it is today and opened a land bridge between Asia and North America.

Europe

Asia

Africa

North America

South America

Australia

Glaciers transported boulders over enormous distances. So-called erratic blocks are left after the ice has melted.

What are glacial valleys?

Ice age glacial valleys form the basis of river networks in northern central Europe. They formed at the edge of glaciers as the meltwaters emerged there, collected, and were finally diverted away. Today, the German rivers Elbe and Spree, for example, flow in glacial valleys. No glacial valleys formed in North America and Asia, as here the north-south incline meant the existence of river valleys (such as the Mississippi and the Volga), which already did the job of carrying away the water.

trapped with the water. Glacial ice, on the other hand, forms from snow that is pressed down over long periods, and thaws and re-freezes again and again. If this process is repeated often enough and more and more snow is added, then firn (containing just 50 percent air) will form. This form of ice gradually increases in density and in the course of thousands of years firn becomes the typically blue or greenish glistening glacial ice that has just 2 percent air content.

temperatures will drop again, and that in 80,000 years' time the Earth could become extensively glaciated once more.

Several miles thick in parts, glacial ice lay on the Earth's surface and thus exerted enormous pressure on it.

What is the difference between glacial ice and normal ice?

The difference lies in the air content. Ice cubes in the freezer compartment form simply by freezing, so that a lot of air is also

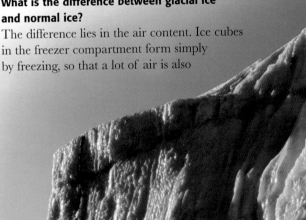

SEISMOLOGY AND VULCANOLOGY: MEASURING THE FORCES OF NATURE

Why do earthquakes occur?

The Earth's crust is not a solid stable mass but is made of seven large and many smaller plates that float on the viscous mantle. These plates are constantly trying to move relative to each other. As a result, massive pressure builds up between them, which can be released when the plates suddenly shift, causing an earthquake. The focus of an earthquake can be just a few miles or up to hundreds of miles below the surface of the Earth. There are around 10,000 earthquakes every year worldwide, but we feel only very few of them.

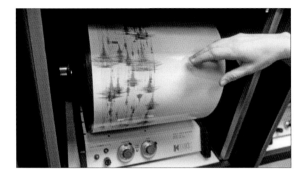

Above: Even the lightest vibrations of the Earth's crust can be recorded with a seismograph.

What were the worst earthquakes ever recorded?

The highest values were recorded on May 22, 1960 in Chile at 9.5 on the Richter scale, and on December 26, 2004, in the Indian Ocean at between 8.9 and 9.3. This latter seaquake triggered a gigantic tsunami, which killed many hundreds of thousands of people. In general, the dangers of an earthquake lie less in the quaking itself than in the resulting catastrophes, whether tsunamis or landslides, fires or collapsing buildings.

Can earthquakes be predicted?

Not really. It is impossible to make an exact prediction of when and where an earthquake will take place. However, scientists can determine the probabilities of an earthquake and predict the regions where they are likely to occur. Researchers try to detect and interpret the signs with the aid of a worldwide network of seismographs, which are used to measure the Earth's movements, and with statistical calculations. If, for example, a danger area has been very quiet for a long period of time, this indicates an increased probability of a big quake. Unusual behavior of animals is also frequently reported before earthquakes. Unfortunately, this

Collapsing buildings, as shown here in San Francisco in 1989, are one of the biggest dangers in earthquakes.

The danger of Vesuvius

Vesuvius, a stratovolcano, is probably the most well-known volcano in the world. It is dangerous because it is dormant for such long periods and then all of a sudden erupts on a huge scale. When it erupted in the year AD 79, it killed the inhabitants of the Roman towns Pompeii and Herculaneum. And in 1631, it claimed around 4,000 lives. The last big eruption was in 1944 at the end of the Second World War. Since this eruption, the volcano has been dormant and statistically speaking another eruption is overdue. Despite the danger in the Naples area, around 3 million people live at the foot of Vesuvius.

does not apply to all earthquakes, so animals are not a reliable warning system.

How did mountains and mountain ranges come into being?

If two tectonic plates meet, one plate slowly pushes itself under the other and folds the other's surface upward. Thus, the Indian sub-continent dug its way under the Eurasian Plate and pushed the Himalayas upward. The same thing happened with the Alps, Andes, and Rocky Mountains. Incidentally, the height of the mountains often tells us how old they are: the higher the mountain, the younger or more active is the process of mountain formation. The oldest mountains, the Caledonian mountain chain, are to be found in the Scottish Highlands, in Ireland, and in Scandinavia. Here the mountains have been significantly transformed and worn down by weather and glaciers over millions of years.

Above: The mighty tsunami that killed more than 200,000 people in Southeast Asia in December 2004 hits the coast of Thailand at Ao Nang.

Left: Vesuvius during the last big eruption in 1944.

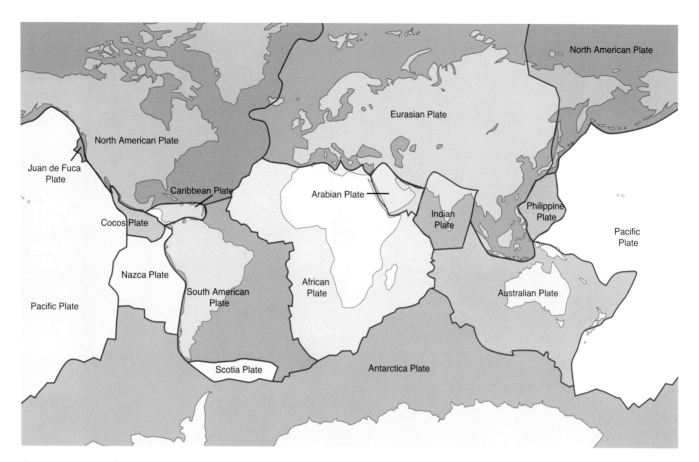

The important tectonic plates are represented in very simplified form on the map. Earthquakes and volcanic eruptions occur mainly on the edges of the plates.

Are all volcanoes the same?

No. Of course they all spew out material from inside the Earth to the surface, but volcanoes can vary considerably in their characteristic form and construction. Scoria cone volcanoes, such as the Sunset Crater in Arizona, consist only of light sediment that erodes easily. Many striking erosion forms can thus be observed on this type of volcano. On the other hand, shield volcanoes spew out thin-flowing lava that spreads slowly around the vent in a circular fashion. Examples of this type are Mauna Loa in Hawaii, or the Vogelsberg in Germany. The most well-known and commonest volcanoes are stratovolcanoes such as Vesuvius in Italy, Fujisan in Japan, and Mount St Helens in the United States. Their slopes are steep and they have a classically conical shape.

Volcanoes can also be distinguished according to their activity. Some have been extinct for millions of years and it seems unlikely that they will erupt again. Others could erupt at any time even if they have been inactive for long periods.

Continental drift

At the beginning of the 20th century, the scientist and geophysicist Alfred Wegener proposed that the Earth's crust moved. He established that the continents of South America and Africa would fit together like two pieces of a puzzle. His contemporaries thought this thesis was audacious. However, more and more fossil finds on the coastlines of Africa and South America, which showed amazing similarity, confirmed Wegener's theory. All the tectonic plates have now been mapped and scientists know, with the aid of satellite measurements, the speed of their movement and in which direction they are going.

Why are there hot springs in Iceland?

Iceland lies exactly on the Mid-Atlantic Ridge and so sits on the border between the American and Eurasian plates. These plates are moving away from each other, or rather, they are breaking apart. On these fault lines, material gushes from within the Earth's interior up to the surface. This is how a long mountain range was formed below sea level in the middle of the Atlantic, the highest peaks of which rise up out of the sea. Volcanism and hot springs on Iceland thus testify to the island's close connection with the interior of the Earth.

HYDROLOGY: WATER, THE BASIS OF LIFE

The Dead Sea has a high salt content due to high evaporation. The salt deposits can be clearly seen in this picture.

Why is water salty or "fresh?"

The water on the Earth is circulating continuously. Over 97 percent of the water is salt water in the seas and oceans and is not drinkable. Every day so much water evaporates that almost 3,000 cu miles (13,000 cu km) is present as water vapor in the atmosphere. The dissolved salts remain in the oceans. The almost salt-free water vapor in the atmosphere condenses, forms clouds, and falls back onto the sea or land as precipitation. On land, the water penetrates into the soil, washes out sodium chloride, for example, and carries this via streams and rivers back to the sea, where the salt can accumulate. Thus, fresh water also contains small amounts of dissolved salts, but in such tiny proportions that it is drinkable and seems "fresh."

Is there enough drinking water to go around?

In principle, yes. Around 2.6 percent of all water on the Earth is fresh water. Of that, by far the biggest proportion (77 percent) is in glaciers and polar ice. The remaining 23 percent is divided into groundwater, rivers, and lakes, from which our drinking water ultimately comes. Even so, this amount should be sufficient for everyone, because the water cycle constantly renews the supply. However, problems are caused by pollutants, which are entering water in ever greater amounts.

How do pollutants get into drinking water?

Nutrients and harmful substances get into the water cycle and therefore into the groundwater via, for example, fertilizers and detergents. Another problem is the residues from medicines that are excreted by humans and end up in rivers and seas. Worldwide, more and more drinking water is becoming polluted and undrinkable.

The Dead Sea

The Dead Sea is a lake between Israel and Jordan that has no outlet streams as it lies around 1,310 ft (400 m) below sea level. The lake is fed by the River Jordan. As with sea water, salt residues have formed over a long period of time in high temperatures as a result of evaporation. The salt concentration is so high that a person can easily float on the surface. As more and more water is being taken from the River Jordan for agriculture and other purposes, the water level of the Dead Sea is continually dropping; the level fell by 3 ft (1 m) in 2007. There are plans to channel water from either the Mediterranean or the Red Sea to replenish it.

Floods

Floods are caused by heavy rainfall or meltwater. In extreme cases they can be catastrophic, but they can also be positive for humans as they leave behind very fertile soils. It is for this reason that flood areas have been favored locations for agriculture since farming began. We attempt to control the effects of flooding by constructing dikes and levees. In the last few years, floods seem to have become more commonplace and severe. Causes for this are climatic changes, building homes on flood plains, and extensive surface sealing, which prevents the water from draining away.

How is wastewater treated?

Pollutants are removed from wastewater in wastewater treatment plants. First the water is cleaned mechanically, i.e. the larger waste (paper, plastic, and so on) is filtered out and removed with giant rakes. Finer particles get stuck in the sand filtration system and suspended particles are deposited in settling basins. Dissolved substances cannot be removed by mechanical cleaning, so the next step is biological treatment.

In this process bacteria are used to digest organic substances and turn them into less harmful substances.

Above: Polluted wastewater is treated again in treatment plants and returned to the natural water cycle.

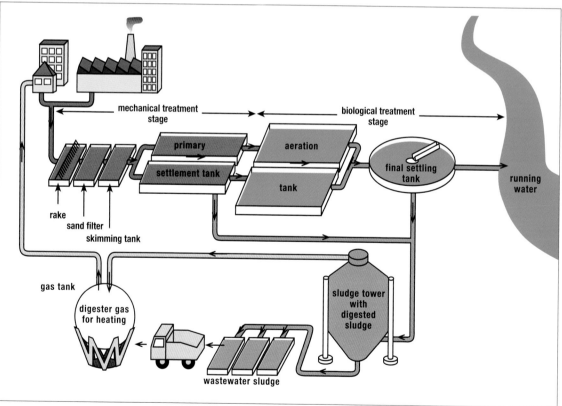

The graphic shows how wastewater is first mechanically and then biologically cleaned. The sludge that is produced can in its turn be used in the production of digester gas, which is used for producing heat.

THE ATMOSPHERE: THE EARTH'S PROTECTIVE SHELL

What does the Earth's atmosphere consist of?

The Earth's atmosphere is an envelope of gases several hundred miles high that surrounds our planet. Up to a height of $12\frac{1}{2}$ miles (20 km) there is that mixture of gases that is essential for survival on Earth: air. Pure dry air consists of more than 75 percent nitrogen molecules (N_2). Oxygen (O_2), which is vital for our breathing, makes up about 21 percent. The noble gas argon (Ar) makes up just under 1 percent and there is 0.04 percent carbon dioxide (CO_2). The remainder is made up of gases that occur only in traces. Apart from the gases in pure air, there are water vapor and suspended particles in the atmosphere. Their content can vary markedly according to time and location.

Why is the atmosphere a prerequisite for the preservation of life?

It not only supplies us with oxygen but also protects our planet in two respects: for one thing, without this protective cover, the Earth would be about as cold as in space and life would not be possible, and for another, some of the Sun's radiation is harmful for creatures, and the atmosphere—above all the ozone layer—filters out the harmful part of the radiation.

The atmosphere is an envelope of gases surrounding our planet. Life on Earth would not be possible without its protection.

The layers of the atmosphere

The atmosphere is divided into distinct layers that are distinguished according to their temperature. The troposphere nearest the ground extends up to a height of over $6\frac{1}{4}$ miles (10 km). Here the temperature falls the higher you go. The stratosphere extends to a height of 31 miles (50 km), where the ozone layer is found, and is distinguished by the fact that its temperature remains about the same throughout its depth. In the mesosphere, between 31 and 50 miles (50 and 80 km) above the ground, the temperature drops again. Above these layers are the thermosphere, which extends up to about 310 miles (500 km), and then the exosphere, which marks the transition to outer space.

What are suspended particles?

Suspended particles such as dust or smoke can be carried over great distances by high winds and can remain in the atmosphere for years. This is how millions of tons of dust from the Sahara Desert came down over Denmark in March 1901, and how the ash particles from the eruption of the Krakatau volcano in Indonesia in 1883 were flung up to a height of 50 miles (80 km) into the atmosphere, and were distributed almost right round the Earth. They caused a drop in the average temperature in Europe the following year, which led to crop failure.

Why is the sky blue?

A ray of Sun is a bundle of electromagnetic waves. It consists of short-wave radiation (in the ultraviolet band), waves in the visible band (from blue to red), and long-wave infrared radiation. If we pass a ray of Sun through a suitable prism, the light splits into the colors of the spectrum as in a rainbow. Likewise, if a beam of sunlight falls onto the atmosphere, it is scattered in varying degrees by individual particles such as air molecules, water droplets, ice crystals, and so on. Blue light is scattered around 16 times more efficiently than red light. Thus, on a cloudless day much more blue light is reflected to and fro between the molecules of air so that to us the sky appears blue.

Why is it getting warmer on Earth?

The effect of the Earth's atmosphere on the temperature of the Earth's surface is similar to that of a greenhouse. Glass lets the short-wave energy of the Sun penetrate almost unhindered into the house so that the soil inside warms up. At the same time, however, the glass is largely impermeable for long-wave heat radiation that radiates from the Earth. The temperature in the greenhouse therefore increases. In the atmosphere it is mainly carbon dioxide (CO_2), methane, and water vapor that play the part of the glass roof. CO_2 forms whenever we burn fossil fuels— through burning off forests, in industry, transport, or domestic use. Humans produce more than 33 billion tons (30 billion tonnes) of the gas annually. The CO_2 concentration has risen from 280 ppm (parts per million) before industrialization to 380 ppm today. The released gas is increasingly closing up the so-called infrared window through which the heat energy can be emitted from the Earth. The greenhouse effect is beginning.

Traffic exhaust fumes and waste gases from industry, etc., lead to smog in certain weather conditions, such as here in Mexico City.

The ozone hole above Antarctica observed in September 2006 was the largest so far, measuring an average of 11.2 million sq miles (29 million sq km).

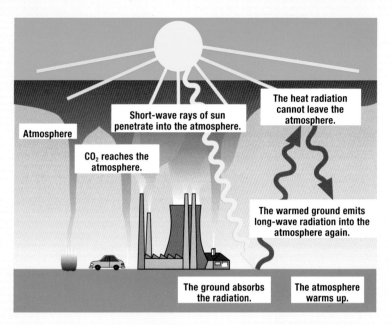

Short-wave rays of sun penetrate into the atmosphere.

The heat radiation cannot leave the atmosphere.

Atmosphere

CO_2 reaches the atmosphere.

The warmed ground emits long-wave radiation into the atmosphere again.

The ground absorbs the radiation.

The atmosphere warms up.

Greenhouse gases, e.g. CO_2, form by burning fossil fuels in industry, in transport, and domestically. They allow short-wave radiation from the Sun to enter into the atmosphere but block the long-wave radiation from the Earth's surface so that the temperature on our planet increases as in a greenhouse.

The burning of fossil fuels produces not only greenhouse gases, but also other harmful substances such as sulfur or nitrogen oxides.

What effect does an increase in temperature have?

The exact effects are unclear. It is expected that extreme weather events such as storms, droughts, or floods will occur more frequently in the future. Visible signs of warming are already apparent in the melting of glaciers, for example in the Alps and polar ice caps. This will lead to a rise in sea levels, and apart from the devastation this could cause, more water vapor will also enter the atmosphere, which in turn will lead to an increase in the warming effect.

Will the ozone hole close again?

In the early 1980s, researchers discovered an area over the Antarctic that has particularly low ozone concentrations. They called it the ozone hole. The cause was identified as chlorofluorocarbons (CFCs), chemicals with a very long life, which had been used for years as a refrigerant in refrigerators and as a propellant in aerosol cans. The chlorine contained in CFCs splits up the ozone molecules and destroys the layer. In the Montreal Protocol in 1987, numerous states promised to get rid of these damaging substances, and this has been successful. However, because the substances are so durable, the ozone layer will only recover marginally in the next 20 years. It is estimated that pre-1980 conditions will not be achieved until the middle of the 21st century.

CLIMATE AND WEATHER

How do high- and low-pressure areas form?

Due to gravity, the weight of the atmosphere exerts pressure on the Earth. The normal air pressure of an air column that stretches from the ground to the upper layer of the atmosphere amounts to about 29.92 inches of mercury (101.3 kPa). Differences in air pressure can form through sunshine, for example. If the Sun shines over a coastal landscape, the air warms up more above the dry land than above the water. The warm air rises above the dry land. Correspondingly, the air pressure rises at high altitude but falls at ground level due to the air escaping here. The result is a balance effect, because the low pressure at ground level acts as a vacuum cleaner and sucks in air from the surroundings. Above the sea, on the other hand, the air masses fall and high pressure forms. Extensive air pressure systems also form dynamically under the influence of the jet stream and Earth's rotation.

Why are there deserts?

Inland desert areas such as the Gobi Desert in Central Asia are situated far from the sea and/or in the rain shadows of high mountain ranges. Moist air drops its rainfall in other regions long before it reaches the desert area, either due to the long distance from the sea or because all the rain gets dropped in the mountains. The monsoon, for example, approaches Asia from a southerly

How does the air move in highs and lows?

The air masses in a high-pressure area (also called an anticyclone) fall, heat up, and generally cause the clouds to break up. In low-pressure areas (cyclones), on the other hand, the air masses rise, cool off, and condense. Incidentally, high-pressure air in the northern hemisphere moves in a clockwise direction, and in the southern hemisphere anti-clockwise. With low-pressure air, these directions are reversed. The same effect tends to occur when water flows out of the wash basin. This is caused by the force of the Earth's rotation, which deflects all moving masses. It is called the Coriolis effect after the person who discovered it.

The Atacama Desert in Chile is one of the driest regions in the world.

direction, accumulates in the Himalayas, and the rain falls on the south side of the mountains. To the north of the mountains, it remains dry. Subtropical deserts are found along the tropics to the north and

south of the equator—the Sahara Desert to the north and the Kalahari Desert in southern Africa. Here, due to radiation ratios and the trade winds in this area, there are distinctive stable high-pressure belts with descending, warming air masses. Such deserts can—as the Sahara shows—extend right to the coastline.

What influence do ocean currents have on the climate?

Ocean currents have far-reaching effects on the climate. The seas store enormous amounts of heat energy and therefore contribute to keeping the larger temperature fluctuations in check. In all the oceans, a constant exchange of cold and warm water masses takes place via a network of currents. The Gulf Stream, for example, carries warm water from the Gulf of Mexico right across the Atlantic to northern Europe, so that on the coast of northern Norway the temperatures are relatively mild even in

Tornadoes can
form anywhere in
certain weather
conditions.
However, they
occur especially
frequently in
the USA.

Where are the coldest and hottest places in the world?

The lowest temperature ever recorded was at the Russian research station Vostok in the Antarctic with −128.5°F (−89.2°C). The coldest inhabited place in the world is the Siberian village of Oimjakon. In 1926 it reached −96.2°F (−71.2°C). The highest temperature recorded, 136.4°F (58°C), was during a sand storm in El Azizia, Libya, in 1922. It was almost as hot in Death Valley, California, in 1913, with a temperature of 134.1°F (56.7°C).

winter. The Humboldt Current, on the other hand, carries cold water from the Antarctic along the western coast of South America to the north. Since the surface water is cold, it hardly ever evaporates even when the Sun shines. The air is therefore hot but dry. As a result, the Atacama Desert in Chile was formed, one of the driest regions on Earth.

How do weather forecasts become more and more accurate?

There is an ever-growing number of weather stations being set up around the world, so the density of the observation network is increasing. New technology is also helping to provide new ways of analyzing weather data, for example by using high-performance computers. The more computer capacity that is available, the more factors can be taken into account when calculating weather scenarios. Besides this, weather satellites are providing more and more accurate data that, in turn, can be analyzed with better programs. All in all, these developments have led to increasingly accurate weather forecasting.

What is the El Niño phenomenon?

The El Niño phenomenon is a distinctive climatic feature that frequently occurs around Christmas time in the Pacific. Normally, a low-pressure system lies over Southeast Asia and high pressure on the coast of South America. As low pressure attracts air masses, a constant wind blows from South America in a westerly direction. At the same time, the wind drives the cool surface water that the Humboldt Current carries along the coast of South America and warms it up. Thus, the sea surface at Indonesia is around 2 ft (60 cm) higher than at Peru and the water is around 18°F (10°C) warmer. The warm water leads to heavy rain and hurricanes in Southeast Asia. In El Niño years, the system oscillates. Due to air pressure fluctuations, the winds are absent, the warm water flows back to South America, and the Humboldt Current is displaced. This results in dreadful weather in South America, with landslips and floods. The causes of the phenomenon are of course natural, but it is possible that with global warming El Niño will occur more frequently and with greater intensity.

Death Valley lies up to 279 ft (85 m) below sea level and the air temperature can reach more than 122°F (50°C).

REMOTE SENSING:
FROM SATELLITE PICTURES TO GPS

How are satellite pictures made?

In principle, they are nothing more than traditional photographs. Earth observation satellites that work with optical sensors are like flying cameras, although they are equipped with outstanding and high-resolution optics. Modern spy satellites can register details of objects that are only inches big. Weather satellites, on the other hand, often have a resolution of several hundred feet. However, they can take infrared pictures, which means that they can record parts of the light spectrum that the naked human eye cannot see. Thus, the equipment of satellites (with specialist cameras and sensors) varies according to their function.

What sorts of satellites are there?

Satellites are distinguished by the type of their orbit around the Earth, the sensors that are used, and their resolution capacity. Some satellites are in a geostationary orbit at about 21,750 miles (35,000 km) above the Earth. They rotate as fast as the Earth and thus always hang above the same spot on the Earth's surface. This is important for

> **Radar images**
>
> Usually optical sensors are used in satellites. However, in space there are also radar systems that send out rays and capture and reproduce their reflections. Reconnaissance of the Earth's surface with radar rays is therefore important because these images provide especially detailed information about the Earth's surface structure. With them, just a few inches of shift in tectonic plates can be measured. These days, radar images are being increasingly used to work on an earthquake early warning system and attempts are being made to further optimize their resolution.

communication satellites (e.g. satellite television), and the pictures we see in weather reports are also made in the same way. Other satellites are designed to be able to observe as much as possible of the Earth's surface. They fly less than 620 miles (1,000 km) above the poles, so that the Earth is constantly turning around beneath them. In this way, they can examine practically the whole of the Earth's surface. In addition, due to their low altitude, a better resolution is possible.

Satellite pictures play an important part in weather observation and make early warnings possible, as in the case of Hurricane Rita in 2005.

A weather satellite (GOES 1) for measuring climate data. It is on a geostationary orbit, i.e. always above the same spot on the equator and rotating with the Earth.

What can remote sensing be used for?

Remote sensing—contact-free sensing of the Earth's surface by airplane or satellite—has many applications. The best-known application is for weather forecasting and monitoring. However, remote sensing data also gives information about physical and chemical combinations in the atmosphere, such as the concentration of pollutants. In addition, the observations can help the emergency services to plan preventative disaster procedures, in that they provide knowledge about the extent of fires and floods and make forecasting of earthquakes and volcanic eruptions possible. Remote sensing data also has a broad application in cartography and geodesy (the science of the size and shape of the Earth by direct measurement), as helpful data gained from aerial and satellite imaging can be used in the mapping of agricultural growing areas or damage to forests, in traffic route planning or municipal developments. And not least, remote sensing is used for espionage and for military purposes in warfare.

This image was put together from numerous pictures of Europe taken at night through the DMSP (Defense Meteorological Satellite Program).

What is GPS?

The abbreviation GPS denotes the Global Positioning System, a satellite-based navigation system, which was commissioned in 1995. It was first developed for military use, but today it is used in cars as very successful navigation systems, at sea, and in aviation. It is also a helpful tool in map-making and land surveying. Its function is based on four satellites that can establish the position of a receiver on the Earth's surface and the speed of its movement at any given time. In order to ensure blanket coverage and continuous contact by four satellites, however, a total of 24 satellites are needed in orbit.

SOIL SCIENCE: THE LIVING SURFACE OF THE EARTH

The Badlands National Park in South Dakota, USA. Advanced soil erosion has left behind an impressive relief.

How are soils composed?

Soils are decomposition layers composed of air, water, and living organisms, formed by the influence of different environmental factors such as climate, the lay of the land, and vegetation. These distinct layers are called horizons.

The topmost layer is the A-horizon, composed of humus, a mixture of minerals and decomposed organic matter, and is well suited as a store for water and nutrients.

Next comes the denser, more mineral B-horizon. Substances accumulate in this lower level as a result of different weathering processes. Mineral layers form with concentrations of clay, and iron and aluminum oxides are released.

The C-horizon forms the boundary with the bedrock on which the soil lies, and consists of lightly broken-up bedrock as well as unweathered rock.

Where are the most fertile soils?

Black earth is considered to be the most fertile soil. It occurs mainly in the northern hemisphere in areas that lay at the edge of glaciers during the ice age. The most important agricultural areas in the world have developed on these soils, such as the Great Plains of the American prairies, the granaries of the Russian, Kazakh and Chinese steppes, and the Börde plains of Central Europe.

What is loess?

Loess is a fine, powdery material that was blown from the moraine and gravel regions during the ice age and deposited in areas bordering glaciers. Loess is rich in minerals and calcium carbonate.

What is permafrost?

Permafrost denotes soils that are permanently frozen. In summer, they thaw only briefly and only to a few inches in depth. Due to the accumulating effect of ground ice, these soils are completely soaked through. They have a mushy consistency and become fluid on the smallest inclines.

Its porosity permits good water storage and aeration. As a result, loess is important in the formation of fertile black and brown earth soils. The biggest deposits of loess are found in China along the Huang He (Yellow River).

What causes soil to erode?

Erosion is a natural process of mechanical wearing away of soils by wind or water. It leads to impoverishment or even destruction of soils.

When it rains heavily, the water that flows away washes channels into the soil. Once a path of least resistance has been created, the water uses it again and again, carrying soil away with it and thus gradually eroding the soil. Plant growth can generally prevent erosion, as root networks hold the soil together.

A frequent cause of erosion is overgrazing of grassland areas by livestock, because this causes plants and their root networks to become damaged. Soil erosion degrades these areas more and more over time, so that they ultimately become unusable, and new grazing areas must be found—and thus the whole vicious cycle is set in motion again.

In the Midwest of the USA it is of course relatively dry, but the soils are fertile when irrigated appropriately.

Fertilizers are used to add nutrients to the soil to increase its fertility.

What are Badlands?

Badlands are a type of arid landscape with clay-rich soil characterized by erosion. There is hardly any vegetation here due to a shortage of water and the loamy condition of the ground. In addition, these areas offer ideal conditions, should there ever be any rainfall, for the water to degrade the soil. Badlands are distinguishable by barren, deeply eroded land and feature channels, furrows, canyons, and gorges. Extensive badlands are found in Montana, North Dakota, and South Dakota, USA, and in Alberta and Saskatchewan, Canada.

VEGETATION: WHAT PLANTS SAY ABOUT THE ENVIRONMENT

Are there only primeval forests in the tropics?

No. Often our image of a classic primeval forest is identical with that of a tropical rainforest. Primeval forest is, however, generally a forest that has remained untouched and natural, one that has not been cultivated, cleared, or changed by humans. Apart from primeval tropical rainforests, therefore, there are also primeval forests in many far-flung regions of the world, for example in Siberia or in the national parks of North America. However, most forests in the world, such as those situated in the central mountainous regions of Europe, are man-made and the result of deliberate forestation.

What are cultivated plants?

When humans first settled, they began to cultivate new, more productive varieties of wild-growing plants. Cultivated plants include economically useful plants as well as ornamental plants. Today, cultivated cereal varieties have little in common with their ancient ancestors. They carry a lot more heads and grain per plant. Cultivated plants are often differentiated according to the areas in which they are grown. Coffee, cocoa and bananas are grown in the tropics, for example, while cotton, cereals, fruit and wine are found in temperate latitudes, and potatoes are grown in the cooler regions. Most cultivated plants that humans were able to breed throughout history disappeared again, as farmers concentrated on breeding higher-performing varieties.

What plants are typical for high mountainous vegetation?

High mountains have very unfavorable climatic conditions, with strong winds, low temperatures, and high precipitation. Additionally, because of the steepness of the terrain, there is often only very shallow soil. This places great demands on the flora. The range of species depends on the height, climate, and type of rock. Above the tree line, for example, the vegetation is normally sparse and the plants become smaller. Grassland is dominant here, with mostly dense, hairy plants such as mosses and lichens.

Sequoias—here a Chandelier tree, one of the famous "Drive-Thru" trees in California—can grow to over 330 ft (100 m) tall and have a girth of more than 33 ft (10 m).

How do plants adapt to their environment?

During the course of evolution, plants have developed different strategies to adapt to the conditions in which they live. Succulents, for example, among them cacti, have developed ways of surviving on little water in regions where rain seldom falls. They are characterized by spines that are often coated with a wax layer in order to lose as little water as possible to evaporation. They do not photosynthesize via their leaves as most plants do, but via their stems. Other plant species have withdrawn to areas that are nutrient-poor but therefore largely free of rival plants. Flesh-eating plants, for example, are found in boggy areas. They have specialized in catching creatures ranging from insects up to small rodents in order to obtain sufficient nutrients, which the soil does not supply.

What are indicator plants?

Indicator plants are plants that have a close bond with certain characteristics of the ecosystem and react sensitively to changes in their environment. Their presence (or their absence) is an important indicator of climatic conditions, air pollutants, or the composition of the soil in which they grow (fertility levels, potential nutrients deficit, pH levels, and so on). They therefore count among the so-called "bioindicators." Stinging nettles, for example, point to high nitrogen content in the soil, and sorrel indicates acid soil.

Why are sequoias so tall and broad?

These characteristics serve as protection against fire. Fires play an important role in the development of sequoias; the conifers' cones will open up only in the heat of a fire, a process necessary for the tree to reproduce. At the same time, however, the trees themselves must not burn, so sequoias have a thick, protective bark that can be up to 12 in (30 cm) thick and their crowns are so high up that the fire cannot reach them.

Cacti are native only to the American continent. They grow in locations where water is rarely available, such as here beside the salt flats of Salar de Uyuni in Bolivia.

As flesh-eating plants, such as this sundew, grow very slowly, they can only survive in areas where they do not have to compete with rivals.

AGRICULTURE: MAKING THE SOIL USABLE

The fields stretch out over the mountain slopes like a patchwork rug in the Tungurahua region in Ecuador.

How long have humans been farming?
At the end of the last ice age, around 10,000–13,000 years ago, humans began to cultivate plants purposefully. The transition phase from nomadic hunter-gatherers to settled farmers (and stock breeders) is known as the Neolithic revolution. Why exactly humans began to farm just at this time is unclear, but certainly the change in climate must have had something to do with it. In addition, due to population growth, new sources of food had to be developed. Farming meant that humans became more settled, as they had to devote longer periods of time to tending the soil and crops.

Where was land first cultivated?
It is certain that farming did not develop in one location but worldwide in several locations at the same time. The oldest farming region is possibly in the Levant, an area in the Middle East to the east of the Mediterranean. Here, along the upper reaches of the Tigris and the Euphrates, is an

area called the Fertile Crescent that essentially includes the modern-day states of Syria, Turkey, and Iraq. It offered prime conditions for agriculture. Research has shown that farming was also beginning simultaneously in China and East Asia at that time. Here there is evidence of a long history of rice and soy cultivation. It is presumed that agriculture developed later on in Central and South America.

Why are soils fertilized?
The fertility of soils depends on the richness of the nutrients in them. Plants extract nutrients from the soil while they are growing, such as nitrogen (N), potassium (K), or phosphorus (P). These are added artificially to the soil to accelerate and improve growth, usually in the form of mineral and organic substances such as liquid manure. More rapid growth, bigger yields per acre, as well as mechanization have led to an increase in the range of nutrients required. However, there is also a risk of over-fertilization. If this happens, the ecological balance of the soil can sustain lasting damage if, for example, the microorganisms die off or the quality of the groundwater is compromised.

What does crop rotation mean?
Soil needs rest phases when no cultivation takes place so that it can recover and build up nutrients

A plantation worker in Guatemala is unloading a coffee harvest that is destined for export. He earns a fraction of the trade price.

again. In ancient times, what is known as the two-field system was practiced, whereby a field would be divided into two, and alternately one half would be planted with grain while the other lay fallow. Later, the more efficient three-field system developed. This system alternated between winter and summer crops and the fallow field, for example. This meant that only a third of the field was unused, which led to higher yields. Additionally, soil quality could be maintained on a long-term basis if different plants were cultivated alternately so that the various nutrients in the soil would not be stressed at the same rate.

In many regions of the world, farmers have no access to modern agricultural technology. A Cuban farmer cultivates his land with oxen.

MINERAL RESOURCES AND MINING: TREASURES FROM THE EARTH

What mineral resources are there?

Fossil mineral resources (e.g. oil, natural gas, and coal) are extracted for generating energy or as a raw material for the chemical industry. Ores (e.g. iron, copper, and tin) are mined for use as a raw material in the manufacture of machines and tools or in electronics and semiconductors. Rocks, clay, sand, and gravel are quarried and used principally in the building industry. In addition, precious stones and metals are used to make jewelry, although diamond, due to its hardness and high dispersion of light, is also useful for industrial applications.

Radioactive elements such as uranium and plutonium are used in atomic energy production.

How do precious stones form?

Precious stones are rarely occurring minerals with varying compositions that are formed from different elements under certain pressure and temperature conditions.

Diamonds, for example, are made of carbon. They form in the Earth's mantle at a depth of more than 62 miles (100 km) in temperatures of more than 1,800°F (1,000°C), and through volcanic activity are carried to the higher layers of earth, where they can be mined.

Rubies (red corundum), on the other hand, consist of aluminum oxide and chrome. They occur very rarely in finest quality, as the chrome that gives them their color also gives them fissures and cracks. In the same way, emeralds are frequently impure

What is the "Great Star of Africa?"

In 1905 in South Africa, the largest rough gem-quality diamond "Cullinan" was discovered. It weighed more than 3,100 carats. It was split up into nine major gems and 96 smaller brilliants. The biggest and heaviest of the diamonds, weighing 530 carats, the "Great Star of Africa" was presented to the then British king, Edward VII, for his 66th birthday. It was incorporated into the royal scepter and can be seen and admired today as part of the Crown Jewels.

Workers on the island of Madagascar look for sapphires, which are washed out of the sand.

More than half of all rough diamonds worldwide are traded in Antwerp. More than 1,500 firms here are dependent on diamond trade.

and typically have inclusions of other minerals. Their green color comes from chrome and vanadium.

For how long have mineral resources been mined?

One of the oldest mines was found in the Ngwenya Mountains in southern Africa. Around 40,000 years ago, humans were mining hematite (iron mica) there. Like ochre, such minerals were mined primarily for their colors and their subsequent cosmetic uses. Iron and copper were being mined for the manufacture of materials as early as 2000 BC, primarily by the Egyptians, who had already developed proven mining skills. However, their main focus was the search for precious stones and gold, the evidence for which lies in more than 700 overburden deposits. Cleopatra's (69–30 BC) emerald mines at Wadi Sikait are legendary.

What makes noble metals valuable?

The expression "noble metal" refers not so much to their value as to a chemical peculiarity of these elements. Such metals do not react with water, and include gold, silver, platinum and mercury or osmium. As with all products, their worth depends on how frequently they occur as well as on demand. Copper, for example, counts as a noble

Three gold prospectors sitting by a gold washer in 1889. The winners in the Gold Rush were mainly the mine owners and the traders.

The most desirable and expensive rubies come from Asia, mainly from Myanmar, Thailand, and Sri Lanka.

metal but is usually not included in a list because it is comparatively common. However, the demand for copper has risen so sharply in the last few years (mainly as a result of the Chinese hunger for raw materials) that the global deposits are almost exhausted. Accordingly, its value has more than doubled since 2001.

What are gold-mining towns?

There were numerous gold finds in 19th-century North America, which led to the Gold Rush. Gold-mining towns, where the gold prospectors could live and provide for themselves, grew up with amazing speed in the vicinity of the finds. These places were rough and lawless. Mainly traders and mine owners grew rich, such as Levi Strauss, who sold jeans to the prospectors. Sacramento, today's capital of California, developed in this way during the Gold Rush in the middle of the 19th century. San Francisco, too, grew as a result of gold finds. Most places shrank back to small villages once gold fever had died down, or even became completely abandoned, as in the case of the ghost town of Bodie in the Sierra Nevada, which once supported a population of 10,000.

Where is El Dorado?

Probably nowhere! The Spanish conquistadors of South America were once fascinated by a legend of a fabulous hoard of gold, which circulated among the indigenous Indians of the Muisca nation. One of the main interests for the invaders (apart from conversion to Christianity) was to lay claim to valuable raw materials for the Spanish crown. At first the Spaniards presumed that the treasure was in Lake Guatavita in present-day Colombia. There were many attempts to drain the lake, right up to the 20th century. A few golden objects as well as coins and precious stones were actually found, but far too few to describe them as treasure.

Why did Antwerp become the diamond capital?

Antwerp became the most important trade center in the world in the 16th century. Technical innovations and the blossoming trade in uncut diamonds led many diamond cutters to settle there. As a result, the industry underwent a period of specialization, with the establishment of diamond bourses, apprenticeship centers, and so on, so that trade could be protected and the increasing requirement for skilled workers could be met. There was another upturn at the end of the 19th century, when diamonds were discovered in South Africa. The Belgian mining company De Beers became one of the most important suppliers of the raw material that was now available in such large quantities that thousands of new skilled workers were needed.

The Cullinan diamond, the biggest uncut diamond ever found, was cut up into 105 diamonds. The nine biggest stones remain in the possession of the British Royal Family.

OIL, GAS, AND COAL: FOSSIL FUELS

When will the oil deposits run out?

The quantity of oil is finite and will therefore be exhausted one day. When exactly this will happen is hotly debated. Scientists, such as the British geologist Colin Campbell, believe that "peak oil" is about to happen: this refers to the moment at which maximum quantity of production is reached and half of the global stocks are used up. Specialists in the big oil companies contradict this opinion. They state that production could be maintained at the same level for several more years. This would be made possible by developing new technologies in the future to open up so-called non-conventional oil deposits that have been economically impossible to exploit thus far. Oil sand, deep-sea oil, and polar oil are included in this category. Ultimately, it remains unclear how big the oil reserves actually are and what proportion of them can be accessed. What is certain is that in the next ten years oil will become scarcer and more expensive.

Why are there oil fields in the sea?

Originally, all oil deposits lay under the seabed, as this is where they were formed. According to the latest theories, oil originated from extinct organic marine organisms. This material was covered by sediment on the seabed and over the course of millions of years was converted to crude oil thanks to pressure and high temperatures. Since the Earth's crust is in constant motion due to the tectonic plates, some oil fields moved, together with the rocks surrounding them, to other regions that were no longer covered by water. Others are still found deep beneath the ocean floors and can be exploited with the aid of oil platforms.

Where are natural gas resources found?

They are normally found in the same places as oil. Natural gas is formed by the same process and therefore almost always occurs with oil. The most important natural-gas-producing countries are Russia and the USA, which together produce over 40 percent of the global output. Some of the traditional oil-producing states in the Middle East, such as Saudi Arabia, the United Arab Emirates, and Iran, also produce natural gas although in smaller quantities. Less well known is the fact that the Netherlands has large fields of gas deposits at

Brown coal does not lie as deep as hard coal and is therefore often mined using the opencast method.

How do coal fires start?

The term coal fire refers to a burning or smoldering of coal seam, coal storage pile, or coal waste pile. Coal fires start through chemical reactions if coal seams come into contact with oxygen. They can occur underground as well as on the surface if, for instance, the seams move upwards due to tectonic movement. Once a fire has broken out, the smoldering flames eat further and further into the seam. The further the fire spreads, the less chance there is of putting it out. Coal fires occur worldwide and are a great problem, especially in China. Marco Polo reported seeing burning coal on his travels along the Silk Route. According to conservative estimates, between 11 and 22 million tons (10 and 20 million tonnes) annually burn off unused in China alone.

their disposal (mainly in the North Sea) and that they are the fifth-largest in the world in terms of output.

How safe is transport through pipelines?

Apart from the traditional means of transport, oil and gas are also transported via pipelines. These networks of pipelines, thousands of miles long, can cross many national borders and even continents. They are usually laid less than 6 ft (2 m) below the Earth's surface, so they are exposed to numerous adverse conditions. They must, for example, withstand temperature fluctuations, corrosion, and even Earth movements.

Although pipelines ensure a comparatively safe means of transport, accidents occur frequently, which can lead to explosions and/or fuel leaks. A further problem arises with third parties—people who try to tap into the pipelines. This happened in 2006 in Nigeria when around 300 people lost their lives after they had bored into an oil pipeline.

What is the difference between hard coal and brown coal (lignite)?

Brown coal and hard coal were formed by the same process but at different periods of time. In locations where deposits of coal are found today, there were ancient forests around 300–350 million years ago (the Carboniferous period). The dead plant parts fell into a swamp where they turned into peat due to lack of air. Sedimentary layers increasingly covered these peat layers over time. The weight of the covering layers acted like a press, which

squeezed the water slowly out of the basic raw
material and first of all formed brown coal.
The longer the process continues and the higher
the pressure, the less water there is in the coal. In
this way, over time the brown coal becomes the
higher-value black hard coal. This changes into
anthracite when subjected to even higher pressure.

What are coalfields?

The term coalfield is used to describe a region that is
characterized by coal mining and frequently also by the coal
and steel industries. In the 19th-century Industrial Revolution
in Britain, Europe and North America, coal became an
important raw material in the production of energy.
Thousands of workers were needed to work at the sites
where the coal deposits were found, not just in the mines
themselves but also in steel works and in other factories that
grew up around the coalmines. These areas became
densely populated, as in the Ruhr area in Germany,
the Midlands in the UK, and the northeast of the USA.
They were the growth engines of their respective countries.
Today, they frequently suffer from problems characterized
by deindustrialization, unemployment, and environmental
pollution. Expressions such as "Rust Belt" point to the
declining importance of these regions.

In Alaska, pipelines
are laid above
ground because
the freezing and
thawing of the
earth would
damage them.

In the future,
deep-sea oil
reserves may be
developed using
giant oil platforms.

POWER PLANTS: THE PUMPS OF THE SUPPLY NETWORK

What types of power plant are there?

Since electrical energy can be generated in different ways, there are different types of power plant. Wind energy plants and hydroelectric power plants convert kinetic energy into electricity. Hydroelectric power plants can be divided into plants that use diversion, impoundment, and pumped storage, and plants that use wave or tidal motion. Thermal power plants are widespread and use steam that comes from the burning of materials such as coal, gas, oil, biomass, garbage, or sludge. Nuclear power plants also belong to the thermal type. In solar plants, the Sun's energy is used for generating electricity.

How does a thermal power plant work?

The principle is the same in most thermal power plants, whatever the energy source. First, the chopped-up raw materials are burned at high temperatures to produce steam. The steam does not come directly from burning, however, but from the heated water that runs in pipes through the evaporator and combustion chamber respectively. Following this, the hot, pressurized steam is carried to the turbines that are fitted with smaller and larger paddles. The turbines are driven by steam pressure in a similar way to a wind turbine or waterwheel. At the end of the process, the remaining heat is extracted from the steam by cooling, i.e. it condenses on the outside of the pipes, drips off as water, is collected and returned to the evaporator.

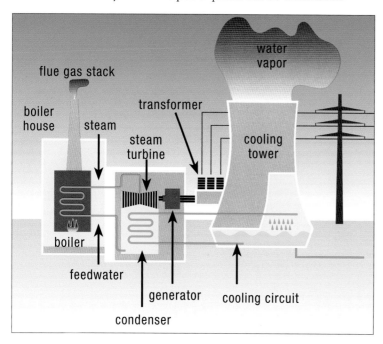

flue gas stack

boiler house

steam

boiler

feedwater

transformer

steam turbine

generator

condenser

water vapor

cooling tower

cooling circuit

Left: Whichever raw materials are burned is unimportant. In a thermal power plant, the burning of raw materials serves only to heat water in order to produce steam. This steam powers the generator via the turbines and the generator converts the steam energy into electricity.

Below: Coal-fired power plants, such as here in Cheshire, England, are among the commonest types of power plant.

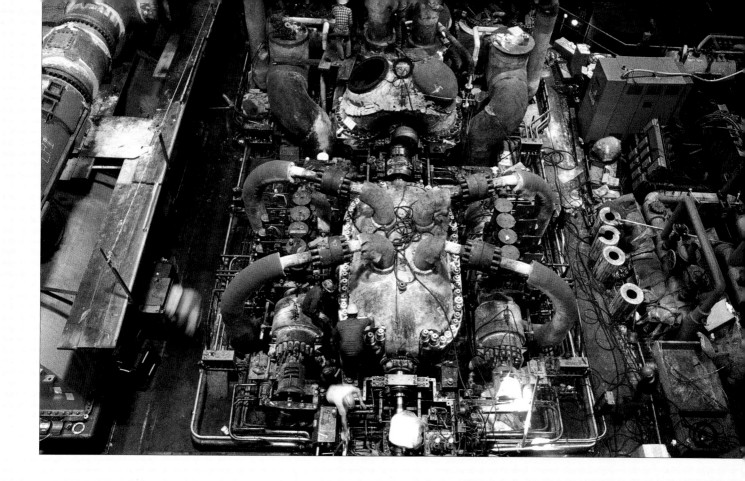

How is air pollution avoided?

Atmospheric pollutants such as soot, smoke, and dust are produced when energy sources are burned. The pollution from power plants is particularly bad due to the enormous quantities of raw materials that are used. Formerly, almost all volatile waste substances entered the atmosphere via the flue stacks but, in the last few decades, emissions have been markedly reduced. Modern filter systems remove dust particles from the smoke, and escaping nitrogen oxides are rendered "harmless" with ammonia, which converts them into nitrogen and water. Sulfur dioxide, which falls as acid rain, is manufactured into plaster using calcium carbonates, and thereby neutralized. Despite great progress in keeping the air clean, however, huge amounts of toxic substances are still pumped into the atmosphere every day, especially as the world's requirement for energy is always growing and far too many countries do not use the most modern technology. A further problem is the CO_2 that is given off in the burning process, which contributes significantly toward climate change.

What does "efficiency" mean?

The efficiency of a power plant tells us how much usable energy can technically be extracted from a raw material. If, for example, thermal energy is converted into electricity, some of the energy output is always lost through waste heat. An efficiency of 100 percent can therefore never be reached, but it is possible to improve the efficiency through technical innovation. For a long time, an efficiency of below 40 percent was typical for brown coal power plants, for example. But modern plants can already achieve 43 percent these days, and a further increase looks possible in the future.

The turbine hall could be called the heart of a coal-fired power plant. The electricity is generated here.

What is a combined heat and power (CHP) plant

CHP plants, also known as cogeneration plants, are often used to supply residential areas or industries with electricity as well as heat. An engine or turbine is connected to an alternator to produce the electricity with the residual heat then used for heating the homes or industrial processes. Their advantage lies in the fact that the residual heat is not dumped as it often is in larger centralized power plants. The CHP plants are therefore more energy efficient. Another advantage is that losses due to electricity distribution are minimized because these generation plants are usually located near the electricity consumer.

NUCLEAR POWER PLANTS: CURSE OR BLESSING?

Why is nuclear power so hotly debated?

This is because the indisputable advantages of nuclear power plants are countered by just as many disadvantages. In principle, a nuclear power plant functions in the same way as a thermal power plant, except that the heat is not produced by burning fossil fuels but by atomic nuclear fission. In this process a vast amount of electricity is produced and no atmospheric pollutants (e.g. CO_2 and sulfur oxides) escape. However, other waste is produced in the form of spent fuel rods. There is radioactive material (uranium and plutonium) in these fuel rods that emits radioactive radiation for thousands of years after it has been used. Additionally, great care must be taken that no radiation leak occurs during the working process. If there is an MCA (Maximum Credible Accident), devastating consequences are unavoidable. Catastrophes such as the Chernobyl disaster in 1986 contribute to nuclear power plants being regarded by many people as extremely dangerous.

Are there nuclear power plants everywhere in the world?

No. The use of nuclear power technology is currently restricted to a few countries. According to the IAEA (International Atomic Energy Agency), there are 435 reactors in operation, 103 in the USA, a further 59 in France, and 55 in Japan. In the whole of the southern hemisphere there are only two reactors each in Brazil, Argentina, and South Africa. Some nations (e.g. Iran) are preparing to use nuclear energy in the future, while others (e.g. Italy and Germany) have closed down their power plants or plan to do so.

Where is radioactive waste stored?

On no account should any radioactive radiation be allowed to leak during interim storage or permanent disposal. However, the substances radiate for thousands of years, so their storage sites must also offer a correspondingly long period of protection. Deep geological layers are thus usually selected as storage deposits. How deep the waste has to be buried below the Earth's surface depends on the strength of its radiation and its half-life. The surrounding rock is also very important when the site is being selected. No water should be allowed

The blue Cherenkov light—shown here in the reprocessing plant at La Hague—occurs in radioactive decay when rapidly moving free electrons travel through the water in the neutralization ponds.

to penetrate into the chambers, or else the containers might be damaged or radioactive material could enter the groundwater. Apart from clay and granite, salt domes also appear suitable for the purpose. As an alternative to underground dumps, it has been suggested that the waste could be disposed of in outer space, but this would be just as expensive as it would be dangerous.

Above: The Sellafield plant in England is controversial due to several incidents as well as discharges of radioactive wastewater into the Irish Sea that borders it.

What happened in Chernobyl?

The town of Chernobyl in Ukraine stands like no other as a synonym for the atomic super MCA. On April 26, 1986, block IV of the nuclear reactor exploded. The causes of the disaster were most probably technical defects and operating errors by personnel.

An experiment was to be carried out on the power supply in the event of a reactor shutdown. To do it, the power had first of all to be turned down and the automatic security system turned off. Whether as a result of personnel failure or due to a technical defect, the power fell far below a permissible level. The test was nevertheless continued and the emergency shutdown was only manually triggered—too late—an hour later. However, this did not lead to the end of the chain reaction (due to a design fault in the reactor), but to short-term acceleration. An explosion was unavoidable.

Apart from the personnel involved, the inhabitants from the surrounding area and several hundred thousand clear-up workers were badly affected. Over 15,000 of these so-called "liquidators" have now died. The long-term effects and the extent of the contamination are still unclear even today. However, thousands of people in neighboring areas have fallen ill with different forms of cancer since then (mainly thyroid cancers and leukemia). Today the region is extensively classified as closed off.

The catastrophe was confined within the damaged Chernobyl reactor. A "sarcophagus" was built around it to prevent radiation leaks.

WATER, SUN, AND WIND: RENEWABLE ENERGY

Wind turbines alone can only partially cover the growing thirst for energy.

What is the difference between fossil and renewable energy sources?

The main difference is in how long they will last. Fossil energy sources are only present for a limited period and one day they will be used up. Renewable energy sources, on the other hand, should, in principle, be available for an unlimited period. There will always be the Sun's radiation, and wind, water, and geothermal power, as far as anyone can judge. Besides that, no atmospheric pollutants result from their use. Wood is also included among renewable energy sources, although its existence is finite. However, it grows again within a relatively short period, i.e. its stock regenerates as long as more is not used up than is grown again. Humans have used renewable energies ever since they were able to light a fire. On the other hand, fossil fuels have been in use for only a few hundred years.

Can the world's energy requirements be met just by renewable sources?

Probably yes, but not straight away. The International Energy Agency (IEA) has estimated that energy consumption will increase worldwide by around 50 percent by 2030. The causes for this are the growing world population and the increasing need for raw materials, mainly in the countries

What is a tidal power plant?

A tidal power plant generates hydropower by harnessing the force of the tidal range, i.e. the change between high and low tide. These power plants are sited in bays that are cut off from the open sea by a dam. The dam forces the water to stream through the turbines located within the dam. If one wanted to make tidal power plants economically viable, there are only 50 bays in the world that could be considered usable as they have a sufficiently high tidal range of at least 16 ft (5 m). It therefore does not make sense to expand the technology in order to replace other power plants. In addition, tidal power plants can have considerable effects on the ecosystems in the marine environment of the area, in that they represent an insurmountable barrier for marine life.

In the tidal power plant at La Rance, France, the kinetic energy of the tidal range is used to produce electricity.

that are taking off economically, such as China and India. All renewable energy sources taken together could certainly cover a large part of the requirement. However, there are problems with economic viability and land consumption. It is not possible, for instance, to erect unlimited amounts of wind turbines, as this could lead to conflict, for example with agriculture and nature conservation, particularly regarding the protection of birds.

Apart from that, electricity producers must be able to cover peak values in consumption at any time. Depending on natural resources available to them, some countries, such as Norway, can cover their whole energy requirement or a large part of it by renewable energy resources. On a worldwide scale, however, alternative energy plants must first become more competitive and thus comparably cheaper. All in all, therefore, the increasing global energy

Dams such as the Glen Canyon Dam in Arizona, USA, enable clean energy production.

or tidal power plants. All types of plant have water flowing through turbines and thus powers generators, which in turn produce electricity. One big advantage with water power is that its energy is easy to store and is almost loss-free. In impoundment power plants, water can be let out of the reservoirs quickly and in huge amounts, as it is required. In this way, very high performance can be achieved in the short term. Electricity from impoundment facilities is thus used frequently to cover peak periods.

Can coal-fired power stations be replaced by wind generators?

Only partly, since locations for wind farms are limited. The amount of wind is not the only factor to be taken into account in this, but also the fact that wind farms spoil the landscape as well as the interests of nature conservation. In addition, even in the best locations there can be days when there is no wind at all and days when it is so stormy that the facilities must be switched off and no electricity is supplied. For such cases, the energy suppliers must keep reserve capacity available. This in turn must be covered by other renewable energy sources or by traditional power plants. Therefore, only a combination of renewable energies can reduce the

requirement can only gradually be covered, step by step, by renewable sources.

How is water power used?

Water power is the most important of all the renewable energy sources. Globally, around 20 percent of all electricity is generated by water power. The energy of the water is exploited in different ways, such as in diversion, impoundment,

The water wheels at Hama in Syria were constructed by the Romans, who already had sophisticated techniques at their disposal for the exploitation of renewable energy.

These days, many houses are equipped with solar cells. Some municipalities even pay cash for environmentally friendly electricity generation.

share of coal and nuclear power in the long term, but cannot replace it completely in the short term.

How is the Sun's energy used?

The Sun's radiation is used in two different ways. Its light energy can be converted directly into electrical energy with the aid of solar cells in the photovoltaic process. This technology is aimed purely at electricity production. A different method is the solar thermal system, in which thermal energy is made usable via solar collectors. The principle is used in single buildings for heating water, but it can also be used on a bigger scale in the form of solar thermal power plants. In such large systems, the Sun's rays are concentrated onto an absorber, in which temperatures can reach to over 1,832°F (1,000°C). Afterwards, this heat can be used again as heat, or be converted via generators into electrical energy.

What does the Kyoto Protocol mean?

The central theme of the Kyoto Protocol is climate protection. In 1997, different countries joined together to sign an agreement that the emission of greenhouse gases should be restricted. However, no guidelines were given as to how the individual countries should reach their targets. Some countries decided to use more nuclear power. Others are trying to make traditional thermal power plants more efficient to reduce harmful emissions in that way. The third possibility, to reduce CO_2 content, involves increased use of renewable energy. Normally, several strategies are used simultaneously in order to do justice to the Kyoto aims. Up to now, however, only very few countries (e.g. the United Kingdom, Germany, and some eastern European countries) have managed to actually reduce their emissions.

The Sun's energy is not just used on a small scale for private households, but also in bigger facilities for electricity generation, such as here at the Chicago Center for Green Technology.

HYDROGEN AND BIOMASS: FUTURE ENERGY SUPPLIERS?

How does hydrogen technology work?
The chemical energy that is released in a controlled reaction of hydrogen and oxygen can be converted directly into electrical energy in a fuel cell. Fuel cells were first developed for space travel, but are also used these days to power vehicles. The advantage compared with combustion engines lies in increased efficiency. In addition, the system produces hardly any pollutants, but mainly water vapor. The disadvantages are that the process is very expensive and the storage of volatile hydrogen is a problem.

What is included in biomass?
Biomass refers to all organic substances that come from plants and animals and are produced by them. In the case of energy generation, we differentiate between energy crops and organic waste. Usually, fast-growing wood and plants with a high content of dry matter are used as fuels. For fuel production, on the other hand, oil crops such as rapeseed are converted into biodiesel, or starchy plants such as sugar cane are used in the form of ethanol. Grass,

Where does hydrogen come from?
Hydrogen (H_2) occurs only rarely on Earth in its pure state. Traces are found in the atmosphere or in volcanic gases. However, the element is found as a molecule component in almost all organic materials, in water, acids, and bases. H_2 can be produced by different processes, for example by electrolysis, in which electrical current breaks up water into oxygen and hydrogen. The most common process is steam reforming, in which steam and hydrocarbon are brought into contact with each other under great heat and high pressure and react with one another.

straw, wood, foliage, dung, organic domestic waste, and sludge are all included in usable organic waste that comes from agriculture and forestry, industry, and private households.

How can biomass be used?
Biomass can be used in many different ways. Solar energy is stored in biomass, as it was turned into

The yellow blooms of rapeseed characterize agricultural land more and more in Germany, not least because it is also used in fuel production.

biochemical energy by photosynthesis. It means that this energy can be released again. Biomass can be used in the form of firewood and wood chips, etc., for heating. Straw briquettes can also be used. In combined heat and power plants fueled by biomass, thermal as well as electrical energy can be generated. Biogas that forms from the decaying biomass is also used as an energy source. Finally, plants are converted into fuel. In Brazil, for example, many cars run on ethanol, which is generated from sugar cane. Even straw can be developed for fuel today.

Are there different sorts of biodiesel?

Yes, because biodiesel is a collective term for all fuels that are generated from plant oils or animal fats. Biodiesel does not contain the pure oils or fats but the fatty acid methyl esters obtained from them. The more viscous oils can be burned in engines but they are not called biodiesel; their use is beset with problems due to their high viscosity. Rapeseed oil methyl ester is used most frequently as biodiesel. Soy oil, sunflower oil, and palm oil as well as residual fats are also suitable sources of biodiesel.

Why rapeseed oil?

As a renewable raw material, rapeseed oil has a much better CO_2 balance than fossil energy sources. Significantly less soot forms in combustion than with conventional diesel fuel and it is more rapidly biodegradable. The use of rapeseed oil is also more efficient compared with other plant oils. Its triumphant advance is connected to its other uses, for example as a lubricant, as a cleaning agent, in cosmetics and in cooking.

The use of fuel cells to power vehicles is environmentally friendly but (up to now) very expensive.

Smaller biodiesel facilities can help to make agribusinesses self-sufficient with biofuels.

Transport routes

Cars

Shipping

TRANSPORT AND SPACE TRAVEL

The 19th century in particular brought revolutionary progress in transport routes and means of transport. The steam locomotive was invented, railways opened up Europe and North America, and the early car manufacturers constructed the first individual transport vehicles. Today, roads, railways, and canals run even through remote areas, bridges cross great valleys and rivers, tunnels break through high mountain ranges and run under the sea. Airplanes link up the continents. Human beings are exploring the depths of the oceans and living in space stations.

Underwater

Railways

TWO WHEELS: BALANCE AND MOVEMENT

When and where was the bicycle invented?

The bicycle is considered the first mechanical means of individual transport. It was invented in 1817 as the velocipede, a kind of walking bicycle, and it would be another 50 years until the invention of the first true bicycle, thanks to a pedal and crank on the front wheel. Chain drive soon followed (transmitted by means of gear wheels from the pedal crank to the back wheel) then pneumatic tires, freewheeling, and gear changing.

The basic bicycle consists of a frame with wheels, saddle, and pedals with bottom bracket bearing. There are three types of frame: diamond frames, so called due to the rhomboid shape, ladies' frames, with a lower-positioned upper crossbar, and so-called y-frames, for bicycles with suspension, such as modern mountain bikes.

How do two-wheelers manage to move with stability and safety?

Two-wheeler cycles are single-track vehicles driven by muscle power or motors. They are balanced by

Today, bicycles are the main form of transport only in China and some African countries.

Why did Karl von Drais invent the two-wheeler?

Baron Karl von Drais, a forestry superintendent from Baden in Germany, built the "draisine" in 1817 as a *Laufmaschine* or "running machine." The front wheel could be steered, and the rider sat between the wheels, pushing against the ground with his or her feet.

The catalyst for this invention can be found in the volcanic eruptions of Mount Tambora in Indonesia from 1815 to 1817. This catastrophe was the cause of a cloud of volcanic ash which reached Europe in 1816/17. The worsening climate that followed ("The Year without a Summer") led to failure of the harvest, famine, and the death of many horses. In these dire straits, von Drais was looking for a horse substitute that would be unaffected by the price of oats. The velocipede was born.

the stabilizing gyroscopic force of the wheels and the shifts in weight and steering by the rider.

What are chain and hub gears?

Both improve the rotational ratio between the back wheel and pedal crank, allowing the cyclist to adjust the speed of pedaling to suit different inclines. In chain (or derailleur) gears, the bicycle chain is led via the derailleur to the cluster of sprockets on the rear wheel axle. The chain may also be guided over one, two, or three different-diameter chain wheels on the pedal axle. Depending

on the number of chain wheels and sprockets on any particular bicycle, between five and twenty-one gears are generally available.

Hub gearing consists of a so-called epicyclic gear box in the hub, which contains an arrangement of sun, planet, and ring gears. These can give up to a maximum of 14 gear ratios.

The draisine was devised by Karl von Drais in 1817. The riders sat between the wheels and pushed off with their feet from the ground.

What are the advantages of a bicycle?

Bicycles continue to be the most economical individual form of transportation. Though in Europe cycling has declined since the late 1950s due to increased prosperity, it is now gaining in importance as a means of local transport due to increased ecological awareness.

What is the role of the motorcycle as a form of transport?

Like the bicycle, the motorcycle is also based on the two-wheel principle. In the past, it was considered

transport for poorer people, and the market has shrunk drastically since the late 1950s, as cars have become ever better value for money. Motorcycles are now a form of transport for leisure and sport, and that is unlikely to change much in the future.

Generally seen as an economical means of transport, for many people today the motorbike represents leisure and freedom, sport and youth.

THE AUTOMOBILE: UNDER ITS OWN POWER

Gottlieb Daimler in 1886 on the rear seat of his motor-driven coach, his son Adolf steering. Horses had had their day!

Who invented the automobile?

Gottlieb Daimler and Carl Benz invented the automobile almost simultaneously. Daimler (1834–1900) studied mechanical engineering and, together with Wilhelm Maybach (1846–1929), designed and built a 1.5 HP gasoline engine. In August 1886, Daimler built this engine into a coach chassis.

However, it is the mechanical engineer Carl Benz (1844–1929) who is considered the father of the automobile. In 1886, he was the first to register a patent for a vehicle with an integrated single cylinder internal combustion engine with 1.1 HP.

Austrian cars of the "Austro Daimler" brand (here a 1932 ADR8 Alpine Sedan) were world famous.

Benz's three-wheeled "Patent Motor Carriage" was not based on a converted coach but was the first original, unified design for a car.

Are there new ideas for fuels for cars and trucks?

Global environmental matters represent the central challenge for humanity in the 21st century. The ecological balance sheets show that of the stress a car places on the environment, more than 80 percent comes from its operation and not from its manufacture.

The main objective of the automobile industry, therefore, has to be to reduce the emissions of the vehicle, in particular CO_2. The industry is concentrating on the further development of present technology on the one hand, and at the same time, with an eye to the future, on means of running future vehicles on energy that can be produced from renewable sources. The research and development departments, therefore, are teeming with "futuristic" designs based on a range of fuels from biogas to biodiesel. Hydrogen fuels and fuel cells are considered a hopeful alternative. Hydrogen burns without toxic by-products and, being a component of water, would be available in sufficient quantities. However, as long as there is insufficient generation of power from renewable energy sources (e.g. sun or wind), environmentally friendly production of hydrogen is impossible, because splitting hydrogen off from water requires a great deal of electricity. Engines using fuel cells to convert chemical into electrical energy are as yet too expensive and their practical use lies in the future. In contrast to electric batteries, fuel cells do not discharge, as they are constantly supplied with hydrogen as a fuel. The cell takes the oxygen needed for the reaction from the surrounding air.

How does an internal combustion engine work?

In 1876, Nikolaus August Otto designed and built the first internal combustion engine. Fuel is burned and heat converted into motion. The engine's pistons move up and down in cylinders (metal tubes), in a four-stroke cycle that recurs constantly while the engine is running.

What are ABS and ESP?

ABS: The Anti-Lock Braking System guarantees that the vehicle can still be steered even when the brakes are fully depressed. The braking power is automatically interrupted for fractions of a second whenever the wheels start to lock up and skid.

ESP: The Electronic Stability Program takes over control of the brakes and engine to stabilize the vehicle when necessary. The ESP receives the required information from sensors on each wheel, a position sensor on the gas pedal, and an angle sensor on the steering wheel. It reacts to both under- and over-steering when the car is going around a bend. For example, in over-steering, ESP throttles back the engine and brakes the front wheel on the outside of the bend, thus returning the vehicle to its proper track.

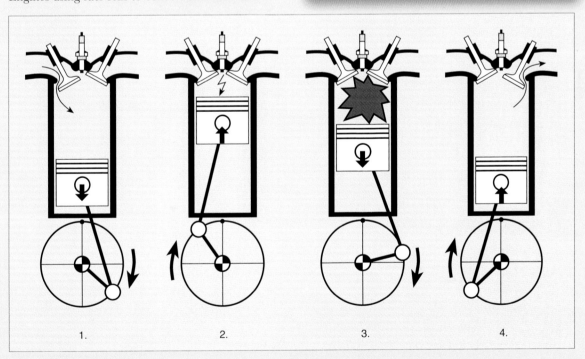

The four cylinders of a four-stroke engine work in the following way:
1st stroke: draws in the gasoline-air mixture
2nd stroke: compresses the mixture
3rd stroke: ignites the highly compressed mixture by means of an electric spark
4th stroke: pushes out exhaust gases

After testing their suitability for everyday use, Nissan brought these ultra-compact two-seater "Hypermini" model electric cars onto the market.

How does an airbag work?

Airbags reduce the risk of serious head and chest injuries. As soon as their crash sensors register an impact, the airbag control device ignites a gas generator. This fills the airbags installed in the steering wheel or in the dashboard on the passenger side, within 30 to 40 milliseconds. The activated airbags support the head and the body and distribute the stress of impact over a large surface area. However, the best possible protection is provided only if the driver and passengers have their seat belts properly fastened at the same time. As well as frontal airbags, side and head bags are also often installed.

With the first stroke, the piston moves down and sucks in a mixture of gasoline and air through an opened valve; at the second stroke, the valve closes and the rising piston compresses the mixture; at the third stroke an electric spark causes the flammable mixture to explode, the gases expand and force the piston down once more. The fourth stroke sends the gases through a second opened valve to the exhaust.

How do electric cars work?

In electric cars, the energy is either carried with or generated in the vehicle. If it is carried with the car, a rechargeable battery serves as a mobile energy source. However, electrical energy can also be generated directly by a system carried within the vehicle: an internal combustion engine, for example, or a fuel cell. To operate the fuel cell, hydrogen must be produced when stationary or carried with the vehicle in pressurized containers.

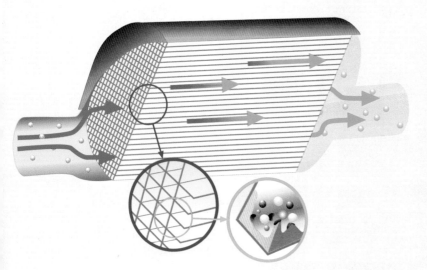

Three-way catalytic converter: the catalytic converter casing (stainless steel) contains a so-called monolith, a ceramic body honeycombed with thousands of channels. This monolith is usually coated with a noble metal (most often platinum). The toxins in the exhaust gases

What is a catalytic converter?

Catalytic converters were known before there were cars. In nature, almost all the chemical actions required for life are catalyzed (e.g. photosynthesis or obtaining energy from food) by enzymes (special proteins). The task of a car's catalytic converter is to convert the exhaust toxins through oxidation or reduction. In vehicles, it works in connection with the internal combustion engine to treat exhaust gases. The catalytic converter drastically reduces the toxic emissions in the exhaust. The converters are manufactured with the precious metals palladium or platinum, which can offset their environmental benefit.

(shown in red) that have not been quite burned up (e.g. carbon dioxide and carbon monoxide) are deposited in the monolith, break down and are ejected in a "clean" state (shown in green).

The electric car is, however, not particularly environmentally friendly. It may not produce any exhaust gases when driven, but indirectly it is a strain on the environment as the electricity required for charging the batteries is for the most part produced in environmentally unfriendly coal-fired power stations.

What are hybrid vehicles?

Hybrid vehicles (the Greek *hybrid* means "mixed" or "of two different origins") combine either a gasoline or diesel engine with an electric motor. For long journeys, the internal combustion engine can be used, and in the denser city traffic the driver can switch to the cleaner electric drive.

What is different about fuel cells?

Fuel cell vehicles tank up with hydrogen or methanol. The fuel cells convert chemical energy into electrical energy and this can power electric motors that are directly coupled to the wheels. Fuel cell technology is today seen by almost all automobile manufacturers as very promising for use in transport.

How do satellite navigation devices work?

These electronic navigators help car drivers find their way around even in unknown cities and regions. Based on signals from the Global Positioning System (GPS), the "navigators" use digital maps to calculate the shortest or quickest route to your destination. They can notify you of traffic jams and recommend ways around, but will also direct you to the hospital, to tourist attractions, and to hotels. Navigation devices installed as fixtures in the car will also use vehicle data such as speed to determine position and plan routes.

Can there be such a thing as an "intelligent car?"

In theory, yes. Although experiments have been going on for years with cars in which sensors survey the road and compare it with stored data, "driverless" cars are not going to appear any time soon. They would be far too dangerous in traffic. In research, however, the technology developed for driverless cars is nowadays used to provide useful support systems for the driver, such as distance warnings for safe parking.

Fuel cell of an electric car. Fueled by hydrogen or methanol, fuel cells turn chemical energy into electrical energy.

TRANSPORT ROUTES:
ROADS, TUNNELS, BRIDGES

Marvels of technology span broad valleys, gorges, or stretches of water. The most famous suspension bridge in the world is the Golden Gate Bridge in San Francisco.

What is "construction engineering?"

The term "construction engineering" refers to the construction of building projects in general. The construction can be above or below ground.

The former is concerned with the planning and erection of building projects and buildings that rise above ground level, while the second covers construction at and below ground level. Among the latter are tunnels and roads.

Pan-American Highway

The Pan-American Highway runs from Prudhoe Bay in the state of Alaska to Ushuaia in the southernmost tip of Argentina. About 18,640 miles (30,000 km) long, this road passes through 17 nations, 4 climate zones, and 6 time zones. Although work began on the first stretch as early as 1925, even today, the Pan-American is not an unbroken asphalt surface. In Central and South America in particular, the highway is often interrupted by stretches of muddy ground and dirt road.

What is the best road surface?

Road surfaces can be asphalt, concrete, paving, or loose material (e.g. gravel). Ever since fast motor vehicles with rubber tires have dominated the roads, asphalt has proved to be the most commonly used surface. Asphalt road surfaces consist of mineral aggregates, with bitumen as the binder. This top layer is only a few inches thick, but the thickness of the whole roadway structure including the foundation totals 20 in (50 cm). Asphalt surfaces will last, on average, for 12–18 years.

What types of tunnel are there?

Tunnels run through mountains or under rivers and canals, and serve as underground routes for subway trains and underpasses for pedestrians, for example. Despite the most modern technology, tunnel construction today is still complicated and expensive.

In general, two types of tunnel construction are distinguished: closed and open. In the traditional closed method, mining techniques are used and geological conditions taken into account. Explosives may be used for excavation, but if the substratum is weak, work usually proceeds with the so-called shield drive method. In this type of construction, earth-boring machines with huge cutting heads drill their way through the substratum, enabling the excavated material to be removed and the tunnel sections to be secured.

Where a shallow tunnel is required, an open type of construction may be used. The tunnel is constructed in the bottom of a trench and then covered over. Such a method might be used in inner-city subway construction.

An almost continuous system of highways, the Pan-American (here in the Atacama Desert of northern Chile) links Alaska with Tierra del Fuego.

What is the Eurotunnel?

When the Eurotunnel began operations in 1994, it enabled the first direct land connection between England and France. With a total length of 31 miles (50.5 km), it is the longest underwater tunnel in the world.

For safety reasons, the tunnel follows a layer of chalk and clay and therefore runs at an average of 131 ft (40 m) below the seabed.

For seven years, the tunnel was excavated from either end by means of huge tunnel-boring machines (TBMs). These TBMs were regular excavating factories. They excavated, removed the excavated material (about 2,645 tons/2,400 tonnes per hour), supported and clad the tunnel sections, and also laid the tunnel rails. Thanks to laser measurement, the two tunnel excavator machines met with a horizontal divergence of just 14 in (35 cm) and a vertical divergence of 2½ in (6 cm).

The Eurotunnel consists of three parallel tunnels: two main tunnels (each 25 ft/7.6 m in diameter) for the trains running north or south respectively, and a service tunnel (16 ft/4.8 m in diameter). The costs of construction, at almost 12.5 billion euros, were twice as high as scheduled. Around 7 million passengers use the Eurotunnel every year. The journey takes 35 minutes.

What are the concrete blocks at the entrance to the Gotthard Base Tunnel for?

The Gotthard Base Tunnel in Switzerland, after its planned completion in 2017, will be almost 35½ miles (exactly 57.091 km) long and will replace the Seikan Tunnel in Japan as the longest tunnel in the world. Concrete blocks are set into the ground at its entrance and along the mountain ridge, marking the ideal route of the tunnel as calculated by GPS. The coordinates of these points have been transposed downwards to the level of the tunnel by calculation. Once the tunnel has been completed, the concrete blocks will be removed. In the future, 200 to 250 goods trains a day are scheduled to travel through this tunnel.

What types of bridge construction are there?

Since prehistoric times, human beings have crossed streams and gorges on primitive bridges and, over the course of millennia, have gone on to span great rivers, sea inlets, and valleys with ever bolder structures of wood, stone, steel, concrete, and steel-reinforced concrete.

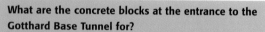

Work on the northward-leading main tunnel of the Eurotunnel. A second parallel tunnel was built for southward-traveling trains.

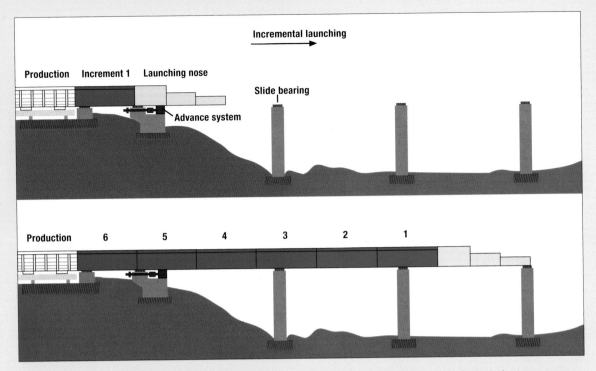

In incremental launching the bridge is built in repeated sections (increments). Each new section, once the concrete is set, is "pushed" forward over the bridge piers together with the already completed increments as the next section is in production in the same concrete formwork. The steel launching nose acts as a support from pier to pier.

In terms of construction, the different types of bridge are continuous girder bridges, where the load and the span are limited, arched bridges supported by an arch, and suspension or cable-stayed bridges.

What are the typical features of suspension bridges?
Supported by steel cables, suspension bridges are used to span broader navigable waters across distances of over 2,600 ft (800 m). Because of the long spans and lightweight nature of the construction, these bridges are relatively flexible, particularly in high winds. For this reason, they are not a suitable design for railways, which need a rigid base.

Supported by bridge piers and tiny coral islands, US Highway 1 runs from the mainland of Florida for about 93 miles (150 km) to Key West.

A famous example of a suspension bridge is the Golden Gate Bridge in San Francisco, completed in 1937, which many people consider the most beautiful bridge in the world. Its main section is ³/₄ mile (1.3 km) long and hangs from two great cables, each with a diameter of 3 ft (90 cm), formed by twisting together innumerable individual cables. Altogether, the Golden Gate Bridge is 1²/₃ miles (2.7 km) long. Many experts said a bridge couldn't be built across the 6,700 ft (2,042 m) strait because of strong, swirling tides and currents, with water 335 ft (102 m) deep at the center of the channel, and almost constant winds. Experts said ferocious winds and blinding fogs would prevent construction and operation. But the engineers proved them wrong.

How are bridges built today?
Mainly by so-called incremental launching, or by the lateral insertion process. In the incremental

Above: "Le Viaduc de Millau" is the tallest highway bridge in the world. Until it was opened, there was no alternative, on the north-south route from and to Barcelona, to the stretch through the Tarn valley, which was subject to traffic jams.

launching method, the piers are constructed first. Then building starts from both ends, initially with a steel girder pushed out to beyond the first pier. The launching nose travels along this girder with the formwork in which the concrete parts are cast, stressed, and finally moved forward. This "incremental" progress of the new bridge sections continues until the bridge is completed.

In lateral insertion, by contrast, the bridge is first completed alongside its future site and then moved into position.

1,230-ft-long (375-m) chains support the body of the Budapest Chain Bridge. Designed as a suspension bridge, it was opened in 1849.

RAILWAYS: AROUND THE WORLD BY RAIL

Which is the largest railway station in the world?

Grand Central Terminal, in the center of Manhattan, is the heart of New York City. Opened in 1913, it has 44 platforms and 67 tracks. The station has two levels; 41 tracks end on the upper and 26 on the lower. Around half a million commuters a day use the station. The four-faced clock above the information booth is a well-known icon of Grand Central.

How did railways get their name?

The railway system is a means of transport based on rails on which specialized trains transport goods and people. Invented more than 200 years ago, it changed transportation more than any previous means of transport.

The railways owe their name to the combination of wheel and rail technology, with mechanical drives and iron rails; this was how the first "railways" were created. "Railway" soon began to be used to refer to the complete transport system, including both route and vehicles.

Who were the inventors of the railway engine?

Richard Trevithick (1771–1833), born the son of a mining engineer, had already observed steam engines as a child, pumping water out of tin and copper mines. As an adult, he concerned himself with improvements to steam engines and in 1804 created the first rail-traveling steam engine in the world. The first public railway was the Stockton and Darlington Railway in England, opened in 1825, which also carried passengers as well as goods.

However, the successful technological breakthrough did not come about until 1829, when George Stephenson (1781–1848) emerged victorious in a race against four other steam engine designs with his first steam locomotive *Rocket*. Without any attached wagons, his *Rocket* reached a speed of 28.9 mph (46.5 km/h).

Why did railways become so important for North America?

While the Europeans, with the aid of the railways, created a completely new but slowly developing transport network, in the United States the railways literally set the course for the future of the country.

Today steam engines only continue to run where coal is cheap, or they pull nostalgic trains such as this train from the Semmering Railway, the first standard gauge mountain railway in Europe.

Manhattan's Grand Central Terminal opened for business in 1913. The tracks, 67 altogether, are on two levels.

In the mid 19th century, the center of the American continent was to a large degree unknown and the route to the Pacific was difficult and could be deadly dangerous. The United States Congress, therefore, decided in 1862 to build a 1,540-mile (2,480-km) railway from Omaha on the Missouri via Sacramento to San Francisco on the Pacific.

Two railway companies received the commission, one starting work in the east, one in the west, and on May 9, 1869, their workforces met in Ogden (Utah). On the following day the last crosstie was symbolically fixed with two gold nails. The first transcontinental railway link was now completed and the way opened for goods and for immigrants.

The Canadian Transcontinental Railway did not follow until 1885, but at 2,894 miles (4,658 km) covered almost twice the distance, running from Montreal to Vancouver.

When and where did electric locomotives begin to dominate the railways?

At the Berlin Trade Fair of 1879, Werner Siemens exhibited an odd vehicle. It was a machine a little over 3 ft (1 m) high, fueled by direct current from the rails, and it drew wagons, conveying 90,000 passengers during the four months of the exhibition.

Mocked in Berlin, the electric locomotive later pushed aside not only its steam rivals, but

Where is the highest railway in the world?

A 710-mile (1,142-km) stretch of track links the Chinese city of Golmud with Lhasa. It crosses mountain passes 16,400 ft (5,000 m) high and more than 620 miles (1,000 km) of the track runs higher than 13,120 ft (4,000 m) above sea level. At Tanggula, at an altitude of 16,595 ft (5,058 m), is the highest railway station in the world.

surpassed its diesel-driven ones. Today, top speeds of 248 mph (400 km/h) are achieved every day in Germany, France, and Japan. In early 2007, the French TGV sped along the tracks at 375 mph (574.8 km/h), setting a new world record for rail vehicles.

What is a tractive unit?

Railway vehicles are run as trains, consisting of one or more wagons coupled one behind the other and drawn or pushed by one or more locomotives. A tractive has its own power unit, either in the front or end wagon or divided among the wagons in a multiple unit train.

The term "tractive unit" covers locomotives, power units, and wagons. In some countries (e.g. Germany), the job description no longer refers to an "engineer" or "train driver," but to a "tractive unit driver."

Built by Robert Stephenson, the steam engine *Invicta* made the first scheduled passenger journey on May 3, 1830.

The French high-speed TGV in Lyon railway station.

Are there different widths of track?

Yes, the railway companies in different countries use different gauges, i.e. widths between the inside edges of the rails on either side. The decision to have different gauges was often made for military reasons: it would prevent an enemy invader from using the country's own rail network.

Standard gauge, 4 ft 8½ in (1,435 mm) wide, is mainly used in Europe. Argentina and India are the main users of the 5 ft 6 in (1,676 mm) gauge, and in southern Africa the Cape gauge (3 ft 6 in/1,067 mm) is used.

Today, gauges of less than 4 ft 8½ in (1,435 mm) make up around 13 percent of the worldwide rail network, with wider gauges accounting for 12 percent, and the European standard gauge for 75 percent.

Is there a future for maglev trains?

The idea has made little progress since the German Hermann Kemper began to concern himself with the development of floating electromagnetic trains in the 1920s. In theory, at least, magnetic levitation trains have numerous advantages. For instance, they are very fast, safe, and environmentally friendly.

In practice, however, things look quite different today. As existing conventional tracks and stations cannot be used and completely new tracks and stations would have to be built, it is impossible to consider wide-ranging use of maglev railways. And trust in their safety has been considerably shaken since the serious accident on September 22, 2006, on the Transrapid test facility in Emsland, Germany, where 23 people died and 10 were injured.

What is the "Indian Pacific?"

This railway line, 2,704 miles (4,352 km) long, crosses Australia from Sydney to Perth and links the Indian Ocean with the Pacific. The climax of the journey, which takes about 65 hours, is the 297-mile (478-km) stretch through the Nullabor Desert. This is the longest absolutely straight railway track in the world—and not a road, river, or person in sight.

Visitors to the Trade Fair in Berlin in 1879 enjoy a ride drawn by the first electric locomotive, designed by Werner Siemens.

Where does the Transrapid run?

After a demonstration of a Transrapid trial vehicle in the early 1970s by the Munich company Krauss-Maffei, the world's first magnetic levitation train approved for passenger transport was introduced in 1979 at the International Travel and Transport Exhibition in Hamburg, Germany.

The current longest Transrapid trial track has existed since the 1980s in the Emsland region in Niedersachsen, Germany, with a total track length of 20 miles (31.8 km).

The first and, up until now, only commercial use of the Transrapid began on December 31, 2002, in Shanghai, China. During the test phase, the maglev train ran at 311 mph (501 km/h), setting a new record as the fastest commercial railway in the world. Scheduled transport began in 2004. Officially, the track was designed only as a test track, but since 2004 its 19-mile (30-km) length has served as a feeder service for Shanghai Pudong Airport. As unofficially made public in March 2007, the city of Shanghai plans to extend the Transrapid track to the site of the World Exhibition in 2010.

How can a train levitate?

In contrast to ordinary railway trains, the maglev train has no wheels but an electromagnetic support and drive system. It runs on a track on pillars that are several feet high, and the train has no contact with the track. It is raised by strong magnets and levitates above the track using the force you feel when pushing 2 magnets of the same polarity together. Electrical coils installed in the track create mobile fields of electromagnetic force. Switched on one after the other, the coils draw the Transrapid along in friction-free motion. The faster these fields of electromagnetic force move forward, the more the train speeds up. Guiding magnets to the left and right of the train keep the Transrapid in the middle of the track.

The Transrapid at the Emsland test facility. The maglev train is currently used commercially as a feeder service for Shanghai Pudong Airport.

SHIPPING AND SHIPPING ROUTES

A giant container ship goes through a lock in the Panama Canal.

How does a captain navigate?

Human beings have always wanted to cross rivers and oceans. Navigation is the art of knowing where you are and setting a safe course to where you wish to go. In the past, navigation was mainly by the stars on the high seas and by the shape of the land near the coasts. Today, modern navigation is based mostly on radar and GPS.

How big is the biggest passenger ship in the world?

As at April 2006, *Freedom of the Seas* was considered the biggest passenger ship in the world. It displaces 154,407 GT (gross tonnage) (140,076 tonnes), is 1,112 ft (339 m) long and 184 ft (56 m) wide, 236 ft (72 m) high and the draft is 28 ft (8.5 m). It carries 4,300 passengers and 1,300 crew on 15 decks.

In April 2008, it was superceded by *Independence of the Seas*, which has similar dimensions, but carries 4,370 passengers and 1,360 crew on 18 decks. However, the *Queen Mary 2*, which is 1,132 ft (345 m) in length, is still the *longest* passenger ship in the world.

What is a supertanker?

Supertankers are ships with a total weight of more than 275,577 tons (250,000 tonnes). Tankers from 330,693 tons (300,000 tonnes) upwards are termed ULCCs (Ultra Large Crude Oil Carriers). Size, however, is not everything: due to their great draft only a limited number of ports can be used by supertankers, and they cannot travel through certain shipping channels, such as the Panama Canal.

What are "knots?"

Abbreviated as "kn," the knot is the measurement of ship speed. It means "nautical miles per hour." A nautical mile equals 6,076 ft (1,852 m). The length of a nautical mile is almost identical to a minute of latitude.

Can ships climb stairs?

A number of navigable waterways cover considerable differences in height. Without locks and ship lifts the St. Lawrence Seaway would never have opened a route to the heart of North America, and it would have been impossible for the Panama Canal to link the Atlantic and the Pacific.

In principle, a lock is a basin closed by doors at each end. The water level is raised or lowered by the filling or emptying of the basin, and the boat or ship within is raised or lowered. Locks have been used to raise vessels up to 98 ft (30 m).

Ship lifts are constructed wherever there is a greater difference in height to overcome and often also because they are more economical than several locks one behind the other. In a lift, the boat or ship is raised or lowered in a great trough. Once the boat or ship has been piloted in, the doors close and the trough rises or descends, together with the vessel and the water. Once it has reached the level of the upper or lower channel, the gates open, and the vessel can continue its journey.

The biggest lock in the world is the Berendrecht lock in Belgium. It is 1,640 ft (500 m) long, 223 ft (68 m) wide, and can contain up to four ocean-going ships and several inland waterway boats.

Covering a lift of 492 ft (150 m), a ship lift to beat all superlatives is currently being constructed at the Three Gorges Dam on the Yangtse River in China. Its trough will be 394 ft (120 m) long and 59 ft (18 m) wide.

Which is the biggest container ship?

According to information from its Danish shipyard, the *Emma Maersk* is the biggest container ship in the world. It is 1,302 ft (397 m) long, 185 ft (56.4 m) wide, has a draft of 53 ft (16 m), and travels at about 26 knots. Officially, the *Emma Maersk* can load 11,000 standard containers. Its engine performance is 108,908 HP.

Where is the biggest inland waterway in the world?

The annual shipping on the Yangtse River in China amounts to 880 million tons (800 million tonnes), making it the busiest inland waterway. This is the longest river in Asia, and it is navigable for 1,740 miles (2,800 km). As the Chinese State Council reported in early 2007, the intention is to extend the navigability of the Yangtse by 2010. A 395-ft-long (120-m) ship lift is to be completed by 2008, able to raise ships of up to 3,307 tons (3,000 tonnes).

The biggest ship lift in the world is being built on the Three Gorges Dam on the Yangtse River, China.

The *Freedom of the Seas* is one of the biggest passenger ships in the world, seen here on its journey up the Hudson to its naming in Cape Liberty, New Jersey.

UNDERWATER: BEYOND THE CONTINENTS

Why do we still talk about the "secrets of the ocean?"

All life on Earth once evolved in the oceans in early prehistoric times. Even today, almost three quarters of the planet's surface is covered by water. Huge areas of water—the oceans—separate the continents.

For a long time humanity was convinced that there was nothing worth finding in the depths of the ocean and, also for political reasons, it turned its attention to space. Only in recent years has it been recognized that almost inexhaustible treasures can be found at the bottom of the sea.

However, it is impossible for any human being to reach great depths without breathing and diving equipment. The enormous pressure of water prevents unprotected descent into the depths: for every 30 ft (10 m) of descent, the pressure of the so-called water column is increased by one bar (1 bar = 14.5 psi). At around 3,280 ft (1,000 m) the pressure is already 100 times what it is on land. To penetrate such depths, human beings need to protect themselves with a steel shell. It is therefore

In the deep-sea diving vessel, the bathyscaphe *Trieste*, Jacques Piccard and Don Walsh dived to a depth of 35,800 ft (10,912 m) in the Marianas Trench.

not surprising that more people have walked on the surface of the moon than have dived in the depths of the ocean.

Who was behind OMI?

OMI stands for "Ocean Management Inc.," an international consortium. The aim of the consortium was to mine several hundred tons of manganese nodules from a depth of 16,400 ft (5,000 m). These potato-sized nodules of ore contain a high concentration of manganese and other valuable metals. The enterprise was successful, and OMI proved that both the concept of hydraulic vertical raising of ore using pumps and also the

Two divers accompany the *Atlantis XI*. On board this submarine, up to 48 passengers can enjoy the marvelous underwater world of the Cayman Islands.

Inside a United States Navy submarine. The bridge is equipped with the most modern technology.

Who holds the deep-sea diving record?

On January 23, 1960, Jacques Piccard, a Swiss deep-sea explorer, and Don Walsh, a lieutenant in the US Navy, dived to the bottom of the Challenger Deep in the Marianas Trench (western Pacific) in the submersible *Trieste*. They reached a depth of 35,800 ft (10,912 m) or, according to another measurement, 37,205 ft (11,340 m). The Challenger Deep was renamed the "Trieste Deep" after this diving record.

The *Trieste* was a free-diving, electrically powered bathyscaphe (*bathus* and *skaphos* are Greek for "deep" and "ship" respectively). Its spindle-shaped float chamber, about 49 ft (15 m) long, was filled with gasoline to give the necessary buoyancy and carried the pressurized sphere for the crew. After the dive, the crew jettisoned the water-filled ballast tanks and, gasoline being lighter than water, the bathyscaphe rose to the surface.

airlift process for fields of manganese nodules are possible. Both systems are like giant vacuum cleaners, sucking up the manganese nodules into freight ships. As yet, however, there has been no subsequent commercial mining project.

What are submarines?

Submarines can travel in the same way as normal ships, but can also dive under the surface of the water and move through the water when submerged. Submarines mainly serve military purposes, but they are also used to explore the oceans. Nuclear-powered submarines can remain under water for months on end and are often armed with nuclear weapons in addition to torpedoes.

In order to submerge, the submarine must take on ballast. Submarines therefore have a double hull with ballast tanks between the inner and outer hulls. When on the surface, these tanks are filled with air. As soon as the diving valves are opened, incoming water drives out the air, the submarine becomes heavier and sinks. To rise, compressed air forces water out of the tanks and the submarine, now lighter, rises. When submerged, submarines are steered by hydroplanes.

An essential element for lengthy submerged journeys was diesel-electric power. On the surface, submarines were powered by diesel engines, and by electric motors when submerged. Nuclear submarines were first constructed in the 1950s. Nuclear power is used to turn sea water into steam, the steam powers turbines and moves the submarine along. In theory, nuclear submarines could remain submerged for indefinite periods of time if they did not have to surface from time to time for supplies. Modern nuclear submarines can move at speeds of around 62 mph (100 km/h).

In 1958, the American submarine *Nautilus* was the first nuclear submarine to travel under the Arctic ice cap.

AIR TRANSPORT:
A DREAM MADE REAL

A typical double-decker plane, as used by Orville and Wilbur Wright for the first controlled motorized flight on December 17, 1903.

Why does a plane fly?

As it is heavier than the surrounding air, in order to fly, a plane requires a force to act against the gravity that draws it back to Earth. This force is created by the uplift provided by the airfoils (the wings). The wings have a strong upward curve on the upper surface, while the underside is flat. The airflow means the upper current of air needs to travel further and flow faster. Low pressure is therefore created on the upper surface of the wing, lifting the plane, dragging it upwards. The pressure along the level and shorter underside is higher, because the air flows past it more slowly.

An essential condition of this rule is, however, that there must be airflow over the wings, which means that the plane must move forward. The faster it flies, the higher the airflow speed, and the stronger the lift.

Which is the biggest passenger plane in the world?

Long before its maiden flight on April 27, 2005, the Airbus A380 achieved world fame as the "Superjumbo" and the "Megaliner" (the internal works name was "Macro-body"). This is the largest wide-bodied aircraft, with two continuous passenger decks and a maximum approved seating capacity of 853 passengers. It was not only the high number of passengers that was decisive in its development,

but also the effective 15 percent reduction in operating costs. However, these aims could only be achieved by the combined use of the most modern materials and construction methods.

The A380 is powered by four Rolls-Royce Trent 900 or Engine Alliance GP7270/7277 engines, each with a thrust of approximately 68,340 lb force (304 kN) or approximately 81,605 lb force (363 kN) respectively. These allow for a maximum traveling speed of 644 mph (1,037 km/h) over a distance of 10,066 miles (16,200 km) and a maximum altitude of 42,979 ft (13,100 m). The abbreviation kN stands for "kilonewton" and in the internationally used SI unit system (Système International d'Unités) it has replaced the old HP (horsepower) unit, which used to measure engine power rather than thrust.

Is the speed of sound constant?

No, it depends on the temperature, the pressure, the density, and the medium in which it spreads. For example, if the temperature is lower, the actual speed of sound is less. If, for example, a plane flies at a height of 6,560 ft (2,000 m) at around 36°F (2°C) at Mach 2 (double the speed of sound), this corresponds to 2,182 ft/s (665 m/s) or 1,487 mph (2,393 km/h). At a height of 9,320 ft (15,000 m) at −68°F (−56°C), however, Mach 2 corresponds

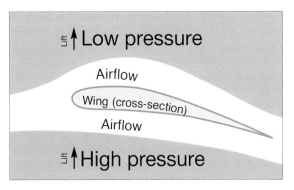

As air moves more quickly over the upper surface of a plane's wing than over the lower one, the air pressure above the wing is lower. The draft this creates provides the necessary lift, keeping the plane in the air.

to just 1,939 ft/s (591 m/s) or 1,321 mph (2,126 km/h).

Which is the most powerful jet engine?

At 568 kN, the General Electric GE90-115B holds the world record for thrust. The special characteristics of the GE90-115B are the fan blades made from composite materials (diameter 10 ft 9 in/3.25 m) that draw 1.77 tons (1.6 tonnes) of air into the engine per second. The GE90-115B is 23 ft 11 in (7.29 m) long and has a dry weight of 18,237 lb (8,272 kg). As indicated by the "B" in the name, the GE90 is used in Boeing planes (777-200LR and 777-300ER).

Why was supersonic travel not a success?

Supersonic intercontinental passenger travel and the passengers on board not having to wear pressure suits—that was a fascinating image. In the mid-

1950s, therefore, the British and French built a passenger plane that would travel at 1,361 mph (2,190 km/h).

In January 1976, Concorde began scheduled flights, from London or Paris to New York in just over three hours. However, public opinion had changed over the years. Concorde was now seen as an embodiment of British and French arrogance. The plane was only allowed to land in New York after lengthy negotiations. In the end, the British and French airlines each employed seven Concordes and, thanks to international jet-set travel, they even made a profit.

"Konkordski"

A few months before the Concorde, the Soviet supersonic passenger plane, the Tupolev Tu-144, made its first flight on December 31, 1968. Although it lacked the sophisticated wings of Concorde, because of its striking similarity to Concorde and because the date of its maiden flight remained unproven, rumors of industrial espionage never quite died down and the plane was nicknamed "Konkordski."

Concorde, the Supersonic Queen! Although the technology is impressive, the fastest passenger plane in the world has been denied commercial success.

The "Beluga" Airbus A300-600ST (Super Transporter). This special version of the A300-600R can transport particularly bulky loads.

Nonetheless, the end came on July 25, 2000. A piece of metal lying on the runway in Paris ripped a tire, fragments of which hit the fuel tank and ruptured electric cables; on fire and unable to achieve sufficient lift, the plane crashed and 113 people died. Flights to New York did resume in 2001 but finally stopped in 2003. Today, the queen of supersonic flight can be viewed in a number of museums.

The lower deck of an A380 with the innumerable bundles of cables and electrical supply lines. New technology and materials have made this "Megaliner" into the most modern of passenger jets.

Why do airplanes get bigger and bigger?

When NASA had to transport ever bulkier goods by air in the 1960s, Jack Conroy and Lee Mansdorf had so-called Stratocruisers converted into giant freighters. As the monstrous converted planes resembled the aquarium fish, the guppy, they conquered the new market as the "Guppy," the "Pregnant Guppy," and the "Super Guppy." The Airbus industry took up this idea to transport parts of planes between its manufacturing locations.

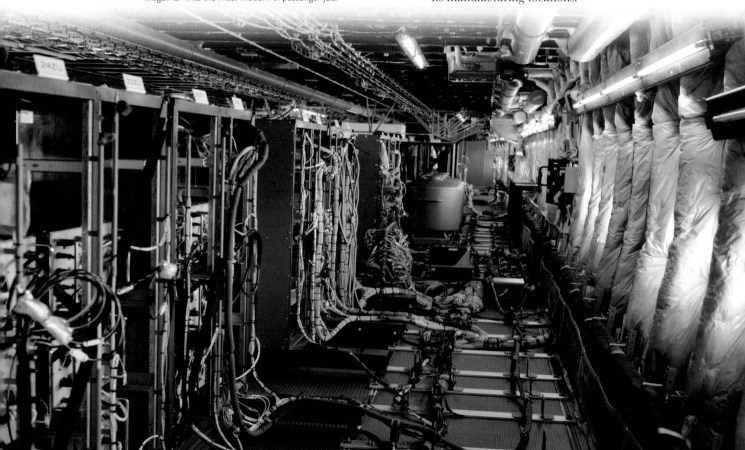

When the Super Guppy became too small for transporting the body sections of the A340, the Airbus A300-600ST, better known as the "Beluga," was created. The Beluga transported about 52 tons (47 tonnes) of cargo in its hold, giving it a cargo capacity of over 49,440 cu ft (1,400 cu m).

Boeing's success story still continues and in the 747LCF "Dreamlifter" it has constructed a special transporter for Boeing 787 Dreamliner assembly groups. Larger than a Beluga, in January 2007 the Dreamlifter for the first time transported 787 components from Japan to the USA. Two Dreamlifters are enough to meet Boeing's full transport requirements for the 787 final assembly line.

Do airships have a future?
As ever more emphasis is placed on economy and freight capacity, airships could be in for a comeback. They are faster than ships and more economical than planes. The value of the potential market in the USA alone has been estimated at around a billion dollars. An example of modern airships is the SkyCat family of the Advanced Technology Group (ATG). ATG supplies the SkyFerry, among other uses, as a ferry for passengers and cars.

Are there recognized safety checks for planes?
In the course of its working life, a passenger plane will fly almost 200 times the distance from the Earth to the Moon and back. Regular overhauls are indispensable to guarantee optimum flight safety. Safety checks are essentially based on so-called operator conditions (e.g. of companies such as Boeing) and internal company measures (e.g. Lufthansa Technik). They extend from pre-flight checks before every flight (this lasts 30 to 60 minutes) to the four- to six-week D-check that covers around 30,000–50,000 working hours. The D-check, during the course of which the complete cabin, for example, is dismantled up to and including the technical equipment, is considered the ultimate in aircraft maintenance.

With a double-decker body, high-tech engines, and the most modern generation of cockpit, the A380 represents an advance into another dimension.

Ground-effect vehicles

The ground effect is created by the movement of an airfoil close to the ground (or to the surface of an area of water). Channeling of the airflow and the resulting rise in pressure increases lift and reduces drag, allowing ground-effect vehicles to move forward as if on a cushion of compressed and, at the same time, eddying air. Although German flying boats were already making use of this phenomenon even before the Second World War (for crossing the ocean on the way to South America, for example), it was not until the mid-1960s that the Soviet Union recognized its military potential. Ground-effect vehicles were known as "Ekranoplan" (gliding planes) by the Soviets.

In the civil aviation market, ground-effect planes were only able to succeed in very small sections of the freight market. New designs are opening up new possibilities in passenger traffic as well; compared to ships, ground-effect planes offer a quieter and quicker journey, and they are more economical and environmentally friendly than planes.

AIR NAVIGATION
AND AIRPORTS

What is air navigation and what work do air traffic controllers do?

Navigation has the general meaning of finding your way in a geographical area. Air traffic controllers monitor air traffic and guide pilots from their starting point to their destination. Using radio and visual contact, they coordinate traffic in the immediate environment of "their" airport and issue permission to take off or land. Approach traffic controllers direct airplanes for landing, while radar controllers coordinate their further flight.

What is the "Tower?"

"Tower" is the prevailing term in air transport for the control tower of an airport. From the tower, air traffic controllers monitor and guide the planes using radar and speech radio.

What are airways?

Airways are the air spaces fixed and monitored by the air traffic control authorities and heavily frequented by air traffic. These airways are marked, along with all the ground navigational aids in their area, on the corresponding airway maps.

What is TCAS?

This collision warning system (Traffic Alert and Collision Avoidance System) will in the foreseeable future avoid collisions and help pilots to find their

The air traffic controllers in the tower of an airport go through very demanding training, are able to use the most modern instruments, and are subject to high psychological stress levels.

way through the skies more independently. Every airplane fitted with TCAS sends out radio signals which are received by other planes. Based on these signals, an on-board computer displays the current air traffic situation and warns the pilot if two or more planes are approaching one another.

What is GNSS?

The navigation systems GPS and GLONAS fulfill the requirements of civil aviation in terms of precision, availability, integrity, and continuity only to a limited extent. The ICAO (International Civil Aviation Organization) has therefore been developing the GNSS (Global Navigation Satellite System) since the 1980s. This is a worldwide satellite navigation concept with the aim of providing optimum flight safety. The EU, USA, Japan, and India have already made great progress with their own GNSS, while other countries are as yet only at the planning and setting-up stages. Worldwide use of a civilian-controlled GNSS is therefore likely only in the long term.

What makes up an airport?

An airport does not only consist of runways, hangars, and the tower. Immediately after landing,

The inside of a Lufthansa Technik maintenance hangar. A Boeing 737-500 is undergoing its four- to six-weekly D-check, which can take up to 50,000 working hours.

luggage or freight is unloaded, the planes are fueled, food and drink is loaded onto passenger planes, and these are cleaned and undergo a short safety check. In the terminals there are check-in desks for passengers and luggage. Luggage and/or freight is guided to the correct aircraft by computer-controlled systems. Despite the most sophisticated security checks on visitors, passengers, and hand luggage, departing passengers can be sure of reaching their departure gate in good time and arriving passengers can generally receive their luggage without too many delays.

What is the purpose of airport security?

Airport security is that part of air travel security which is generally concerned with preventing terrorist or other criminal attacks on aviation. On their way to the flight gate, passengers and crews are checked with metal detectors for dangerous items and luggage is X-rayed for weapons or explosives.

Which is the biggest airport in the world?

Four airports share the superlative title. The airport with the most runways (seven!) is Dallas-Forth Worth in the US State of Texas. The greatest number of passengers passed through Hartsfield-Jackson Atlanta in the US State of Georgia in 2004 (84 million passengers). Frankfurt-am-Main in Germany offers the most international connections, while London Heathrow has the most international flights and the greatest number of international passengers.

What is a vertiport?

A vertiport is an airport in an urban center that can be used by helicopters and other aircraft able to land and take off vertically.

What is a hub and spoke system?

It refers to the concentration of air traffic in large airports. Representing the basic structure of commercial air traffic networks, the result looks like a wheel, with passengers and freight being transferred at the "hub" (the large airport) and the "spokes" representing the feeder services.

London Heathrow Airport has the most international flight connections in the world and the largest number of international passengers.

SPACE TRAVEL: THE WAY INTO SPACE

So that damage caused on launching can be inspected, the Space Shuttle is approaching the ISS with its hold open.

How are astronauts chosen and how do they prepare for their work?

There is hardly any field in science and technology that has had as high a public profile as space travel and its rapid development over the last 50 years. The first astronauts and cosmonauts made solo flights and were in space for just a few hours. Today, there are always several people living and working on board the ISS (International Space Station), and they sometimes remain there for months at a time.

Apart from excellent general health, a scientific and technical university degree in fields such as materials science, atmospheric research, life sciences, planetary observation and research, astronomy and stellar physics is an essential basic qualification for any astronaut. The European Astronaut Center (EAC) is in Cologne, Germany.

What is the work of NASA and ESA?

The abbreviations NASA (National Aeronautics and Space Administration) and ESA (European Space Agency) refer to the American and European space agencies. While the ESA is concerned solely with civil space research, NASA does not completely separate military and civil aviation research. The vision and aims of NASA are, as it declares, to

Space walking. Powered by his own jetpack, US astronaut Bruce McCandless is floating on his way to work in space.

"boldly expand frontiers in air and space to inspire and serve America and to benefit the quality of life on Earth." This gives rise to its mission,

"To understand and protect our home planet, to explore the universe and search for life, to inspire the next generation of explorers..." (NASA Mission Statement).

What are Space Shuttles for?

A Space Shuttle (Orbiter) is a reusable transport vehicle that can return to Earth, landing like a plane. Only American Space Shuttles are used for manned space missions, and they transport astronauts and materials to the International Space Station (ISS).

What is the International Space Station (ISS) for?

The ISS was built by international cooperation and is not quite completed but has had people living in it since November 2000. Planning goes back to the 1980s, but construction did not start until 1998. Even incomplete as it is today, the ISS is the largest object created by human hands orbiting the Earth. In a stationary orbit of about 218 miles (350 km), it circles the Earth every 92 minutes. The station is scheduled to be completed in 2010 and will then be four times the size of the Russian Mir Station, brought to Earth in a controlled descent in 2001. The ISS will weigh over 518 tons (470 tonnes) and be 34 ft (10.5 m) wide, 262 ft (79.9 m) long, and 289 ft (88 m) deep.

The ISS is in practice a space laboratory. There are plans for long-term experiments on biological systems in weightless conditions. There are also plans to install a centrifuge to simulate the gravitational attraction of various planets. This research, together with the long periods spent on board by the crew, will contribute to testing how human beings can survive in space or on other planets for longer intervals, and will also aid scientists' understanding of outer space in general.

Are there space tourists?

After the break-up of the Soviet Union, the Russian space industry was desperate for sources of funding. The first customer interested in a flight into space was Dennis Tito, an American multimillionaire. In April 2001, he purchased a ticket to the ISS for 20 million US dollars and became the first space tourist.

A year later, the South African Mark Shuttleworth followed, as did another American, Gregory Olsen, in October 2005. The first woman tourist, Anousheh Ansari, an American of Iranian descent, flew to the ISS in September 2006. On April 7, 2007, the American millionaire Charles Simonyi took off for a 12-day stay in the ISS.

Responsibility for the ISS is shared by several countries. The US is constructing the living quarters, centrifugal module, energy supplies, life-support systems, communication and navigation systems. Canada is providing a 53-ft-long (16-m) robotic arm. The ESA (European Space Agency) and Japan are to build a laboratory and Russia is to provide two research modules, living quarters, and Sun collectors. Other components will be supplied by Brazil and Italy.

What is "Progress?"

It is the name of an unmanned Russian space transporter which since 2001 has provided the ISS with supplies of equipment and fuel. In contrast to

Launch of the *Discovery* Space Shuttle from the Kennedy Space Center at Cape Canaveral, on its way to the ISS.

The Baikonur Cosmodrome. A space capsule and an unmanned Progress space transporter being prepared for launching at the Russian space facility.

sent to burn up in a controlled manner in the atmosphere.

It is usual for a Progress to deliver a total of 2.8 tons (2.5 tonnes) of freight, including food (586 lb/266 kg), fuel (2,470 lb/1,120 kg), oxygen (112 lb/51 kg), and private packages and medical equipment for the astronauts, both for the current crew and for future ones. Fuel can be pumped across, but all the other goods have to be carried by hand through the narrow docking ring into the ISS. Also among the supplies for the ISS are the most varied kinds of technical instruments.

Does weightlessness make you ill?

No, but the human body does frequently react to weightlessness with space sickness caused by confusion of the sense of balance. The symptoms

the Space Shuttle, it is not reusable. After docking at the ISS, its freight is unloaded and stored in the station. Over the following months, the Progress is loaded with waste, then released from dock and

Under construction since 1998, the ISS is the largest object made by human hands to orbit the Earth. NASA's ISS budget for 2007 amounted to 1.8 billion US dollars.

Working in
weightless
conditions. Several
hours of physical
training a day
form part of
the program,
as here on board
the *Endeavor*
Space Shuttle.

(dizziness, nausea that can lead to vomiting)
fade over time with adaptation to the state of
weightlessness. Long periods of weightlessness (two
months or more) lead to the human body adapting
to the lessening of stress, especially in the spine and
legs. Bone and muscle mass and the volume of
blood are reduced. This does cause health problems
for astronauts returning from space, as numerous
TV and filmed reports after landing have shown.

Why is re-entry into the Earth's atmosphere dangerous?

To prevent astronauts from burning up on the
return to Earth when they re-enter the atmosphere,
they are insulated by a heat shield against
the enormous friction heat produced during
aerodynamic braking. The outer surface of the
Space Shuttle reaches temperatures of between
698°F and 2,300°F (370°C and 1,260°C) during this
phase of the descent, and the nose cone and front
airfoil surfaces become even hotter.

To deal with such stresses, the endangered areas
are protected with exactly fitted heat shield plates.
These measure 6 in × 6 in (15 cm × 15 cm), are
a few inches thick, and are made of impregnated
graphite with a pigmented coating of borosilicate.
This guarantees the right ratio of heat absorption
and radiation. Tiles covered with a similar coating
insulate the areas less subject to heat stress.

Are there space travel stations?

The Americans, Europeans, and Russians have space travel
centers, a kind of space travel station. NASA has the John
F. Kennedy Space Center at Cape Canaveral in Florida, the
Europeans have the Centre Spatial Guayanais at Kourou
in French Guyana, and the Russians have the Baikonur
Cosmodrome in Kazakhstan.

On February 1, 2003, presumably due to a
damaged heat shield, the Columbia Space Shuttle
broke up on re-entry into the Earth's atmosphere,
killing its crew.

Are robots used in space?

There are always tasks that are too dangerous or
too difficult for the astronauts. As early as 1981,
a Space Shuttle made a journey into space with
a "Canadarm." This robotic arm, Canada's
contribution to the space program, has a reach of
more than 50 ft (15 m) and can move up to 293 tons
(266 t). The construction of the ISS would have
been impossible without the Canadarm.

Robots are also playing a vital role on the planet
Mars. In December 2007 NASA said its robot on
Mars had found evidence of a past environment
perfect for microbial life. But such missions are
highly risky and similar efforts have failed.

DSL

Computer technology

Internet

◀ Radio

▲ Television

INFORMATION TECHNOLOGY

Information Technology (IT) has become a core element of modern industrial societies. Today, music, documents, and pictures can all be sent effortlessly around the world and at a speed which could only have been dreamed of not so very long ago. Cell phones can reach every last corner of the Earth and the internet and email link the entire world. However, the basis of barrier-free communication was founded over 120 years ago, when Heinrich Hertz discovered electromagnetic waves. Electromagnetic waves are indispensable for wireless, radio, television, telephones, and computers. Without them, there would be no global telecommunication.

Cell phones

Music

RADIO: THE BASIS OF MODERN TELECOMMUNICATIONS

The Sky Tower television tower in Auckland, New Zealand, is a "terrestrial" (i.e. Earth-based) transmission station.

What are radio waves?

Radio waves are electromagnetic waves, i.e. simultaneous oscillating electromagnetic fields. These waves do not require a medium of transport. Unlike sound, electromagnetic waves can also pass through a vacuum (in space at the speed of light). However, materials which conduct electricity (including air and metals) can slow down the waves so they can be fully shielded.

Wavelength is the distance between two similar and adjacent points of the wave (e.g. the wave crests or its troughs). Another measurement, frequency, gives the rate of rhythmic wave repetitions per second in units of hertz (Hz). One hertz corresponds to one oscillation per second.

Today, data transmission via radio waves is more important than ever. Broadcasting stations use these waves to transport television, radio, navigation systems, and telephone signals into virtually every corner of the Earth.

How long is a long wave?

A long wave (which is also used in sound radio) has a wavelength of between 1,100 yds and 6 miles (1 km and 10 km), a short wave is between 11 and 110 yds (10–100 m). In comparison, the microwaves used in cell phones are between 0.04 and 39 in (1 mm and 1 m) in length.

What different types of sound radio are there?

In addition to analog antenna radios and cable networks, today there are also other kinds of transmission method. DAB (Digital Audio Broadcasting), which transmits radio signals digitally, is becoming increasingly important. The abbreviation DAB-T refers to terrestrial DAB, i.e. Earthbound transmission via sender masts and antennas. DAB-S refers to satellite transmission. People who receive digital satellite television or DVB-S (Digital Video Broadcasting Satellite) can also hear radio this way. Radio can also be listened to over the internet. Unlike conventional radio, the quality of digitally broadcast programs is good regardless of the transmission method (see also "What is Streaming Audio?" on page 281).

What are electron tubes and what is a transistor?

Among other things, tubes were and are used to strengthen electromagnetic waves transmitted over antennas. Transistors are semiconductors, i.e. electronic devices whose resistance is changeable. The transistor fulfills the same purpose as the tubes, but in a much smaller space. It does not have to be heated in advance to be ready to operate. Transistors can be mass-produced industrially and their small size has made it possible to manufacture much smaller devices than was previously possible. Additionally, their low energy requirements are a further advantage when compared with tubes. Today, tubes have been almost completely replaced by transistors.

Can I listen to my home station when I'm abroad?

Listening to home radio stations is no problem over the internet and almost all big radio stations now broadcast at least some of their programs on the web. Broadcasting via antennas is mostly limited to the home region, with one exception: in the case of short-wave radio, waves of between 3 and 30 MHz are reflected back from the uppermost layer of the atmosphere (the ionosphere) and can sometimes be received worldwide.

A "Fliver," one of the radios from the early days of telecommunications. A tube, the regulation resistor, a coil, and a condenser are the basic components.

What is streaming audio?

Streaming means continuous data transmission into a computer network. Usually, streaming is spoken of in connection with the internet. Unlike other processes, in the case of streaming, data can be continuously read even while it is being transmitted. The user does not have to first receive the entire data packet, but can continuously call up information (e.g. music, videos), provided that the data transmission is fast enough, via DSL (Domain Specific Language), for example.

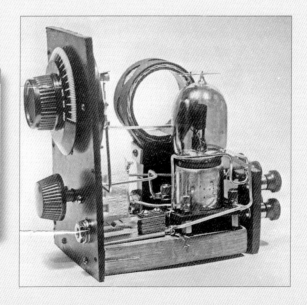

Satellites transmit radio signals worldwide. The geostationary satellites always send and receive from the same point above the Earth.

What networks are there for cell phones?

The first Europe-wide standard was GSM (Global System for Mobile Communications). In addition to the original GSM 900 which dates back to the beginning of the 1990s, there now exists the GSM 1800 (GSM 1900 in the USA and Canada) which can be used far beyond Europe's borders. A third standard offers significantly higher transmission speed: the UMTS (Universal Mobile Telecommunications Service) network. This system transmits data via CDMA (Code Division Multiple Access), broadband radio technology which, in addition to speech, can also send pictures and other large data packets. UMTS also makes mobile internet surfing possible and is the worldwide standard.

What can a cell phone do?

In addition to the original function—making telephone calls—cell phones can now do much more. They can take photographs, manage personal data, act as a Walkman for entertainment, navigate using a GPS (Global Positioning System) receiver with satellite support and they can be used to access

What is a SIM card?

A SIM (Subscriber Identity Module) card is a small chip that is put into the telephone. This storage card recognizes and registers users on the network and also acts as a phone book. You get one when you sign a contract with a cell phone service provider or by buying it in a Pay-As-You-Go plan.

Terrestrial transmission stations are also found in difficult terrain such as here on Rossbrand mountain in the Austrian Alps.

CELL PHONE TECHNOLOGY: ALWAYS CONTACTABLE

How does mobile technology work?

Mobile technology is primarily a wireless radio-telephone connection which can send and receive radio signals either via a transmission tower and antennas or via a satellite. However, in actual fact this term also includes many other types of radio services which can be picked up on mobile receivers, such as shipping radio services, data services, or amateur radio. In mobile technology, signals are sent on frequencies between 300 MHz and 30 GHz.

Cell phones are becoming increasingly multifunctional. Taking photographs with them is now standard.

the internet. In future, this list of functions will increase. Equipment with built-in flashlights is already on the market, as well as phones which allow you to control technical installations remotely, such as central heating and alarms. It would therefore seem highly likely that, in future, cell phones will replace all the other small handheld computers on the market.

What is roaming?

If you telephone within a single mobile network, the smallest spatial area is a radio cell connection. The change to a different cell within the same network is no problem. However, to go from one network to another (or abroad), elaborate hand-over procedures are required. Exchanging and invoicing the cell phone calls becomes more complicated. The telephone companies agree contracts with each other to clarify these technical and financial questions in what are called roaming agreements.

Through play, the children of the information age have lost any fear they might have of new technology.

You can only phone a home network from a foreign network if such a roaming agreement exists between the two.

How do pre-paid phones work?

For this type of cell phone, the customer buys a certain amount of talk time in advance and uses this credit to pay for calls. The advantage of this is that no fixed contract is agreed, no basic fees are incurred, and the user retains full control over costs. The disadvantages are (mostly) higher prices per minute of talk time and the risk of not having any credit left to pay for an urgent call.

What do PIN and PUK mean?

Personal Identification Numbers (PIN) are given out with any new contract by telephone companies and others (e.g. credit card companies). This secret number identifies the authorized owner of the cell phone and must be given each time the phone is switched on. To prevent theft, if the wrong PIN number is keyed in more than three times, the telephone is locked. In this event, a number that is provided in the contract, the PUK (Personal Unblocking Key), is used to unlock the phone.

Can emergency calls be made without a PIN number?

Yes, calls to the emergency services can be made on all cell phones, even on prepaid phones that are out of credit or if a person has forgotten their PIN number. This is what to do: dial the international emergency number 112 and press the connect

button on the phone (often the green key). Even without the phone's PIN, you will be connected to the nearest emergency center.

Can cell phones be used with any SIM card?

No, currently the use of many cell phones is restricted to a single network. Since the price of the phones often includes a contract with a specific service provider, the phones are provided with what is called a net lock. These phones can only be used to make calls from a specific network and the customer is bound exclusively to the relevant provider. Prepaid contracts that include a cell phone in the price are often provided with a SIM lock. Normally, in the first two years, the user can use this SIM card and phone only in the provider's network, although during this time the phone can

Cell phones which make calls via satellite can literally reach every corner of the world.

The SMS (Short Message Service) has earned a secure place in electronic communications.

be unlocked (for a fee). After two years, the phone may be unlocked free of charge.

Can a cell phone be located?

Yes, the cell phone constantly sends signals to the operating network, so its approximate location is always known. Furthermore, with the help of special services or software, the precise location of a phone can be determined—without the user noticing, and even if the phone is not in use. These services can be used, for example, when trying to locate missing persons. Some companies have also made it possible for the precise location of a phone to be identified by GPS, either for self-protection or, for example, as an electronic babysitting device for children. These companies are normally independent of the cell phone companies.

What is Bluetooth?

Bluetooth is a wireless data interface for short-range distances of up to about 33 ft (10 m). It enables cell phones, PDAs (Personal Digital Assistants, which are small, handheld computers), and other electronic devices that are in close proximity to each other to exchange data. Bluetooth devices transmit in free-to-use 2.4 GHz ISM radio bands (Industrial Scientific Medical bands). However, there can be interference from other devices. Bluetooth is a joint development by several large electronics companies and is today the standard used worldwide in computer and communications technology.

What do SMS and MMS mean?

SMS (Short Message Service), a system originally used only by network engineers until being made available to the public, is a by-product of data transfer via cell phones. Today, SMS or text messages can be sent not only via cell phone networks but also on landlines and over the internet. A later development, MMS (Multimedia Messaging Service) allows pictures and text to be sent between cell phones.

Right: The construction of installations for messaging services has resulted in whole forests of masts.

This term is used to describe electromagnetic radiation caused by technology in the environment. The key radiation sources are electrical equipment and transmitting devices (e.g. televisions, radios, cell phones). Due to the growing concentration of devices, people are exposed to an ever-increasing radiation created by electromagnetic fields. It is accepted that these electromagnetic fields cause localized heating in human bodies, but consensus has not been reached on any possible adverse effects on human health. The accepted level at which electrosmog is considered to become a serious health hazard varies greatly from country to country.

TELEVISION AND DVD: WINDOWS ON THE WORLD

Two important transmitters in one picture: a terrestrial broadcasting mast and a satellite.

How are pictures sent to the television set?

Originally, television pictures were transported to television sets by means of analog, electromagnetic waves via transmitters and receivers (antennas). Nowadays, individual transmission areas are as a rule supplied by digital terrestrial antenna television, DVB-T (Digital Video Broadcasting Terrestrial). In addition, satellites transmit television programs via digital (DVB-S or Digital Video Broadcasting Satellite) or analog radio waves, particularly in isolated areas or between countries. Another electromagnetic transmission of television signals is provided by analog and digital cable networks, for example cable television and DVB-C (Digital Video Broadcasting Cable). Television over the internet, or IPTV (internet Protocol Television), is also becoming increasingly important.

How do pictures appear on the screen?

In cathode ray tubes (CRTs), electrons travel from one terminal (a cathode or negative terminal) to another (the anode or positive terminal). They are then deflected by magnetic fields onto different points of the screen, where they strike a fluorescent layer.

The increasingly widespread use of LCD (liquid crystal display) technology is based on the properties of polarized light. If a voltage is applied to a tiny cell containing liquid crystal, it changes the polarization of the light passing through it. The applied voltage can thus control whether light passes through the cell or not, thereby switching a tiny dot of light on and off.

A plasma screen uses ionized gas and thousands of electrodes sandwiched between two glass plates to create a picture. Each picture element (pixel) is addressed with a pair of electrodes. When a current flows across each pixel, the ionized gas emits colored phosphor light.

Plasma, LCD, and laser: have tubes had their day?

Conventional cathode ray tubes are increasingly being replaced by other components which come with smaller casings. The flat LCD screens also produce a sharper picture and are flicker-free. One disadvantage of the first LCD screens, namely low contrast, has been greatly offset by the use of TFTs (thin film transistors). A TFT allows flat-screen electronic switching but one is needed for each color, so there are three transistors per pixel. Plasma screens can be manufactured in much larger sizes than LCD screens and both offer excellent picture quality. However, the glass plates in these screens are relatively fragile. Neither type of flat screen shows any distortion at the edge of the screen, so in this respect they are more precise than tube screens.

Soon the market will see a new generation of screen types, based on a proven invention: laser TV. Similar to projectors (or beamers), in these devices the picture is produced on the screen using laser technology. The manufacturers promise significantly improved and cost-effective picture quality, compared with LCD and plasma technology.

Why are there different types of picture format?

For a long time, the standard format for televisions was the size ratio 4:3 (width:height). This was because the cathode ray tubes were difficult to produce in other sizes, and movie theaters have been using formats such as 16:9. The new TV technology known as HDTV (high-definition television, see below) uses 16:9 as standard, not least in order to be able to show motion pictures which are "unpruned" or free of black lines.

What does "HD ready" mean?

HD ready is a new, worldwide television standard that has also been broadcast in Europe for some years. HDTV is a high-resolution system being offered on the market in two screen resolutions: 720 or 1,080 vertical lines per picture. The

At the world's biggest technology show, CeBIT in Hanover, a manufacturer presents the latest generation of plasma screens.

720 version already offers twice the number of pixels than the existing PAL (Phase Alternating Line) standard does, and enables significantly increased picture quality. For HDTV, a new technology is recommended, known as HDMI (High Definition Multimedia Interface). This interface transmits digital picture data with digital sound data. After a very short time, HDMI has already replaced the DVI (Digital Visual Interface) standard (where digital video data is combined with analog sound).

Is there a standard DVD?

No, currently several different formats co-exist. Since its introduction, the DVD (Digital Versatile Disk) has been constantly expanded and improved. Recently, HD-DVD (high-definition DVD), HD-VMD (high-definition Versatile Multilayer Disk) and Blu-ray disk (BD) were competing to be

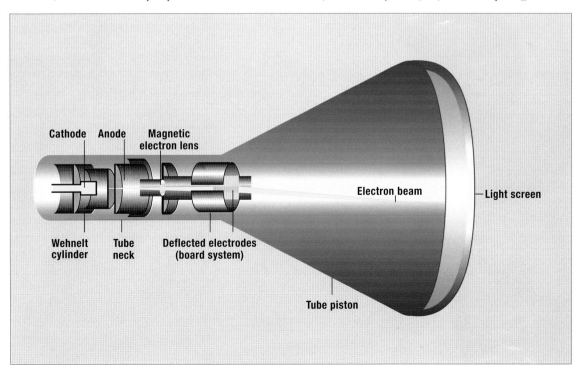

Cathode | Anode | Magnetic electron lens

Electron beam — Light screen

Wehnelt cylinder | Tube neck | Deflected electrodes (board system)

Tube piston

The diagram shows the structure of a conventional picture tube.

the successor to the DVD on the market; BD seems to have emerged as the winner. The greater storage capacity of DVDs compared to CDs is possible because the DVD uses a shorter wavelength laser (red) compared to CDs (infra-red) and also a better lens. Combining these factors means that the spot that reads the data on a DVD is about $^2/_3$ of the size of the CD spot. This means that the tracks that the spot runs along can be closer together, and that the "pits and lands" in which the data is encoded can be shorter. Multiplying this together gives a DVD several times the capacity of a CD, around 4.7GB. Also, DVDs are designed to be able to have two layers, and also possibly two sides. This means that DVDs could have 4.7GB, 9.4GB, of 18.8GB capacity, depending on the combinations of layers and sides.

Can any DVD be played on any equipment anywhere?

No, DVD manufacturers encode their products with a regional code, the effect of which is that

Always present: consumer electronics play a central part in everyday life.

The DVD is the established standard. Showing movies or recordings on magnetic tapes in the home has all but disappeared.

a DVD purchased outside Europe, for example, cannot be played or viewed on most European DVD players. The reasons are all marketing ones: cheap imports must be prevented and DVDs cannot appear on the market before the relevant movie premiere. Furthermore, different versions of movies require regional guidelines, to comply with the various child protection laws or censorship standards. Currently, there are eight different regional codes, six for different territories, one unoccupied, and one for international territories (the high seas, space, and extraterritorial zones).

Can I record a DVD myself?
Yes, some kinds of DVD format can be recorded onto, such as DVD-R (recordable DVDs) and DVD-RW (rewritable DVDs). However, you have to use a DVD recorder; DVD players cannot record. Some better recorders also have hard disks for storing programs, and some have two tuners so that you can be watching one program live at the

same time as recording another, or you can record two programs at the same time while watching a pre-recorded program.

What does the future hold for video technology?
In the near future, the movie rental business will probably continue to be developed over the internet (as well as via mail order video stores). Further competition for video rentals comes from the "video on demand" system which could well dominate the market in future. Here, the customer has the possibility of finding and playing a movie over the internet, either for a limited time or for a fixed number of showings.

When producing data storage media, clean room conditions are required. Even the slightest contaminant makes DVDs unusable.

COMPUTERS: MUCH MORE THAN CALCULATORS AND FOR PLAYING GAMES

At the heart of a piece of electronic equipment: the individual components are put on circuit boards and interconnected.

What is the binary system?

Computers (among other things) count using a binary numeral system that can represent any desired number with the figures 0 and 1. Thus, multiples (powers) of 2 are used and also the 0 and the 1 ($2°$). Counting is done from right to left. For example, the number 14 can be expressed in the following multiples of 2: 8 ($2 \times 2 \times 2 = 2$ to the power of 3) plus 4 ($2 \times 2 = 2$ to the power of 2) plus 2 ($1 \times 2 = 2$ to the power of 1). Thus, in the binary system the number 14 is represented by 1110. From right to left, it reads as no 1, a 2, a 4 and an 8—altogether 14. The advantage of this method lies in the fact that in computers all numbers can be represented by two coordinating points, i.e. with yes/no, in/out, or available/not available.

What do digital and analog mean?

Analog technology is the process of taking an audio or video signal and translating it into electronic

What does hardware and software mean?

Hardware means the actual computer machine and any of its peripheral devices (i.e. all of the equipment connected to the computer). Most of the hardware is unseen and enclosed in a case or chassis. The umbrella term "software" is used to cover all computer programs, and these can be divided into two groups: system software (such as operating systems, organization and service programs) and application software (e.g. word processing and graphics programs, games, etc.).

pulses. The newer digital technology breaks the signal into binary code—a series of 1s and 0s—transfers it to the other end where another device (phone, modem, or TV) takes all the numbers and reassembles them into the original signal.

What is a computer made up of?

As a rule, the so-called "Von Neumann architecture" is used. This comprises five main functional units: the arithmetic or computing unit, the control unit, the memory, the input and output units, and the bus or wiring system.

The core hardware component of a PC is the primary circuit board, which is also known as the motherboard or mainboard. This contains the interconnections for a whole range of central electronic components, including:

- the computer's central processing unit (CPU) which controls the computer
- the memory or RAM (Random Access Memory) for direct access by the user
- the BIOS chip (Basic Input/Output System) which stores the programs that open up on the computer as soon as it is switched on or booted up
- the bus system of cables which transports signals and data between the individual components of the computer
- expansion cards (e.g. for graphics, sound, or networks)
- additional interfaces to connect to external equipment, such as CD or DVD players

Data is stored on a hard drive, a rotating disk with magnetic surfaces on which data can be written and read.

A PC also consists of output devices, such as a monitor (i.e. one or several screens) and a printer, along with various input devices such as the keyboard, mouse, or touch screens (contact screens which register pressure from a finger touching underlying sensors and through which data can be inputted), as well as many other types of externally connected items.

What are microchips?

Microchips are integrated circuits or electronic components, assembled on one wafer of silicon, which enables many millions of transistors to be made on the tiniest surface. Previously, individual electronic components were set out and linked on a circuit board. The continual decrease of this circuit to the size of a chip is what has made modern computer technology and electronics possible. Twenty years ago, a transistor was twice the size of the top of a matchstick. Today, billions of transistors

In the binary system, for every power of 2, a specific place is allocated as shown in the table below.

Powers of 2	2^6	2^5	2^4	2^3	2^2	2^1	2^0
In the decimal system	64	32	16	8	4	2	1
1 in the binary system is							1
2 in the binary system is						1	0
4 in the binary system is					1	0	0
8 in the binary system is				1	0	0	0
16 in the binary system is			1	0	0	0	0
32 in the binary system is		1	0	0	0	0	0
Of course, intermediate values can also be represented, e.g. $3 = 2 + 1$ ($2^1 + 2^0$) and $19 = 16 + 2 + 1$ ($2^4 + 2^1 + 2^0$).							
3 in the binary system is						1	1
19 in the binary system is			1	0	0	1	1

The binary system is one of the main ways in which computers calculate. The basis is powers of the number 2.

Computers and computer-aided learning are having a huge influence on education—and not just in schools.

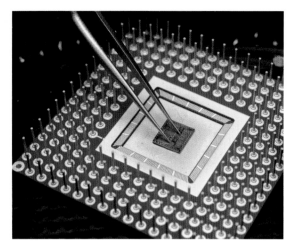

could fit onto the surface of a chip measuring less
than ½ in² (1.25 cm²) in size.

Why do I need an operating system?

The term "operating system" means software
that the computer requires in order to be able
to operate, i.e. to manage the data stored on it
and to communicate with the equipment connected
to it, inputting and outputting data. Among other
things, the operating system provides the user
with a visual interface to enable them to manage
information and input and output data. It thus
acts as a sort of translator between the language
of machines and that of humans.

How does a USB work?

A USB (Universal Serial Bus) is a data bus
or subsystem that allows peripherals to be
connected using a single interface. An advantage
of the USB is what is known as hot plugging
or hot swapping. While operating, connections
can be switched off and then turned back
on again. Additionally, a USB can be used
to provide power to equipment with low
energy consumption. The USB 2.0 connection
is currently the standard, having replaced the
old standard 1.0 (1.1).

What is virtual reality?

In addition to the real world, devoted computer
users often seek out an alternative electronic or
"virtual" world. Computer games make up a large
part of this. These can be roughly divided into two
groups: "jump and run" games, where a type of
problem is described pictorially and in which the
main concern is to defeat opponents on relatively
non-violent levels, and the "ego-shooter" games
in which players have to try—with a good deal of
violence—to defend their (pretend) existence against
virtual enemies, as well as enjoying simulations of
various kinds. Role play and strategy are included
here in addition to flight simulators and car racing.
In this realm, whole virtual parallel worlds exist
and some users spend more time here than in the
real world.

THE INTERNET: THE DIGITAL WORLD

Are the internet and the www the same thing?

No, although the terms are often used interchangeably, they are not the same thing. "internet" refers to all the interconnected national networks, the "worldwide web" being just one of these. Other services are, for example, email, the electronic mail service, TELNET, which is another type of internet protocol (see "Is HTTP a language?" page 294), and IRC (internet Relay Chat), which is a text-based network for real-time chat over the internet with more than one participant. The reason the www tends to be understood as the internet per se is undoubtedly due to how widespread it is; the majority of surfers use this service.

What is a home page?

A home page or starter page is the first page you see when visiting a website. It acts as the entry point or portal for the site. On it you will find "buttons" that you click to access other pages on the site and to find more detailed information elsewhere on the worldwide web.

Tim Berners-Lee (born 1955), the founder of the worldwide web, an internet-based hypermedia initiative for global information sharing, at the Massachusetts Institute of Technology (MIT) in Cambridge, Massachusetts.

What do the terms "upload" and "download" mean?

These terms refer to the direction in which data is going on the internet, either being sent (uploaded) or accessed (downloaded).

When downloading from the internet, data is transferred from the server to the internet user's computer. Conversely, if a person has their own website and wants to post their own most up-to-date information, achievements, or dates, etc., on this website, then this data must be sent from the person's computer to the server. This is called an upload.

The home page of Google: the internet search engine is one of the most "clicked" in the world.

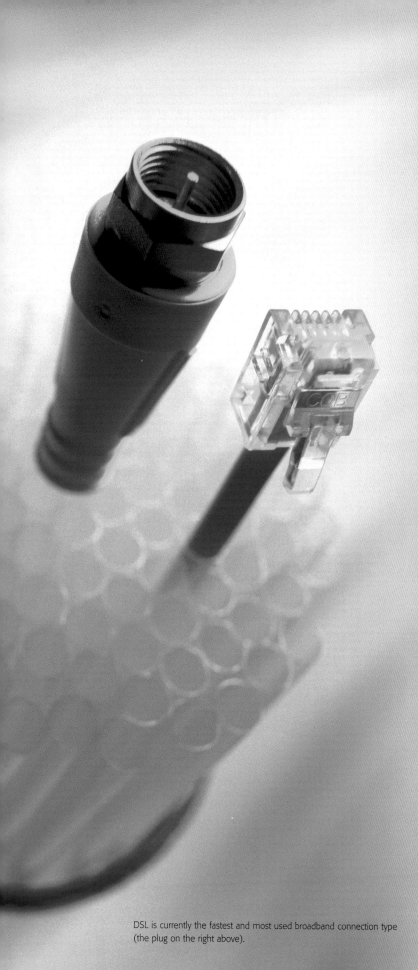

DSL is currently the fastest and most used broadband connection type (the plug on the right above).

News services: at the CIA headquarters in Langley, Virginia, a worker monitors their own network.

Is HTTP a language?

No, HTTP (Hypertext Transfer Protocol) is a protocol that sets out the rules governing how information is exchanged on the worldwide web. This protocol acts as the go-between for internet users, i.e. between a surfer on their own PC (the client) and the data provider (the server), as well as between the several intermediaries among them, such as proxies, gateways, and tunnels. The client making an HTTP request is referred to as the user agent. The responding server is called the origin server.

Who invented the internet?

In 1958, ARPA (Advanced Research Projects Agency, now known as DARPA) was founded in the United States by the US Department of Defense. A decade later, ARPA had the use of a (initially countrywide) network, comprising four computer centers. This network, known as ARPAnet, was the forerunner of the internet. Its development created a single base for different data transmission mechanisms, which in 1973 became known as the internet.

How quickly can you surf?

The speed at which web pages can be downloaded to clients' screens depends first of all on the transport capacity of the relevant cable connection. Analog transport over telephone lines and a modem, which converts computer signals from digital to analog, is the slowest and is hardly ever used nowadays. In comparison to this, ISDN (Integrated Services Digital Network) telephone lines offer a much faster download speed. However, the fastest current connection to the internet is DSL (Digital Subscriber Line), which offers the fastest download speed of all.

What is a WLAN?

This acronym stands for Wireless Local Area Network, which means a cable-free local network. WLAN uses radio waves to enable communication between various computers. Thus, the computer can be used in different floors of a building or in different buildings. A central transmitting and receiving station, called a router, controls the individual participants on the network. WLANs are used both for private networks and for internal company networks. Since the radio waves can penetrate stone walls, every computer within range can pick up the signal. This creates a significant security risk. In order to prevent people from surfing free of charge on someone else's internet account or gaining unauthorized access to other computers, data may be encoded before being transmitted by WLAN. There are various different encoding systems available for this.

What is a hotspot?

Within public WLAN networks there are so-called hotspots, usually available to users for a charge.

These are places where one can make a radio connection to the internet from a laptop or a PDA (Personal Digital Assistant, a small handheld computer). Internet cafés, hotels, public buildings, and transport hubs such as airports and train stations are examples of hotspots.

What are computer viruses?

With the great triumph of the internet, a new form of criminal activity has emerged: accessing somebody else's computer and networks. Malicious programs (known as "malware," from the words "malicious" and "software") are normally spread through file attachments, for example via infected emails or through visits to disreputable websites. Malware can cause damage such as data loss or the dissemination of sensitive information, servers can crash, and PCs can be put completely out of action.

The main types of attacker are:
- viruses, which, like biological viruses, replicate themselves, spread on a massive scale, and damage computers

Surfing the net: internet cafés all over the world offer their customers access to the digital information world.

Pure comfort: home banking, where financial transactions are carried out over the internet, is growing at an enormous rate.

The dark side of the information age: the "I love you" virus infecting a computer in 2004.

- Trojan horses, or "Trojans," which embed themselves in apparently harmless software; the most advanced of these evil-doers can work constantly in the background and use espionage software or "spyware" to disseminate personal data and passwords
- worms, which are transferred by software but can also send themselves by email.

Fundamentally, it is very risky to surf the internet without having a consistently updated virus protection program, or to open emails from unknown senders.

Do firewalls make surfing safer?

Firewalls protect networks and computers from unauthorized access. There are two different kinds. Personal firewalls are a software tool to protect computers from viruses and other attackers. Network firewalls are those that protect computers or routers (which connect different networks) between the trustworthy internal (e.g. company) networks and the (external) internet. In both cases, all ingoing and outgoing data is checked for viruses and, if found, these are destroyed. Firewalls ensure a relatively high degree of data security, but do not dispense with the need for virus scanners.

Is online banking safe?

In principle, yes. Banks and credit card companies use different techniques to safeguard financial transactions over the internet. In addition to SSL (Secure Sockets Layer) protocols, which encode the data concerning a payment transaction, customers are given a Personal Identification Number (PIN). A single-use transaction authentication number (TAN) for each payment provides additional protection.

Am I anonymous on the internet?

Anonymity on the internet is not automatically guaranteed. Every computer that is connected

Surfing, learning, playing, chatting: teenagers take the digital world for granted.

to the internet receives an "IP" (internet Protocol) address from the service provider, which is something like a telephone number. As a rule, private individuals receive a new IP address every time they connect to the internet. Servers, on the other hand, have fixed addresses. Using these numbers, every computer can be located on the internet and identified, for example when investigating a criminal offense.

What is a browser?

A web browser is a computer program that displays websites. Using a browser, web pages can be visited but not changed. In contrast, with what's known as an editor, data can be changed on a website.

How can we protect children from inappropriate web pages?

There are special filters available for this. Such software can block access to sites with undesirable content. Most of these filters are based on regularly updated lists from the relevant known providers. These filters are already included in most browsers.

How do you find pages on the internet?

Websites with search functions, known as "search engines," search the internet based on the user's keywords and list relevant web pages. By clicking on a listed page's link, the user can view the actual web page and associated site. Another possibility are links located within websites themselves, which are connections leading to other websites.

Can phone calls be made over the internet?

Yes, with what is known as VoIP (Voice Over internet Protocol). Using this and paying an internet flat rate, telephone calls can be made at no extra costs. VoIP-suitable telephones can be connected directly to a network. Conventional telephone equipment must be connected via a VoIP router.

DSL data networks can carry considerably larger quantities of data over the internet than traditional cables.

MUSIC:
THE DIGITAL ERA

From vinyl to polycarbonate: optical disk data storage has completely replaced records.

How does sound get onto the CD?

Music data is stored in the form of concentric tracks reading from the inside to the outside of the CD (Compact Disk). The tracks are made of tiny microscopic indentations ("pits") and bumps ("lands"), which are pressed onto the disk. In the industry this is done by what is called glass mastering, comparable to stamping. After molding, the CD, made of polycarbonate, is coated with an aluminum layer on one side.

In the case of home CD burning, the polycarbonate (which has already had its reflective aluminum layer pressed on) is partly heated with a laser to create the pits and lands.

How does a CD player work?

A laser scans the CD and reflects off the aluminum layer on the back of the disk, reflecting differently depending on whether it falls on a pit or a land. Then the digital signals are converted into analog. A player only reproduces the music. A CD burner can be used both to produce CDs and to play them.

What is copy protection?

Not every type of data storage media can be copied. The copy protection on CDs, DVDs, and the internet is there to prevent the unauthorized copying of music and video data and to protect copyright.

However, one of the largest software manufacturers and provider of a popular MP3 player—together with one of the biggest record labels—has offered MP3 data without copy protection since April 2007.

Dr. Theodore H. Maiman operated the first working ruby laser (Light Amplification by Stimulated Emission of Radiation), thereby creating the basis of modern laser technology.

What is DRM?

In order to stem the illegal copying of music data on the internet, several online music shops have set up DRM (Digital Rights Management).

This is simply usage restriction, in order to protect copyrights. A code can be embedded in the data, which can then establish how often a title is played, copied, or burned onto a CD. Data with DRM restrictions can only be reproduced with special programs or equipment which supports the process.

What is an MP3 player?

MP3 (officially called Audio Layer 3) is an encoding format that has been adapted to suit the limited range of human hearing (between 20 Hz and 20 kHz).

Music data is compressed using a mathematical algorithm in order to store the audio data on the

Digital watermarking

The use of digital watermarking is a further measure to try and prevent the unauthorized distribution of music from online stores. For example, data such as copyright information can be built into the music, which is encoded in a way that is inaudible to the human ear and which does not adversely affect quality.

restricted volumes of a CD. In order to do this in a standardized way, MPEG (ISO-MPEG) regulations are applied. MPEG stands for Moving Pictures Expert Group and refers to a cooperation between companies and institutions regarding coding and compression standards.

There are other digital audio players in common usage such as flash-based players, non-mechanical solid state devices that hold audio files on internal flash memory or removable media called memory cards. Basic MP3 player functions are commonly integrated into USB flash drives. Another competing device is the hard drive-based player, or digital jukeboxes, which have higher capacity and can hold thousands of songs. But MP3 players have become the recognized industry standard.

How do I load up my MP3 player?

There are two basic ways to load up an MP3 player. You can either use download portals from the internet (either free of charge or for a fee) onto the PC, or you can produce them yourself using a specific software program to "rip" your music CDs, compress them, and store them on the computer.

Afterwards, these can be copied onto the MP3 player. Depending on the model, you can either burn a CD-R (Compact Disk Recordable) and play that on the player, or use a USB interface to copy the data directly from the computer onto the hard drive or flash memory of the MP3 player.

The Walkman has been replaced. Thanks to data compression, MP3 players can store much more than a magnetic tape ever could.

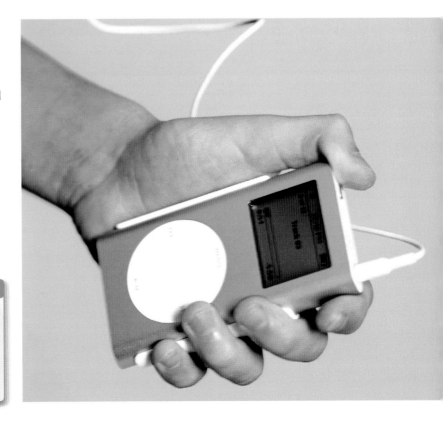

INDEX

intestinal pacemakers 193
ionization 101, 172
ions 69, 86, 87
iron 19, 74, 77, 84–5, *85*, 233
    cast iron 85
iron pyrite 93
isotopes 73, 125
ISS (International Space Station) 274, 275, 276, *276*
IUI (intrauterine insemination) 203

jellyfish *139*
jet engines 269
joints, artifical 107, 187, 189
Jupiter 48, 49

Kalahari Desert 222
karyotypes *152*
kelp 134
Kelvin, Lord *45*
kerosene 110, *111*
kidney failure 190
kidney stones 177
kingdoms 120
knots (nautical) 264
koala bear 129
Koch, Robert *131*
Krakatau 218
krypton 72, 100
Kyoto Protocol (1997) 245

Lab-on-a-Chip (LOC) 204
lactic acid fermentation 158
Lactobacillus 158, 159
lactose tolerance 161
Lake Pontchartrain Causeway 258
Lamarck, Jean Baptiste de 125, 127
larynx 182
lasers *38*, 39
    dental treatment 185
    eye treatment 180–181, *180*
    laser endoscope *178*
    laser TV 287
Lavoisier, Antoine Laurent 67
LCD (liquid crystal display) 286
Le Viaduc de Millau 259, *259*
Leeuwenhoek, Antoni von 130
legumes 98, *98*
lemons 86, *86*, 95
lenses 38, 119, 180, 181, *181*
    gravitational 39, *39*
Leonardo da Vinci 42, 163
levers and pulleys 13
lichens 122
life, origins of 116, 208
light 36–7, 39, 59
    colors 36, 82–3
    electromagnetic radiation 36, *37*
    infrared 172
    reflection 82
    refraction 38, *59*
    speed of 46, 47, 56
    ultraviolet 172
    wavelengths 36, 37, 82
light bulbs 100–101
    energy-saving 101, *101*
lightning *34*, 35
    ball *34*, 35
lightning conductors *34*, 35, 107
lignite 236–7
limestone 93, 208
Linné, Carl von *122*, 123
liposuction 196, *197*
Lister, Sir Joseph 167
lithium *12*, 45, 72
lithotripsy 177, *177*
litmus paper *87*
Lobstein, Jean-Frédéric 200

locks (waterways) *264*, 265
loess 226–7
Lorenz, Konrad 146, *146*, 148

macular degeneration 181
magic acid 87
magic mushrooms 136
maglev trains 262–3, *263*
magnets 15, 17, 33, *33*, 44–5, *44*
magnification 38–9
malaria 138, 155
maned wolf *127*
manganese 266–7
marble 93, *93*
Marianas Trench 267
marmots 137, *137*
Mars 48, 49
mass 16, 17, 20, 25, 47, 50
matches 78, *78*, 79
matter 16–21, 47, 53, 56, 58, 59, 64
    aggregate states 74–5
    antimatter 20, *20*, 21, 53
    conversion into energy 20, 21, 58
    creation 21
    dark matter 54–5
    force 16–17
    mass 16, 17, 20, 25, 47, 50
    see also atoms
Maybach, Wilhelm 251, 252
medical technology 7, 8–9, 164–205
meiosis 151, *152*
melanin 77, 202
Mendel, Gregor Johann *150*
Mendeleev, Dmitri Ivanovich 73, *73*
Mendel's rules 150–151
mercury (element) *7*, 66, 67, *67*, 85, 101, 184
Mercury (planet) 48, 49
mesons 25
mesosphere 218
metabolism 64, 112, 116, 145, 172
metamorphic rocks 209
meteoric rock 209
meteorite strikes 208, *208*
microchips 105, 291–2, *292*
microscopes 38–9
microscopy 119
microtechnology *188*, 189
microwaves 37
Mid-Atlantic Ridge 215
milk 161
Milky Way 13, 49, *49*
Miller-Urey experiment 116
minerals 92–3, 232–4
mitochondria 118
mitosis 118, *118*, 151
MMS (Multimedia Messaging Service) 284
mobile phones 282–5
molecular biology *168*
    forensic 199
molecular pathology 198
molecules 40, *40*, 70, 71, 75, *108*, 117, 170
    molecular infectious diseases 112–13
Möller, Johann Diedrich 119
monocots (monocotyledons) 133
monsoon 221–2
Montreal Protocol (1987) 220
moraines 211
motorcycles 251, *251*
mountain formation 214
mountain vegetation 228
MP3 players 298, 299, *299*
MRI (magnetic resonance imaging) 172–3, *172*, *173*
muons 24

mushrooms 136, *136*
mutagens 128
mutations 127, 128, 161

NASA (National Aeronautics and Space Administration) 274–5, 277
natural gas 232, 235–6
navigation 264
Neanderthals 140, *140*, 141
nearsightedness *181*
neon 72, 101
neon tubes *100*, 101
neophytes 145
neozoes 145
Neptune 48, 49
nerve prostheses 204–5
neutralism 143
neutrinos 19, 24, *54*, 55
neutrons 18, 19, *19*, 24, 26–7, 27, 28, 52, 73
Newton, Sir Isaac 13, *13*
nidicolous animals 147
nitrates 98, 99, *99*
nitric oxides 96, *97*
nitrogen 98–9, 101, 218, 230, 239
nitroglycerine 78
Nobel, Alfred 78
noble gases 72
noble metals 233–4
nuclear energy 15, 28
nuclear fission 15, 20, *21*, 28–9, 240
nuclear force 15, 58
nuclear fusion 30–31, 51, 52, 53
nuclear power plants 15, 28–9, 31, 238, 240–41
nuclear resonance scanning 172–3
nuclear submarines 267
nuclear weapons 20, *21*, 47

obesity 160
obstetrics 167
ocean currents 222–3
ochratoxins 112
oil 110, 111, 232, 235, 236, *237*
oil fields 235
Oort cloud 49
operating theaters *194*, 205, *205*
optics 38–9, 59
ores 232
organelles 118
Otto, Nikolaus August 253
Ötzi the Iceman *141*
overgrazing 227
oxidation 67, 76–7, 77, 78, 95, 109, 111
oxygen 69, 74, 76, 77, 90, 91, 95, *96*, 118, 121, 135, 218
oxygenation 81
ozone 96, *96*
ozone layer 96–7, 218, *219*

pacemakers 192–3, *192*
Pan-American Highway 256, *257*
paper 109
Paracelsus 67, 167, 169, *169*
paraffin 110
paramecium 121
paraplegics 188
parasitism 142
particle accelerators 21, *25*, *26*, 44, 54, 55
Pasteur, Louis 159
paternity testing 154–5
pathogens 112–13, 121, 132, 168
pathology 198–201
    gynecopathology 198
    molecular 198

Pavlov, Ivan *148*, 149
Paxton, Joseph 162
PDAs (Personal Digital Assistants) 284, 295
penicillin 167
periodic table 66–7, 72–3
periodontitis 185
Perl, Martin L. *24*
permafrost 226
perpetual motion 42–3
pesticides 143
PET (positron emission tomography) *20*, 21
pH value 86
pharmacy 168–9
phenotype 129
Philosopher's Stone 66
phishing 297
phloem *134*
phosphates 89, *89*
phosphorus 78, 98, 230
photons 21, 25, 36, 56, 58, 82, 101
photosynthesis 82, 98, 121, 122, 130, 133, 135, *135*, 136, 247
phylogenetic tree of life *122*
physics 7, 8, 10–61
picobiliphyta 122
PIN (Personal Identification Numbers) 283
planets 48, 49
plant feeding system 98–9, 134
plant kingdom 120, 133, 135
    see also vegetation
plant structure 133, *133*
plasma 32, *34*, 35, 74
plasma screens 286, 287, *287*
plastic surgery 196–7
    cosmetic 196–7, *196*, *197*
    reconstructive 196
plasticizers 103, *103*
plastics 102–3
platinum 73, *80*
plutonium 28, 69, 232, 240
polar icecaps 220
pollen, pollination 134, 135, *135*, 138
pollution 216, 239
polymers 102, 105
porcelain *106*, 107
positrons 20, *21*, 27
potassium 98, 230
potassium chlorate 78
potato chips 109, *109*, 112
power bikes 251
power plants 238–41, 242
precious stones 92, 232–3
precocial animals 147
predator-prey relationship 142
prehistoric man 140–141
primeval forests 228
principle of independent assortment 151
principle of least action 58
principle of segregation 151
principle of uniformity 151
prions 112–13
processed food 161
proctoscopy 178
prokaryotes 117, 120, 130
prostheses 107, 167, 186, *186*, 188, 204–5
    endoprostheses 186
    exoprostheses 186
protective instinct 149, *149*
proteins 80, 98, 112, 118
protists 120, 121
protons 18, 19, *19*, 24, 25, 26–7, 28, 30, 32, 51, 69, 72, 86
PVC 102, 103

quadriplegics 204
quantum physics 56–7, 59, 68

PICTURE CREDITS

This is a Parragon Publishing Book
This edition published in 2008.

Parragon Publishing
Queen Street House
4 Queen Street
Bath BA1 1HE, UK

Copyright © Parragon Books Ltd 2008

ISBN: 978-1-4075-2529-7

Printed in Indonesia

Authors
Physics and chemistry: Dr Christoph Hahn
Biology: Dr Ute Künkele
Medical technology: Ulrich Hellenbrand
Geoscience: Dr Alexander Grimm
Transport and space travel: Horst W. Laumanns
Information technology: Ralf Leinburger

German edition created and produced by: ditter.projektagentur GmbH
Project editor: Irina Ditter; Proofreader: Kirsten E. Lehman
Picture editor: Claudia Bettray; Design: Claudio Martinez
Lithography: Klaussner Medien Services Gmbh

English-language edition produced by Cambridge Publishing Management Ltd
Project editor: Diane Teillol; Translators: Susan James, Kate Landenberger, Eithne McCarthy; Copyeditor: Anne McGregor; Layout: Julie Crane
Proofreader: Kelly Walker; Indexer: Marie Lorimer